Living wit the bomb
the bomb

By the same author

Depression: the Way Out of Your Prison

LIVING WITH
THE BOMB

Dorothy Rowe

Routledge & Kegan Paul
London, Boston, and Henley

First published in 1985
by Routledge & Kegan Paul plc

14 Leicester Square, London WC2H 7PH, England

9 Park Street, Boston, Mass. 02108, USA and

Broadway House, Newtown Road,
Henley on Thames, Oxon RG9 1EN, England

Set in 10/11½ pt Century
by Inforum Ltd, Portsmouth
and printed in Great Britain
by Cox and Wyman Ltd,
Reading

Library of Congress Cataloging in Publication Data

Rowe, Dorothy.
Living with the bomb.
Bibliography: p.
Includes index.
1. Nuclear weapons—Psychological aspects.
2. Antinuclear movement.   I. Title.
U264.R68   1985   172'.42   85–2304

British Library CIP data also available

ISBN 0–7102–0477–9

CONTENTS

Animal Voices

'I'm not going to look,' the Ostrich said,
'I shall bury my head in this lovely sand
And not let anything spoil my day:
If I shut my eyes, it will go away.'
And a shadow slanted across the land.

'Oh, don't be so daft,' the Monkey laughed,
And he flicked a flea from his matted hair.
'It's not going to happen – at least, let's hope.
I've looked it up in my horoscope,
And it said the future looked fine – so there.'

An artiodactyl ungulate –
All right then, a Hippo if you prefer –
Who lay in the mud said, 'Let's talk sense:
We've got to have missiles in our defence,
And everyone knows these things deter.'

The blind and the bland and the seeming strong
Were all of them wrong and all obtuse;
But then they were creatures not trained to think,
And tamely they tottered towards the brink.
The kind that are human have no excuse.

ROGER WODDIS

PREFACE

This book is a sequel to my *Depression: the Way Out of your Prison*.[1] When I wrote that book I knew that the essential part of the key to the prison of depression was forgiveness – forgiveness of oneself, of one's past and future, and of other people – but I also knew that a study of forgiveness, in all its complexities, would have overloaded a book which I wanted to make compact and readable. Moreover, I knew that I needed to do some more thinking about forgiveness. I knew a lot about unforgiveness; I was not sure that I understood the process of forgiveness.

One of my readers, Margaret Ballard, saw the deficiency in my *Depression* book and wrote to me. She said,

> *I daresay you will receive hundreds of letters about the book, and hope that this one won't be an imposition but there's one aspect of depression which I feel you didn't tackle in the book, and I would like to ask you about it.*
>
> *In common with many people I'm sure, I find the chief source of my depression/unhappiness is the appalling cruelty in the world and my total lack of power to do anything about it. You say in your book that we must forgive people before we can escape the prison of depression, but if we forgive the people who cause dreadful pain to laboratory animals, or those who abuse their children, or those who torture political opponents, how are we to effect any change in their behaviour? And surely you agree that we should effect some change in such behaviour – not that we should just accept it? You*

*did touch on this matter in the book but didn't do more
than mention it, so I would be very interested to hear how
you feel it can be dealt with.*[2]

Why is there so much appalling cruelty in the world?
Cruelty is not just to those we call our enemies but cruelty to
ourselves and the world we live in. For is it not cruel that we
have created for the human race a future which could be as
brief as 4 minutes but will be no longer than 150 years. A
nuclear war, triggered by national pride or mere computer
failure, could eradicate most of us in four minutes and the rest
of us in a nuclear winter and its aftermath. Even if we avoid
this, the rate at which we are despoiling the planet, cutting
down the trees on which our oxygen supply depends, polluting
the oceans, killing the life that exists in our rivers and lakes,
disrupting the delicate network of life on earth, means that if
we do not come to our senses and seek to preserve rather than
destroy, then this planet will be unable to continue to support
human life for much longer.[3] Meanwhile, as our population
increases so does the devastation by natural disasters, created or aggravated by the stripping of the forests and the
poverty which forces more and more people to live in disaster-
prone areas. Attempts to relieve or eradicate the problems of
poverty and population founder on the rocks of greed, corruption and a system of international banking whose stability is
undermined by the massive debts of the Third World countries.

The warnings are there all the time for us to see. The planes
fly overhead, the missiles are installed. Our newspapers,
radio and television show us in words and pictures what
cruelty we inflict on one another, either directly by killing and
maiming, or indirectly by allowing such cruelty to continue.
Some of us heed these warnings and try, in ways which seem
puny and ineffective, to alter the course of human history so
that the human race will not only continue to exist but will
live with greater love and understanding. However, most of
us are ignoring the warnings and go on living our lives as if all
is well and life will continue forever on this bountiful planet.
But denial of reality, that is, lying to yourself, is the most
costly error you can ever make. Reality does not become

unreal. You do. Our present world is full of people who are unreal to themselves, who do not know themselves. It is they who will destroy us all.

Marshall McLuhan argued that communications technology had turned this world into a 'global village'. Now Derrick de Kerckhove of the McLuhan Program in Culture and Technology is arguing that, while the technology of the bomb can destroy us, the myth of the bomb, the emotions the presence of the bomb can arouse in us and the stories we create to order these emotions, can unify and save us. He wrote,

> As an applied technology, the bomb is absolutely useless, but as the source of unconditional planetary collaboration, its presence is essential . . . the bomb is . . . the helpless consequence of a grotesque disproportion between the legitimate development of technology and the fairly primitive level of our social development. The planet today presents a collective case of 'arrested development' akin to those mathematical prodigies who are incapable of reaching the average levels of social adjustment. The scale of the disproportion may be what is required to bring us back to our senses.
>
> What is required of us is neither very much nor very difficult. All it would take now to get out of danger would be to raise our 'nuclear consciousness'. And everybody from the Mexican street peddler to the Manhattan bureaucrat or to the Marseilles fishmonger can do something about that without so much as lifting a finger. The bomb is saying the same thing to everybody.[4]

I do not share Derrick de Kerckhove's optimism. What is required of us is very difficult. Just as our bodies require oxygen and food to grow and live, so do we as people need to live in groups and to define ourselves in terms of who is in and who is outside the group. We are unaware of much of this complex process just as we are unaware of much of the functioning of our bodies, and just as a fish would find it difficult to understand its relationship to the water, so we find it hard to understand our relationships to one another. Yet it is the way that we relate to one another, how we form groups and define ourselves and our enemies that has brought us to the brink of extinction as a species. We may, like the dinosaurs, be trapped by the very conditions of our existence, and so perish like the dinosaurs. But we have one advantage which, perhaps, the dinosaurs did not have – the capacity for self-reflection. We can choose to look at what we are doing and so choose to change the way we behave. However, change is a risky business and many people prefer not to take that risk. Change means admitting that you might be wrong; change means forgiving and forgetting; change means living with greater insecurity and uncertainty. That is why most people refuse to reflect upon themselves and their lives but instead insist that they are right and others wrong. An inability to see alternatives is regarded as a virtue and admired as a strength.

If we could realise that we must find alternatives to our way of living if we are to survive, then we could begin by looking at how we live our lives in families and contrast with this how we live in our religious, racial and national groups. There are many similarities, and some of them are unnecessary and destructive. We need to examine how we bring up our children, and live with the knowledge that, if we are to survive, we must not do to them what was done to us. We need to understand why we need enemies and to ask, 'Do we need enemies *that much?*'

In this book I have tried to describe what is happening to us, as individuals, when we know of the peril we are in and deny it. I have tried to show, from many different perspectives, how we can live only as a member of a group, and what a price we have to pay for this. I have tried to show how foolish it is not to question the assumptions on which we base our lives – assumptions about the necessity of competition, about the differences between men and women, about security and freedom – and how foolish it is to construe forgiveness as a weakness and revenge as a strength. Forgiveness is not a virtue, but merely a sense of grace which comes from self-knowledge.

What I have not tried to do in this book is to give all the statistical information to back my contention that we are facing extinction as a species. There is a plethora of books and scientific articles on this where readers can find the facts. But facts never alter attitudes, and it is attitudes which are important. Neither have I much to say about the governments of the USA and the USSR, except to deplore the foolishness of the old men who run them. Each nation is so entrenched in its view of itself as all-good and the other as all-bad. For Americans and Russians to see one another as ordinary people sharing common desires, concerns and anxieties many changes would need to be made, but perhaps not so many changes as would be necessary in some other countries for their inhabitants to see themselves as having common concerns with the rest of the human race. For this reason I have written about India and Japan, countries which contribute largely to the Bombs which threaten us, India through a burgeoning population and the possession of the Nuclear Bomb which may trigger a nuclear war with Muslim nations, and Japan, an industrial giant who consumes the earth's resources with little regard for the needs of other races and other species. The power to destroy us all does not reside solely with America and Russia.

To change or not to change is the choice which confronts us all. Choosing not to change means choosing death. Choosing to change means choosing life.

Chapter 1

'I WAKE UP CRYING'

*In recent months we have learned that nuclear war, even
on a limited scale, would bring a lengthy spell of extreme
darkness and cold. The phenomenon of a 'nuclear
winter' could well cause, through freezing and
starvation, as many ultimate casualties as the immediate
war itself, while the long term environmental injury,
especially in terms of our capacity to feed ourselves,
could readily prove equally critical. Moreover, while the
war and its direct destruction would probably be
confined to northern mid-latitudes, the broader scale
repercussions would likely extend much further,
afflicting most if not all nations of the global
community.*[1]

I read this one bitterly cold winter day, the kind of dreary,
grey day when I always curse the English for not doing
something about their weather. It is not the cold that gets me
down. It is the greyness that seems to go on for ever and ever.
By February it is very easy to indulge myself in those
thoughts of anger, despair, and self-pity which destroy hope
and courage and can lead to the black pit of depression. So
then I have to pause to look at the green shoots which promise
daffodils and swallows, and remind myself that February is
only four weeks long and that spring is on the way. But when I
think of a nuclear winter, a winter where we would not know
whether it would ever come to an end, when the illnesses we
suffered would be much worse than the colds and influenza of
an ordinary winter, where the trees and plants would be

shrivelled and no bird would sing, I think, 'I hope I don't survive the bomb.'

This is what many people think. Here in England everyone lives within the range of a potential bomb site, and this horrible fact is often taken as a source of comfort. I often hear myself and other people saying, with a smile, 'My war will be a short war.' Not all Americans, I find, believe that a nuclear war could be fought in Europe and leave America untouched. Some know that such an event would mean for them a slow death. They would agree with the man, a father of three young children, who said to me,

> I saw that film, *The Day After* and I thought that could be me, driving along the road and seeing the mushroom clouds go up. I don't think it's a good idea, going into a bunker and then perhaps coming out after and finding your family dead. It would be better, like a friend of mine said, to get your family all together and stand outside.

When I asked Margaret Ballard how she coped with living with the bomb she replied,

> *'The only honest answer I can give you as to how I can manage to live with the possibility of it is that I don't think about it, because to do so is too frightening. This doesn't work all the time, of course, and frequently I have appalling visions of what it would be like if these weapons were used (I've seen newsreel films from Hiroshima) but I never feel that there is anything I can do to prevent the mad politicians and military men from doing what they please. Twenty years ago I joined CND and went on marches, but I'm cynical and have lost hope now and so don't go anymore. My only hope is that, when the bomb drops, I'll be right underneath it and don't have to take weeks to die.'*[2]

The inevitability of trouble and disaster provokes in some people laughter and wit, the 'gallows humour' which has always been an effective tool for survival. Through humour we can ridicule our enemies and so reduce their power over us. By laughing at our troubles we can reduce them to a more

CHRISTOPHER LOGUE'S

True Stories

A spokesperson for Buckingham County Council has said that after a lengthy search on the part of its Civil Defence Planning Officer, the Defence Committee has concluded: "The safest place to be when the bomb goes off is in the cellar of the local pub. Our plan is to draw up a list of people who will be useful after the disaster. They will be mustered in the pub's cellar. There is no better hiding place."

Responding to this suggestion. Mr Barry Warner, manager of the Prince Albert, Branwell, is offering places in his cellar for £10. "Nobody is getting into the cellar unless they have a £10 ticket. Either way, I'll do well out of it. Having bought your ticket, you can drink as much beer as you like – I mean they can't drink much in 4 minutes, can they?"

INFORMATION: Daily Telegraph 24.12.1983; *ibid* 5.12.1983; Wantage Herald 11.12.1983; Guardian 9.12.1983; Mirror on Sunday 11.12.1983; Weekly Focus 27.11.1983; Bankok Post 11.12.1983.

manageable size, and by sharing a joke we can re-affirm the strength of our group and so gain courage. Laughing at the ridiculousness of human endeavour can give us the power to continue in that endeavour. Laughing at what frightens us can make us less afraid. So we joke about the end of our world.[3]

But there is something bizarre in laughing about the destruction of our world and something peculiarly morbid in wanting to die in a nuclear holocaust. In ordinary life it is wise to laugh at our troubles and it is human to hope for a short, painless death, but in ordinary life life goes on. In ordinary life we can laugh at our troubles because we have hope that life will be better if not for ourselves then for those we love. In ordinary life we can come to imagine and so accept our own death because we know that, although we must die, some part of us will go on living through our children, those who knew and loved us, and through our work. That is ordinary life. But we no longer live an ordinary life. We face not merely death but extinction. Should we laugh at those troubles of the world which threaten to remove all hope from the world? Should we wish for a brief, painless death when what perishes with us are those people and institutions which gave our life significance and continuity? Laughing at troubles can become unthinking callousness, and wishing for an easy death can be not so much a longing for the peace of death as a disgust with life.

There are many people who so hate their fellows that they long to see them destroyed. Such people are not just those who cry, 'Death to the infidel!' and then send young boys to walk across minefields and to absorb poison gas. Many ordinary, otherwise decent people feel such disgust with the human race that they see some merit in any event which would remove such undesirable and unsuitable people from the world. Then, they feel, the world would be a better place. If the disgust they feel for human beings includes themselves they see themselves as deserving such a death as well as welcoming the peace of death.

But saying yes to death is a very dangerous thing to do. Welcoming death, however far away we see that death, has an insidious and destructive effect on how we live our lives. 'What is the use?' creeps in, and with that a sense of hopelessness and purposelessness. Whenever the end of some event is in sight we can find it very easy to cease from the effort necessary in relation to that event. Some people give up studying a day or two before an examination. Some people cease to care for their appearance as soon as the first signs of ageing appear. The hospital where I work is to be closed in seven years' time. When I asked for a burglar alarm to be installed in the Psychology Department to protect very expensive computer and video equipment I was told that it was not worth doing because our building was to be pulled down when the hospital closed!

Such a way of thinking leads some people to argue that we do not have to worry about the destruction of our forests, the pollution of our waters, the extinction of whole species of animals and plants because sooner or later everything will be destroyed. This kind of hopelessness in adults is dangerous. It imperils and sours their lives as well as the lives of those around them. But such hopelessness in children is even more tragic. For them, turning away from life to face death is not an embittered reaction to an unsatisfactory life but a realistic assessment of their future. Many children are well informed about the stockpiling of nuclear weapons and the dangers that this entails. How do they live with this? How do they see their future? What should the adults around them say to them? When I was a child in Australia during the Second World War I was well aware of the danger we were in of being killed or taken prisoner by the Japanese, and for many years after the war I had terrifying dreams about Japanese soldiers. But all through my wartime childhood I was being told by my father, my teachers and by government propaganda that after the war, which we were certain to win, life would be splendid. Alongside the fear there was hope. The hope that was instilled in me was to some extent unrealistic. It took me some time to realise that the good things in life would not fall into my lap and that I had to work for them. But this unrealistic hope enabled me to take what I now see, looking back, as enormous chances. When one has hope security is not so important.

But my generation was the last to grow up with that hope for the future. My friend Ron Janoff of New York University, some thirteen years my junior, told me of how vividly he remembered reading an article when he was seven in 1951 about the results of a hydrogen bomb being dropped on New York. He lived in Newark, New Jersey, and the effect of that article on him was that he made no plans for the future. He grew up living from day to day. It was not until he went into therapy that he learned to face the fear of imminent death and to risk making plans. Now he watches over his four-year-old son with tender care and risks some hope.

Another American friend, Susie, a vibrant twenty-year-old

from California, who had learned about the suddenness of
ordinary death as a child when her mother died of a heart
attack, and the randomness of death when her younger
brother in his teens died in a freak accident, said to me,

'It blows my mind. To think that one button – just one
little button pressed and that's the end of everything.
You know how you go along in your own little bubble,
and you used to be able to do this, just go along in your
own little bubble, not taking notice of anything else, but
now over you is this big bubble, and it's there all the
time and you've got to take notice of it. I usen't to make
any plans at all. I thought, "It could finish any time, so
what's the point?" I do make some plans now, a year or
two ahead, that's all.'

Jim Carse, also at New York University, told me that his
sons, in their early twenties, say to him, 'Dad, you were lucky.
When you were young you had a future.' What does a father
say to that?

How do we live if there is no security and no hope? How do
parents guide their children when none of us knows what the
future will be? Jill Tweedie wrote,

*When I talk to my own teenage son, our mutual
helplessness under nuclear government enforces an odd
democracy, the democracy of childishness, but it lessens
my ability because my experience has become invalid,
irrelevant. All the truisms are no longer true – train, get
a job, stick to it, don't waste your time, think of the future
and so on – the words taste stale in my mouth. 'Look at it
this way,' he says, 'I wouldn't mind being a furniture
designer but I don't want to be designing furniture when
the bomb falls, do I?' What is the answer to that, apart
from further cliches? 'I'll travel,' he says, 'See the world
before it's gone.' I can only nod, weakly.*[4]

Some of us, when we look at our children, do not simply feel
weak and helpless. We cry. Not ordinary tears of pity and
rage, but wrenching, terrible tears that seem to come from
the bottom of the soul and encompass the whole world. Grief
of a kind we have never known before. An overwhelming grief

which comes upon us suddenly. A chance word, a television image, and we are seized and wracked, tight with pain, beyond words. One mother said, 'Out of a deep sleep I wake up crying.'

Those of us who cry like this usually cry alone. To show such grief to others would not do. Joanna Macy said,

> *When the prospect of collective suicide first hit me as a*
> *serious possibility – and I know well the day and hour*
> *my defenses against this despair suddenly collapsed – I*
> *felt there was no one to whom in my grief I could turn. If*
> *there were, and indeed there were, for I have loving,*
> *intelligent friends and family – what is there to say? Do I*
> *want them to feel this horror too? What can be said*
> *without casting a pall, or without seeming to ask for*
> *unacceptable words of comfort and cheer?*[5]

How can we try to deal with this terrible despair? Some of us try to deal with it by action. We join the Campaign for Nuclear Disarmament or one of those plethora of action groups which my irreverent journalist son calls 'Gay Whales Against the Bomb'. We go on marches and wave banners. We camp outside missile bases or we send food and money to those who do. Some of us make brave, angry gestures and get ourselves ignored by the media and arrested by the police. Some of us study hard and can, at the sound of the word 'deterrence', produce facts and figures about warheads, missiles and megadeaths. Joining a group and sharing our concerns can bring some comfort, but joining together to fight the arms race is far from simple. How can we convince others of the rightness of our cause?

The starting point is to make other people aware of the terrible dangers which threaten us. No matter what witty jokes have been devised about the nuclear threat the truth which has to be faced is sombre, allowing of no simple solutions, and leads easily to despair. Anyone who wants to discuss these matters runs the risk of appearing morbid to his listeners and thus undermining the credibility of the message. We are more likely to believe statements made by a person we see as having special knowledge and power. The special knowledge is not as relevant (I have often

from *Beyond a Joke* by Brick, Spokesman 1983[6]

seen nurses being greatly impressed when a consultant gives
his opinion, not just on his medical specialty, but on politics,
the incompetence of administrators, the youth of today and
the foolishness of religious belief) as having prestige in the
eyes of the listeners. In America a person gains prestige with
gaining success, and the sign of success is optimism. Thus
anyone whose message is pessimistic cannot be successful,
and anyone who is not successful does not merit attention.
When I visited the 40+ Club in New York (a club established
for those executives who had been 'let go', or, as we say in
England, 'made redundant', euphemisms for being sacked
from your job) I found that these men and women dared not
show the sadness and despair they naturally felt. To do so
would make them appear even less successful than they were.
Moreover, a successful person never presents a problem without at the same time presenting the solution. A morbid
message which contains vague solutions like 'get rid of nuclear weapons' or 'universal love' does not come in a form
likely to attract the attention of most Americans.

In England optimism as a sign of success is not so necessary
– verbose eccentrics with pet hates are popular media figures
– but a quiet cheerfulness is considered to be the correct way
to present oneself, from the 'stiff upper lip' of the upper classes
to the 'can't complain' of the working class. The appropriate
reaction to any threat to the country's safety is a demonstration of cheerful patriotism – 'the Falklands spirit' with its

memories of 'the Dunkirk spirit', our brave British soldiers, the Queen on the balcony at Buckingham Palace and people talking to one another in the underground. Any message to the effect that a nuclear war would be one which the British would not win is quite unacceptable.

Just as pessimism is unacceptable, so is anger. Society deplores a display of anger, especially if the person displaying the anger is a woman. Anger is so unfeminine. Standards must be maintained. In England the Greenham Common women have earned more unfavourable notice because they ignore society's rules about how women should behave than because they oppose the installation of cruise missiles in England. The vice-chairman of Ratepayers Against Greenham Encampments, Alex Hutcheon, wrote to the *Guardian*,

> Sir – The local inhabitants of Greenham are enraged about the women who are polluting a beautiful part of Berkshire. The violence perpetrated by these squatters on the residents of Newbury and district when they are opposed is well known here and it is also a fact that they are driving the ratepayers and their families from the local swimming pool and leisure centre because of their disgusting and unnatural behaviour.
>
> It appears not to be generally known that these illegal squatters' campsites are inhabited by itinerant squatters at various intervals and that they have a house at their disposal a short distance away. They do not spend all their time huddled around fires and suffering the ravages of weather. They cut wire fences, vandalise road signs, council vehicles and private property – and Bruce Kent supports this!![7]

People who worry about untidiness and the unseemly behaviour of women protesting against the installation of nuclear weapons are not likely to be affected by any reasoned arguments which show that more than a part of Berkshire is in danger of being polluted by worse things than squatters' camps and vandalised road signs. After all, facts never alter attitudes.

I was reminded of this not long ago when I went to a

theological college to talk to the students about people who get depressed. During the discussion I mentioned how the experience of depression was universal, found in all races and cultures and in recorded history. One of the students queried this. He was, he said, from South Africa and it was well known that the Bantu people never got depressed. Black people, he explained to me, were not affected in this way. I replied that I thought that this could not be the case, and I quoted research in transcultural psychiatry to support this. I ended by talking about the work of a friend of mine who in Kenya studied the incidence of depression among women and the relationship between leprosy and depression. If blacks in Kenya got depressed I could not believe that blacks in South Africa did not. All through this account the student regarded me seriously and nodded. A year later I returned to the college to talk to a group of students about counselling depressed people. The student from South Africa was in the group and towards the end of the session he asked me the same question – did I not know that the Bantu race were impervious to depression, that they were happy-go-lucky people, unaffected by the kind of things which affect white people in South Africa and cause them to become depressed. I was astounded. This man had spent over a year in a theological college whose teaching emphasises pastoral care and a compassionate awareness of human suffering, yet he still believed that black people do not feel pain in the way that white people do. I said very shortly, 'Well, in the pictures I've seen of them standing beside their bulldozed houses they don't look very happy', and then I went on, again, to give him all the facts from the transcultural studies which show the universality of depression. At the end of the session he came up to me to thank me for an interesting talk and to say goodbye. He was returning to South Africa to take up his ministry. As I drove home I wondered whether I had taken refuge in facts rather than do what I should have done, that is, make him look at the reality of the situation, that he had given his allegiance to and received the blessing from a church whose founder taught that while suffering is universal so is God's love. If he truly acknowledges this, if he acknowledges that black people suffer just the way that white people do, then he could not return to South Africa and accept

the way of life there. He would not be able to minister to his
white congregation and ignore what was happening to the
blacks. He would be forced into dangerous action or
anguished impotence and, in either case, isolation. Thus his
belief that black people do not feel pain has nothing to do with
facts. It was a defence against despair.

Why hadn't I said this to him? I looked at myself and
acknowledged that the reason I had not challenged this man
was because theological students are so *nice*, so proper and
kindly in their behaviour, so *vulnerable* that I did not want to
upset them. In terms of personal vanity, if I did upset them
they might not go on seeing me as a kindly woman who gives
good advice. But more, if I had challenged the South African
student I would have been doing more than challenging one of
their colleagues. I would have been challenging them. How, I
would have been asking, do you reconcile God's power and
love with the existence of suffering? If God is all-powerful and
all-good, why does He allow suffering? Does the existence of
suffering, be it the dispossessed and starving blacks in Africa
or the well-fed whites in Europe weeping helplessly as the
nuclear weapons take away their children's future, show that
God is not all-powerful, or that God does not care, or, perhaps,
that God does not exist at all? When we question God's
attitude to suffering we have to question our own. How do we
live with the immense and seemingly endless suffering in the
world?

We can acknowledge the existence of suffering and work to
abolish it. But suffering goes on and on. Despite the efforts of
good men and women to feed the starving, one natural or
man-made disaster follows upon another, wrenching people
in the Third World from their homes and their crops. In my
small way I spend hours trying to help one suffering person
release himself from the painful experiences of childhood, and
then I see in the world around me society inflicting on small
children the same experiences – the sins of the fathers being
visited on the children. The women of Greenham Common
protest as one cruise missile launcher goes by, and they know
that across the Atlantic the missiles are pouring from the
factories. Acknowledging suffering and trying to combat it is
very dangerous. At any moment courage can give way to
despair.

We can, like this man from South Africa, deny that suffering exists, or such suffering which to acknowledge would
make us feel uncomfortable. We can feel a well-contained
concern for starving children in Ethiopia or Bangladesh or for
the vanishing whales in the South Pacific and give a tidy
donation to Oxfam or Greenpeace, but suffering which encompasses us and which cannot be ameliorated by a donation
to a worthy charity is infinitely harder to bear. Joining an
anti-nuclear weapons group does not produce a glow of virtue
like giving a donation to the Save the Children Fund. What it
does produce is a flood of information – magazines, pam-
phlets, books, videos, T-shirts, car stickers, badges – all of
which give endless facts about nuclear warheads and missiles
and guns and tanks and planes and ships, and facts about
forms of death and destruction which go beyond the capacity
of our imagination to encompass.

Recently Leeds City Council produced a booklet called
Leeds and the Bomb which describes what would happen if a
one megaton groundburst hydrogen bomb hit the Town Hall.
I know Leeds well – my son went to college there and now
works for Radio Leeds – so I know what a large, solid city it is.
The massive Town Hall and the buildings around it were built
by the Victorians and they built to last. The booklet tells me
that,

> Only a minute after a one megaton groundburst
> hydrogen bomb hit the Town Hall *very little of Leeds
> would remain standing*. Immediately on detonation
> there would be a blinding flash of light and deadly
> nuclear radiation would be emitted. Within three
> seconds an intensely hot fireball some 9,000 ft across
> would be formed. The familiar mushroom shaped cloud
> would then rise into the sky. A blastwave travelling
> faster than the speed of sound and winds of up to 200
> m.p.h. would then spread outwards across the city.
> Within hours radio-active fall-out would come down on
> most of the city.[8]

The booklet goes on to describe what would happen, suburb
by suburb, out to the beautiful countryside which surrounds
Leeds. The booklet had already told me that a one megaton

bomb is seventy times more powerful than the one which destroyed Hiroshima. I find Hiroshima hard to encompass in my imagination and I have been there. I try to imagine Leeds after a bomb, and all I can see is the Leeds I know – rain-swept streets, crowds of people, terraced houses, blocks of flats, cars and buses battling the one-way system through the city. How can I imagine all that destroyed?

It is no wonder that some people react with disbelief. Such things are not possible. Some people react with anger. The Tory councillors in Leeds, like those in Lincoln for which a similar pamphlet was produced, condemned the booklet, saying it was a waste of public money and created unnecessary anxiety. Children, they said, should be protected from such knowledge. The people who get angry like this are those who acknowledge the existence of the nuclear arms race but only to say that it is necessary, for we have enemies and we must arm ourselves against them. Not to do so is to risk losing not just our lives but our country and our democratic way of life.

Most people, I find, deal with the threat of nuclear war by simple denial. When I asked Liam Hudson, one of the most original thinkers that the profession of psychology has produced, how he lived with the bomb he answered with one word, 'Denial'. My agent Andrew Best said simply, 'I'm an ostrich.'

However, some people do not deny the threat of nuclear extinction but build it into their system of thinking. Those people whose view of life is profoundly pessimistic see the nuclear threat as confirmation of their beliefs, while many people of various religious faiths see the destruction of the earth as a necessary part of the Divine Plan. Some see nuclear weapons as essential to their country's safety, while some expect a nuclear war and plan to survive in an aggressive and primitive way.

Each way of reacting to the threat of nuclear war – disbelieving and denying, objecting, or welcoming for either patriotic or religious reasons – has implications for the way we live our lives. It is not just that everyone who pays taxes is making a contribution to the arms race. Deny it though we may, the fact is that we are now in danger of eliminating ourselves as a species so that, as Jonathon Schell said, *'Only the stones and stars, and whatever algae and mosses have made it through, are present to witness the end.'*[9] Whichever way we react to this knowledge affects us in our everyday lives and in the lives of our children.

Chapter 2

'IT'LL NEVER HAPPEN'

Coming home from school one day my daughter brought me a riddle: 'What is the difference between ignorance and apathy?' I began to answer her question seriously, literally, with definitions and distinctions. But she interrupted me. Shrugging her shoulders, she laughed, 'I don't know and I don't care.'[1]

Our world is full of a multitude of things, all constantly moving and changing. We cannot possibly notice everything that is going on around us. If we did we would be overwhelmed by sensations. Instead, we have to select what we notice and attend to. This means that we can often fail to notice something which will affect us seriously – like the smell of burning in the kitchen, a packet of white powder in our daughter's bedroom, a newspaper article on a change in the tax laws. Events like these will eventually force us to pay them attention, and while we may regret that we did not notice them earlier we often comfort ourselves by saying, truthfully, 'I was too busy with other things.' Again, while we do attend to many things, we do not inform ourselves fully about everything we notice. I find the functions of the English Inland Revenue beyond my comprehension, so I leave my tax affairs in the hands of someone who says he understands these things. However, when it comes to the functions of the National Health Service, my employer, I make sure I am as fully informed as possible. The difference in my attitude is not simply because as head of a department of clinical psychology I want to do my job as well as possible. The difference is one of trust. I trust my tax man. I don't entirely trust the people who run the National Health Service – the administrators, the consultants, the government officials and the government itself whose concern for our health service is somewhat limited.

When it comes to all the matters to do with the dangers of nuclear weapons it is hard to imagine that anyone in Europe and North America has not noticed something. For many people the dangers seem far away – 'over in Europe, not here in the States' or 'not in my lifetime'. Some people may be simply misinformed. Some people gain what information they have solely from government sources because they trust the government to look after them and tell them the truth.

In England people born during and after the Second World War have known only a system of government aimed at providing adequate care and protection for everyone. Whenever the present Tory government makes, or threatens to make, any reduction in the level of care and protection the objections to this contain cries of disbelief. How can a government not ensure that everyone is adequately fed, clothed, housed and have health and educational needs met? For many people in England it is inconceivable that the government should choose not to provide these things. They forget that such provision is, in historical terms, very recent, about forty years, and, in geographical terms, very rare. Few governments see their primary duty as to care for their people. Most governments see their primary duty as keeping themselves in office and their people in order. Nevertheless, many people in England, having known no other form of government, assume without questioning that their government is looking after them in all matters of life and death. They may grumble about the cuts in the National Health Service, but they believe that the National Health Service is an institution like the Church of England, which may change but never disappear. Where matters of national defence are concerned they feel the same confidence in the government. The government will look after them, and while the government may not tell them everything (national security is very important) what the government does tell them is true. This simple, trusting attitude is sometimes mixed with a nostalgia for the

from *Where The Wind Blows*[2]

Second World War. Raymond Briggs, in *Where the Wind Blows* showed two such people.

Their tragedy was that they believed that their government would protect them. They followed the government's advice on how to survive a nuclear attack, and they perished.

In America criticism of the government on matters of defence can be considered unpatriotic, and patriotism is for Americans one of the highest virtues (if not the highest). Such patriotism demands that the government be regarded as (on the whole) truthful and honest. Recent discoveries that former governments, like those in Britain and Australia, have sought to conceal evidence that the test firing of nuclear weapons produced levels of radiation which later caused the deaths of many people from cancer may create unease in some people, but is dismissed by many. How could the government lie to us on such important matters?

What they and others like them forget is that while our governments may be relatively truthful with us over matters to do with living in a peaceful world, all matters to do with the defence of our country are to do with *war*, and in war the first casualty is truth.

Of course, many people know this. I was discussing these matters with one man, an automotive engineer reduced by the recession to working as a garage mechanic. We mentioned the bunker which our District Council have built to protect themselves in a nuclear war. He pointed out to me that the information we were given about this bunker, particularly about the provision of radio equipment, was incorrect. He said, 'They think we're stupid. They tell us rubbish and expect us to believe it.'

There is an unfortunate tendency in some people when they gain power, be they presidents, prime ministers, government officials or even consultant psychiatrists, to despise those people for whose care they are responsible. They forget Abraham Lincoln's wise warning, 'You can fool all of the people some of the time, and some of the people all the time, but you cannot fool all the people all the time'. But, when it comes to lying, people in power are no different from the rest of us. *Provided you have a good memory, you may be able to lie to other people and get away with it, but if you lie to yourself you are in trouble.*

Psychoanalysts call lying to yourself *denial*. Otto Fenichel, in his *Psychoanalytic Theory of the Neuroses*, began his account of denial with 'The tendency to deny painful sensations and facts is as old as the feeling of pain itself.'[3] A talent for denial has certainly played a major part in the survival of the human race.

"I've had a good life—seventy-five years of self-deception."

PUNCH December 8 1982[4]

No doubt our cavemen ancestors ignored physical pain and the threat of death as they were hunting for food while in the cave the women comforted themselves and their children saying that outside in the dark there was nothing to be afraid of. By denying fear we give ourselves and others courage. But if we deny our fear without understanding what it is that we are afraid of we can make some bad mistakes. If we are to save ourselves we must look our peril in the eye and know what it is that we are denying.

When it comes to looking our nuclear peril in the eye not everyone is prepared to do this. Some people want to know what it is. Many do not.

When I was thinking about this one day I realised that my introduction to the nuclear threat was actually a demonstration of the two attitudes to danger, curiosity and denial. In 1945 I was fourteen and in my second year at Newcastle Girls' High School. I was, in fact, in 2A. At that school the girls were put into classes according to their intellectual and academic ability. At the end of their primary school years they had to compete for a place at the Girls' High School and, once there, examination marks determined which class each girl went into. In my last two years at primary school I had an energetic and enthusiastic teacher, Mrs Peebles, who was determined that her girls were not merely going to High School, they were going to get into the A class. To achieve this with me she would hit me with a ruler and call me 'Careless Connie' ('Conn' was my birth name) whenever I made a mistake. But she did encourage me to write, and she called my essay on a seagull 'the best composition she had ever read', so I forgave her the sharp pain of the ruler.

I did pass the examinations and went to High School where I had to wear a horrid uniform, never speak to boys, and behave in the quiet, obedient manner demanded by the women who were our teachers. By my second year at that school I had learned to fear my teachers even more than I had feared Mrs Peebles. In 2A the teacher who frightened me the most was Miss Coombes. She taught us physics and chemistry. She walked with the help of a stick and sat at the teacher's desk on a raised dais while she taught, but her cold fierceness produced more silence and obedience in class than more physically active teachers. She would dictate notes and we would copy these carefully into our books and then memorise what we had written. One passage we copied down was *the* definition of the atom: '*The atom is the smallest part of matter which cannot be divided.*'

I remember being in our dining room at home and reading in the *Newcastle Morning Herald* about the dropping of the atom bomb on Hiroshima and the splitting of the atom. I was puzzled, and discomforted because here was something I didn't understand. In those years I was always putting my poor, ignorant mother right on all sorts of matters and I would not admit that I did not understand or know something. So I went to school wanting to know but not daring to ask what splitting of the atom meant. The other girls in my class were curious too, and we waited for Miss Coombes to tell us. We stood respectfully when she came in, leaning heavily on her stick as she mounted the dais and settled herself into her chair. She told us to sit down, take out our chemistry books, and then she went on dictating the chemistry notes she had begun in our previous lesson. We looked at one another, wondering if one of us would dare to ask Miss Coombes what had happened in Japan, but no one did. Later, in the play-ground, I was infuriated to discover that in 2B (the class I despised most, more than 2C, 2D or 2E) Mrs Wylie, their physics and chemistry teacher, had abandoned her prepared lesson and had devoted the whole lesson to explaining about the atomic bomb. I was so annoyed I didn't stay around to find out what Mrs Wylie had actually said.

I knew why Miss Coombes hadn't told us about the atomic bomb. At that school the teachers were always right. They would not want to admit making a mistake or not knowing something. Mrs Wylie was an exception. She was married, and that was a very rare thing for a woman high school teacher in those days. It marked her out as something of a maverick. But I could not expect Miss Coombes to admit error or ignorance or to make any sudden changes in her pro-gramme of teaching. Her job was not to help us understand life and the world we lived in. Her job was to get us through exams. An all-female school which ignored males and sex would have no difficulty in ignoring the atomic bomb. We were asexual females leading industrious, orderly lives. What happened in Japan was no concern of ours.

No doubt my teachers, including Miss Coombes, meant well and wanted to protect us from the dangers of the world, but pretending that such dangers did not exist was no protection. The dangers of sex and war remained with me. For the first, I found that the delights outweighed the dangers, but the danger of the other made a dark counterpoint rhythm all my life. At university I and my friends, most of them ex-servicemen, worried about being called up for service in the Korean War. Australians were involved in the Emergency, as it was called, in Malaya, and then came Vietnam and con-scription for young Australian men. I could see that war dragging on for so long that my son would become one of the conscripts. Life in England, I found, put more physical dis-tance between us and the incessant wars in Africa, Asia, the Middle East and Central America, but the danger did not lessen. I am always amazed when I hear people saying how nuclear weapons have preserved the peace for the past thirty years. I know that I live in the eye of the whirlpool, and that the eye of the whirlpool can shift at any moment.

Nevertheless, for some years I did not give much thought to the increasing dangers of a nuclear war. I noted but did not concern myself with the various events to do with nuclear issues. During the Cuban crisis I waited with some anxiety but with my then usual disbelief that anything really bad could happen to me. Not long after something bad did happen to me personally, and I discovered with considerable pain that I did not have a charmed life. Something really bad could happen to me at any time.

Such a discovery affected every aspect of my thinking and feeling. I became more aware of the brevity of life, and of the threat which could make my brief life even briefer. When I moved to Lincolnshire in 1972 I was constantly reminded of the danger by the roar of Vulcan bombers overhead, carrying their nuclear warheads. I knew that the airfields nearby would be early targets in a nuclear war. I watched Nevil Shute's film *On the Beach* on television (I had avoided seeing it when it first came out in 1957, the year my son was born) and I saw with horror the terrible lie it contains. Australians (or any people for that matter) will not behave that well when facing extermination. They will not queue obediently for their pills and then go home quietly and take them and die. Some might, but they will find it hard to avoid the wild, violent drunken party that would celebrate the end of the world.

Even with the avoidance of the question of how people behave when they do not want to die but feel helpless to prevent it, *On the Beach* had a powerful message. I felt that I should do more. I joined the Campaign for Nuclear Disarmament, not because I agreed with their advocacy of unilateral disarmament but because I wanted to support the way they kept going the questioning about the wisdom of having a nuclear defence. I went on a CND march one summer's day in London and saw that the crowds there were mainly young people with a sprinkling of elderly people. The middle-aged must have stayed home to tend their gardens and their careers.

This was my first inkling that there were many people who regarded themselves as sensitive, caring people and yet who denied that there was any problem where nuclear weapons were concerned. That this was so was brought home to me most strongly at the International Congress on Personal Construct Psychology at Boston, Mass. in 1983. At the end of each of these congresses which are held every two years the delegates have a meeting to assess the success of the congress and to plan future congresses. At this meeting in Boston it was generally agreed that the congress, apart from some small problems, had been a success. Arguments started when it came to deciding on the venues for future congresses. Delegates from Australia complained that the congresses were held only in the United States and Europe. They demanded that congresses be held regularly in Australia. The British delegates countered with the argument that they found it hard enough to get the money to go to the States. They couldn't afford to go flying to Australia every two or four years. The arguments went on, and finally it was conceded that the Australians had a point. It was agreed that in 1985 the congress would be in England, in 1987 in Honolulu, and, after that there would be a regular alternating between the States, Europe, and the South Pacific. This discussion took the planning of the conferences into the 1990's and beyond. I watched this discussion and was amazed. The delegates seemed to be seeing their future stretching before them with no more problems than getting research grants and travel expenses. No one said, 'All being well,' or 'God willing' or 'Touch wood'. No one said, 'If we are all still alive.'

Since then I have been asking various psychologists how they managed to live with the threat of nuclear war. Some, usually those just entering the profession, acknowledge the existence of the danger and their anxiety about it. One young man said, 'I worry about it a lot. I always think about it when I'm making plans for my future.' Some psychologists, usually those in the middle of their careers, deny the problem and are surprised that I have asked. It is curious to hear people, whose job involves deciding whether another person is mad, advocating what we regard as the measure of madness. A person who is 'out of touch with reality' is 'psychotic' (we don't like using simple terms like 'mad' but that is what 'psychotic' means). Somehow, in the thinking of these psychologists, it is crazy to deny your immediate surroundings and to claim that the Russians are using powerful rays to insert wicked thoughts in your mind, but it is not crazy to pay attention to your immediate surroundings and to deny that the Russians really do have nuclear weapons targeted on your home.

Some psychologists, however, acknowledge the painful conflict between denial and the implications of full awareness. Roger Power, the father of two small children, said to me,

'Most of the time I deny it – unless something happens to remind me. Then I have to think about it. Some of my friends are preoccupied with it all the time. But I can't take that on board. If I did it would destroy my life. But it's on the edge of my world all the time. There's no intellectual answer to the whole nuclear business. The only answer is a scream.'

What Roger is describing here is the conflict between the pain of intelligent awareness and the dulling of the pain by the stupidity of denial. 'People,' said Fenichel, 'become stupid when they do not want to understand.'[5] Maintaining such stupidity requires the constant effort of dulling one's wits. Other people have to join in the deception. They have to agree when we say to them, or show by our actions, that 'If I know about it I'll have to worry about it, so don't tell me.'

Agreeing to deny and to deceive so as not to worry is commonplace in ordinary life. In the family I grew up in the most important rule was 'Don't tell Mother anything that would upset her.' We meant it kindly – Mother would have an asthma attack if she got upset – but Mother was a person of fixed opinions and many things upset her, so the longterm effect of this rule was the destruction of all intimacy. Conversations in our house were always superficial and repetitive. We lived our lives elsewhere. I would argue with my mother what clothes I should wear or whether I would get my hair cut, but I would never ask her to share my anxieties about how I should live my life. By denying to her by my actions that I had such anxieties I could deny to myself that such anxieties existed. I told myself all would be well, and blundered on.

Something similar is happening today in the way that many people are dealing with their anxieties about a nuclear war. Whenever I have the opportunity to speak or write to an 'agony auntie' I ask how frequently their readers raise questions about nuclear issues. The usual answer to this question is, 'Hardly ever.' Marjorie Proops of the *Daily Mirror* wrote to me to say,

> *I was fascinated by your question about my readers'*
> *anxieties over nuclear war. The fact is that very rarely do*
> *people mention it. Letters are sent to the Editor or to our*
> *Public Opinion Column about people's fears but the*
> *number of letters isn't very high. I think that people are*
> *afraid to put their fears into words or even to think very*
> *seriously about the subject. Perhaps it is too horrendous*
> *to think about and perhaps ordinary people feel so*
> *helpless. The average citizen who writes to me is much*
> *more likely to be worried about cuts in her Social*
> *Security benefit or the fact that she has a drunken*
> *husband who knocks her about. I dare say if, like you, I*
> *asked them direct questions about their anxieties*
> *concerning nuclear war they would all say they fear it*
> *but they certainly don't express it in letters to me.*[6]

Since the people who consult me are anxious and we have to discuss what makes them anxious, I usually ask them about what fears they may have about a nuclear war. Miss Taylor, a woman in her sixties, who said of herself, 'I'm a worrier. I've always been a worrier. I'm always getting myself worked up over something,' gave a typical answer. She said, 'I never think about it. If it happens, it happens. I never worry about it.'
'What do you worry about?'
'Myself. My concerns.'

This same attitude was what I found when I travelled in India in 1983 and asked my Indian friends what they worried about. Money was a great problem, and the government, and, most important, the burgeoning population. Friends in the Himalayas worried about the vanishing forests, and friends in Chandigarh worried about trouble in the Punjab and the threat from Pakistan. When I asked them how they felt about the threat of nuclear war they indicated that that was my problem. Nuclear war was something which belonged to Europe. That a nuclear war in Europe would, if nothing else, pollute the Indian atmosphere, that India was spending a great deal of money on what is euphemistically called a 'nuclear capability' and that Pakistan was well on the way to getting its own bomb were all matters which they could not worry about. They had more pressing concerns.

Many of the Americans whom I asked about their reactions to the nuclear threat were surprised at my question. It was not an issue which concerned them immediately. Their attitudes are reflected in the American media.

American newspapers, like the newspapers of all other countries, are more concerned with domestic rather than foreign news. On my last visit to the States the major domestic concern seemed to be the approaching Mother's Day. Every paper was filled with enormous advertisements for suitable presents for Mother, who was invariably presented as young, slim, beautiful and immaculate. Old, fat, ugly, untidy mothers apparently do not exist in America. I searched for the news between these advertisements and found some, but very little, to do with nuclear issues. In *USA Today* I was very taken with a story about the possibility of India exploding another test bomb in the Great Indian Desert. A map showed where the Great Indian Desert was, and an insert map showed where India was![7] It would not be necessary for an English newspaper to show where India was. The English would know. They would also know that the Great Indian Desert borders on Pakistan, and that Pakistan will not take kindly to India exploding a bomb there. Such an event will only spur the Pakistan government to increase its efforts to obtain the bomb.

The mental maps we carry in our heads are often very different from the geographical features of the real world. When I was talking to undergraduates at the University of Lincoln-Nebraska about the nuclear threat, one woman student said, 'Of course, you people in Europe worry about these things because you're much closer to where wars are being fought than we are.' I quickly checked my mental map of the world. I was sure that Lincolnshire, England, where I live is much further from Beirut and the border of Iraq and Iran than Lincoln, Nebraska, is from Nicaragua and El Salvador. (My copy of the *Readers' Digest Great World Atlas* shows that Lincoln, Nebraska, is about a thousand miles closer to Central America than my Lincolnshire village is to Lebanon.) A psychologist at Miami University, Oxford, Ohio, explained to me,

> 'People here think that nuclear war here will have nothing to do with them. Europe is a long way away. So is Central America. The newspapers here are very much to the Right. Anything to do with nuclear issues gets very little coverage. Just a small paragraph, nothing more. People here just don't know very much about it.'

When issues are presented by the media in America they seem to be wrapped in the general message which minimises the dangers or which assures that everything is going to be all right. I was surprised to see 'The Story of the Atomic Bomb' included in the Ripley *Believe It Or Not* programme.[8] I have been reading and, later, watching Ripley since I was a child, but I have never regarded it as a source of real knowledge. After all, the name tells you that you don't have to believe it. The required response to Ripley is simply, 'Amazing' or 'Gosh' or 'Fancy that'. You are not required to question, comment and remember. The programme on the atomic bomb showed, with original newsreel film, how the first atomic bomb was built and dropped on Hiroshima. The greater power of the atomic bomb over all other bombs in 1945 was described with solemn pride, the size of the destroyed city was stressed, and one scarred victim and the shadow of a person vapourised in the blast were shown, but nothing was said to draw attention to the extent of human suffering the bomb caused, or to the fact of how small the first bomb was in comparison with present bombs, or to the issues of life and extinction which now face the human race. Instead, the film ended with the confident voice of the presenter saying, 'August 6, 1945 marked the start of the atomic age' in the same way as he could have said, '1940 marked the start of the antibiotic age'.

An article in *Science Digest*, a journal clearly devoted, like the *Readers' Digest*, to making us feel happier and more secure, purported to show that 'as missile accuracy increases, nuclear arsenals shrink, and the twin menaces of fallout and nuclear winter recede.'[9]

The author of the article, Robert Jastrow, described how the emerging technology of computer-guided missiles 'make the Pershing 2 ten times more accurate than any other American or Soviet missile now in the field. The precision of the Pershing 2 warhead is a revolutionary advance – a quantum leap – in missile development.' He argued that,

> Nuclear weapons – especially large weapons – are very undesirable from a military point of view. In fact, some experts believe they are not militarily usable at all. If used on the battlefield, nuclear weapons tend to contaminate the terrain and prevent the occupying troops from advancing. If employed in 'surgical' ICBM attacks against military sites, they generate radioactive fallout that kills innocent civilians. If used in large numbers against cities, they stir up great clouds of radioactive dust that can poison the lands of the attacking army. And there is the specter of nuclear winter.
>
> So, for all these reasons, if nuclear weapons are not needed, they will not be used. The major powers will always keep some large nuclear weapons in reserve as a deterrent to genocidal missile attacks on their cities. But every truly military task that is assigned today to a nuclear block-buster – the destruction of a missile silo, a command post, a fuel depot or an ammunition dump – will be assigned in the future to a smart warhead carrying a very small charge of nuclear explosive. Eventually, as the first generation of smart warheads evolves into second and third generations, and accuracies improve from dozens of yards to yards and then to feet, the small nuclear weapon may give way to an ordinary charge of TNT. These changes will not eliminate war, but they hold the promise of delivering the world from the threat of a nuclear holocaust.

What Robert Jastrow seems to be overlooking is that so long as nuclear weapons exist, the threat of a nuclear holocaust exists. He also overlooks the fact that, while an infallible computer has yet to be invented, human error is with us always. Like the man in the Feiffer cartoon, he prefers the illusion of happiness to truth.[10]

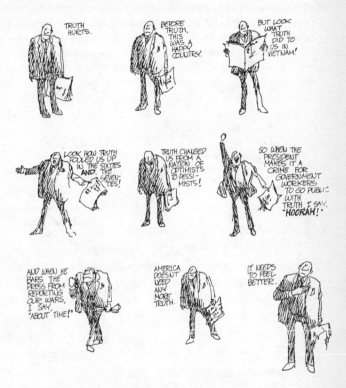

I asked my friend Stephanie who lives in South Africa how she managed to live with the threat of nuclear war. She wrote to me and said,

'Last year, when I saw members of my family in England, I was astonished to hear that the younger members do not expect to live beyond 50 (and expect to spend that time unemployed, despite academic and other training). I was filled with guilt. Despite the fact that I am one of the very few people in this country who listens to the World Service regularly, who reads the

Listener, the *Sunday Times* and the *New Scientist* (although usually many weeks after publication) the threat never seemed very real to me. Most people do not listen and do not read anything but what the South African Broadcasting Commission and local newspapers put out. The SABC is a government organ, while the newspapers, though excellent, are so bound by rules that they have to be very careful what they print. When I returned from England, gloomily full of the nuclear threat, people I spoke to said they were grateful to be so far south on the tip of this large continent. None seemed to have any notion of the effect of a holocaust on our country – imagining perhaps that the northern hemisphere might disappear without trace while we continued as normal, which of course is impossible because, apart from anything else, of our dependence on gold as a source of income.

'The reason why the nuclear threat seems so remote is that we have so many other things to worry about. The atmosphere is always tense and fearful, and all whites are overcome with guilt. This shows itself in various ways – unspeakably selfish and undisciplined driving on the roads, by whites, and increasingly by members of other races now that trucks and buses are all driven by the latter and now that they are increasingly able to afford private vehicles. The road accident rate, exacerbated by excessive consumption of alcohol, is enormous, to the extent that we now have slots on our horrible television about drinking and driving, and courtesy and care while driving. It is shown by manic spending, luxury living among whites, and rashes of fraud, embezzlement, etc. on a grand scale. It is shown by the ownership of firearms and a terrible jumpiness and fear which results in accidental deaths and a good many suicides (often embellished by fathers killing wives and children before killing themselves). In a different way this "millenium psychology" is demonstrated by the sudden mushrooming of evangelical "born again" movements popping up all over the place, building huge complexes (with shops, sport facilities, saunas, etc) and attracting thousands of mainly white adherents. One sees them all over town, with fish symbols on their cars and often the fish worked into the notices over places of business. Every week they put huge advertisements into the paper promising miracles, signs following healings and proclaiming that Jesus wants you to be successful in business. One of the slogans is that it is not what you do but who you know (i.e. you should be a member of the Jesus old boys' association) that matters. As a result of this terrifying manifestation the established churches are competing and the charismatic wings of most of them are growing very fast.

The fear is of being swamped by blacks, and of having to pay for what has been done to them over the centuries . . . I think a lot of the fear and tension arises from people knowing they have done wrong (by voting for the new constitution which excludes the blacks from government and restricts them to the 'homelands') and burying their heads hoping against hope.

I could go on and on. But you see, like everywhere else, we are warped and torn here by fear and tension about things happening on our own doorstep. It is no wonder that the nuclear threat either seems mercifully remote or else is seen as a final straw "too ghastly to contemplate" which would blow everyone's minds if it were added to everything else. I imagine that the film *The Day After*, now showing in our cinemas, seems like S.F. and is lumped with *Star Wars* as a sort of fantasy.'[11]

from *Beyond a Joke* by Brick, Spokesman 1983[12]

Even so, there is evidence to show that, with the help of Israel, South Africa has acquired and tested nuclear weapons.[13] Brick's cartoon could now be reversed to show the Southern Hemisphere disappearing.

In 1984 I proved to myself that the world is round and not all that large. In July of that year I boarded a plane and flew east. I kept on boarding planes and flying east (with a few excursions north and south) and eventually arrived back home. On the way I talked with many people.

In Hong Kong those people whose attention was not completely taken up with family matters or by the necessity to pass examinations focused solely on 1997, the date when the English mandate ends and China takes over the colony. Nuclear matters concerned them as much as their massive pollution of their air and water, that is, not at all. As a psychologist colleague there said to me,

> With respect to your interest in gathering material about the threat of nuclear warfare, I wonder if you will find much concern here. The 'public' obsession is what happens to Hong Kong in 1997. There are thousands of people here who have had personal experience of that euphemism 'conventional warfare' in China or Indo-China, and who find global destruction beyond the range of convenience of their construct system.[14]

On a very short visit to south China I asked my guide, a young woman, how she felt about the nuclear threat. She said that for her there was no problem. There was some danger in north China, but there in the south she felt quite safe. What she had to worry about was improving her English and getting a better job.

In Singapore I was told, 'We are too busy making money to worry about a nuclear war.' The concern with making money in Singapore is not so much a greed to amass possessions as a social requirement to be able to buy a home in a country where housing is very expensive and to work hard in a country where age and infirmity is a responsibility of care by relatives and not by the state, and where a disinclination to work is seen as a most reprehensible lack of moral fibre. The country's enemies whose presence helps to cohere this multi-lingual, multi-racial society are seen as not far away – the Vietnamese who may sweep down the Malay peninsula and, out of envy and spite, wrest from the citizens the fruits of their labours. The social climate of Singapore, in response to government policy, forces people to work for the future rather than enjoy the present. Living life like this, most people would find it very hard to contemplate a future where there was no future and all one's work was wasted.

Now in the Land of Oz a joke is being told, 'There was a nuclear war, but they forgot to bomb Australia.' This joke combines the secure belief in 'The Lucky Country', 'She'll be right, mate,' with the anxiety that where it is all happening is somewhere else. This anxiety is partly envy and partly the fear of being patronised, dismissed as 'mere colonials'. There is also the anxiety that what is happening is too complex for Australians to understand, and there is the anxiety that life is not as simple and straightforward as it ought to be. Mickie de Stoop, who does a very popular phone-in programme on Radio 2GB, Sydney, told me of the anger and abuse her one session on the nuclear threat provoked, so much so that she was not keen to repeat the exercise. Australia has some of the world's largest uranium deposits, and in the pre-emptive reasoning of many Australians, to be against the mining of uranium is to be anti-American, and to be anti-American is to be pro-Russian, a 'Commie ratbag'.

Living in Fiji should be like being in heaven, but it isn't. After Captain Cook had found Fiji (the Fijians living there might protest that it wasn't lost, but to no avail) the British benevolently took it into their Empire and proceeded to exploit it. When the Fijians proved reluctant to undertake the arduous work needed in the sugar plantations the British brought in Indians, and then, following the Empire's precept of 'divide and rule', encouraged the Indians and the Fijians to maintain their separate identities and their differences. The principle of 'divide and rule' is enshrined in the country's present constitution (in their parliament, 20 seats for Fijians,

20 for Indians and 12 for general electors) and, while the two peoples live peaceably side by side (intermarriage is rare) trouble, so some citizens of Fiji told me, will come in the next ten years over who owns the land and who will have work. So their government points to Russia as the enemy and bans all contact with the USSR. Though there is some anxiety about the Japanese dumping nuclear waste in the Pacific, and some resentment against the French ('a lot of Fijians died liberating the French') for nuclear testing at Mururoa and Fagataufa Atolls, the danger is seen as Russia, but a mysterious danger, since, 'here no one has seen what a Soviet looks like'. Meanwhile the indigenous trees vanish for firewood, the goats and the sacred cattle nibble at the dry grass, the newly planted pine trees promise quick money but fail to hold the precious rainwater, while the mountains lie like dying lions.

I was in Mexico on September 1, the date when the President makes his *Informe*, his report to the nation. This year the news was good. The end of the financial crisis was in sight (never mind that to earn the approbation of the international banks the poor in Mexico, who number 42 per cent of the population, had to become poorer, and that rich Mexicans were still getting their pesos out of the country). Things could only get better. Financial stability would match social stability. After all, as I was told, 'Mexico has had its revolution'.

But revolution is not far away from Mexico, revolutions and counter-revolutions in which Russia and the US take a keen interest. It is this interference which Mexicans fear. There is the fear of 'conventional' warfare where competing nations supply more and more dangerous forms of chemical warfare. There is the fear that the US government, having failed to learn from their experience in Vietnam will try to end all conflict in Central America 'once and for all' and resort to nuclear weapons.

Many Mexicans, having to deal with the daily problems of inflation, unemployment and poverty, and, in Mexico City, the problems of increasing numbers of people, inadequate housing, too many cars, poor roads, an insanitary water supply, floods in the rainy season and dust in the dry, look no further than these for their worries. But some, especially the young, educated people, view the future with alarm. Alicia Hammer, of Fondo de Cultura, told me, 'So many of the young people feel there is no point in studying or working for a career or marrying. They feel they have no future.'

Such a future may combine with the fatalistic view of life which Eileen Haley told me she finds in her students at an agricultural college. We discussed the ecological problems in Mexico, and she commented that the students 'don't see themselves able to band together to do something'.

In the National Arts Museum in Mexico City is a painting by Jose Maria Velasco of the view a hundred years ago from the Shrine of the Virgin of Guadalupe looking across a grassy plain to the small town that Mexico City then was, and beyond that a lake and the peaks of Ixtaccihuatl and Popocatepetl. Now the city has engulfed the Shrine in its houses, traffic and smog and stretches far to the south. I climbed the Latinamerica Tower and looked out over Mexico City. It reminded me of the setting of Hiroshima – a flat plain of a city surrounded by high mountains – but not just a city vulnerable to nuclear destruction; it was already being destroyed by its self-generated pollution.

So, all over the world, people are busy worrying about their own immediate concerns (and they have plenty to worry about) rather than face the stark truth that these concerns, like their lives, are in peril. It is always easier to worry over small matters than large. This can be a sensible thing to do, so long as we still acknowledge the existence of the large concern. But if we deny the large concern then we are in trouble.

Just what kind of trouble we get in may depend on how we experience our existence and how we fear our annihilation. By 'annihilation' I do not mean nuclear annihilation. In a nuclear war we die, and we can fear that kind of death as we fear every other kind of death. However, to die we have to live, to become a person and to have a place in the continuity of life. For each of us there is something far worse than death, the mere death of a body. It is the annihilation of the whole person, a wiping out, a negation of the individual. We know that this can happen and our body stay alive. All of us came close to experiencing this kind of annihilation when we were small children, when the adults around us ignored, humiliated, punished, betrayed, and abandoned us. We all experienced these things to some greater or lesser extent. We fought back, protecting ourselves by devising all kinds of defences which then became our characteristic ways of behaving. Some of us survived with a strong sense of our own identity and with confidence in our ability to protect ourselves in flexible ways from threats of annihilation. Some of us survived, but with a sense of not quite knowing who we were and with a system of defence whose rigidity precluded an easy adaptation to adult life. Some of us were virtually annihilated in childhood and grew up as 'as if' characters, people who feel that they are nothing but playing roles which other people expect of them, an act without an actor.

Just as we know what this kind of annihilation is we also know what our sense of existence is. We rarely put such knowledge into words, indeed, it is very hard to find the right words to express such knowledge, but it underlies every choice we make. We know that for every moment of our lives we have to create our existence by finding the conditions which allow us to exist and by avoiding the conditions which will annihilate us. But to maintain a sense of continuity in ourselves and to see the world as having a reality and solidity on which we can depend we have to forget the fact that we create ourselves and the world in which we live. Such forgetting is necessary for day-to-day living, even though we know quite well that no two people are the same and each person sees the world differently.

When I am trying to find out why a person behaves as he does I always try to find some way of discovering how that person experiences his existence and fears his annihilation. For instance, a woman, Cheryl, was telling me about the argument she and her husband were having over their car. He wanted to buy a new, expensive car, and she wanted to keep the car they had. She said, 'He always wants a new car every year. It's not as if new cars get that much better each year, but they always cost more. It's such a waste.'

The way she said 'waste' made me feel that this related to something important and was not just a passing comment. I asked, 'Why is it important not to waste money?'

'Of course it's important,' she said, 'we're not poor but we're not all that well off. John just doesn't know how careful I've got to be. He leaves all the money matters to me. He doesn't realise how difficult it is to make the money go round.'

'Why is it important to make the money go round?'

'Well, I've got to look after the family. The children need so many things, and I want the children to have a good life.'

'And why,' I asked, 'is it important for the children to have a good life?'

'I want them to have a better life than I had. I didn't have much of a childhood. My mother never spent money on me, only the bare necessities, never bought me a present, anything. I know she was short of money, but she could have, sometimes, bought me a present, just something to show she loved me.'

'That's why you want to have money to buy your children things – to show that you love them?'

'Yes.'

'Why is it important to show your children that you love them?'

'So they'll love me, of course. That sounds terrible, doesn't it? I suppose they should love, without me giving them things, but that's what I feel. I couldn't bear them to hate me the way I hated my mother.'

'Why is it important for your children to love you?'

Cheryl looked at me as if to say, 'What a stupid question!' but out of politeness she struggled to find an answer. 'So we're all together, a family, so I'm near them. I couldn't bear it if they didn't love me.'

'What would happen to you if your children didn't love you, if your family didn't want you or if something happened to them and they disappeared?'

She was horrified. 'Oh, I couldn't bear that. I can't bear being on my own. I've always got to have someone with me, even if it's only the cat. I couldn't be on my own. It's unthinkable.'

What Cheryl was saying here was that she experienced her existence as being part of a group. Any event which threatened to expel her from the group and to isolate her threatened her whole existence. It could annihilate her. Thus every choice she made, from deciding how much to spend on the weekly groceries to putting up with an aggravating husband and selfish children was based on her knowledge that she could exist only as part of a group. Isolation would be a fate far worse than death.

In contrast to Cheryl is my colleague Mick McHale. Mick is a Nurse Therapist and we occasionally talk together about his work. One day he asked my advice about one of his clients. This man was showing the symptoms of Huntington's chorea and Mick was wondering whether the client should be told this. Such knowledge would have tremendous implications for the man and his family.

Mick said, 'It would make a lot of sense to him if I could explain to him what's going on.'

I asked, 'Do you think it's important for him to be able to make sense of it?'

'I think so.'

'The way you said "make a lot of sense" sounds as though that's very important for you.'

'Yes, it's very important. It helps give me a sense of direction and cuts down on some of the confusion, so I know where I'm going.'

'Why is it important to know where you're going?'

'If I don't know where I'm going I get confused and chaos seems to reign in my life and I find that very uncomfortable.'

'What would happen to you if chaos reigned in your life?'

'It's difficult to imagine, because throughout my life I've always tried to gain order, but the thought is so terrifying that, the sense of confusion, I'd be so desperate, I'd just want to opt out, if there was that much confusion and chaos, and I knew I couldn't sort it out, I'd kill myself.'

'You spoke of having a sense of direction. Why is that important?'

'If I have a sense of direction then I can achieve something, and then people pat me on the head and tell me what a good boy I am and that makes me feel good.'

'Why is it important to have people pat you on the head and say what a good boy you are'

'It makes me feel wanted and loved.'

'Suppose there was no one to pat you on the head would you still go ahead and do those things or would you lapse into chaos?'

'In the short term I'd go on, hoping they might change. In the long term, I'd do something I'd still get a pat on the head for. I'd just shift the focus. There's always somebody around who wants something done for them.'

'If there was nobody around at all would you still go on?'

'Yes, I could do that. Reward myself. Not so much fun.'

'That kind of striving for achievement – I always call that clarity – clarity as against chaos. Does that make sense to you?'

'Yes, very much.'

I then asked Mick which for him was the more real, his internal or external reality, what went on inside him or what went on around him.

He said, 'Internal reality is far more real. I tend to believe that far more than my external reality.' He went on to say that while he wanted approval when he did actually gain it it no longer meant anything to him. 'I think the difference is, if I've got things sorted out and I know when I've done a good job, I can reward myself, but if it's on the periphery of that, if I'm not sure whether I've done a good job or taken the right direction, then it's very important and I really appreciate it.'

'So getting approval makes things more clear for you.'

'Yes.'

Thus Mick showed that, while he did not depend on other people for his sense of existence, as Cheryl did, he needed other people for their approval and affirmation. Neither Cheryl nor Mick could live without other people. Nor can any of us.

Cheryl and Mick here illustrate the two ways in which people experience their existence and fear their annihilation. We could call them 'extrovert' and 'introvert', although these words are heavily loaded with other meanings. However, it does seem that the human race does divide into two groups, depending on how they perceive their internal reality (what goes on inside them – thoughts, feelings, images) and their external reality (what goes on around them). These differences can be described in different ways. Psychoanalysts describe the differences in terms of preferred methods of defence – extroverts prefer repression and introverts isolation – and the implications of this. An important measure on the Rorschach inkblot test is the balance between the actual characteristics of the blots (the colour and shading) and the fantastical characteristics imposed on the blots by the person looking at them (movement and texture). For instance, if you look at a blot and see, say, some red and yellow flowers you would be responding to the shapes and colours on the card you are holding in your hand. But if you look at a blot and see, say, some furry bears playing with a ball, the movement of the bears and the impression of the fur would be your response to something inside you. The actual card in your hand is neither moving nor furry. A very different kind of psychological test, the Weschler Adult Intelligence Scale, was used by John Gittinger and his colleagues in the American Central Intelligence Agency to establish whether a person was an 'Internalizer' or an 'Externalizer'. On the basis of various ratios of scores on the sub-tests of the WAIS Gittinger developed an elaborate system of personality assessment which the CIA used to identify possible agents and to predict the behaviour of significant foreigners, for instance, how Krushchev would react in the Cuban missile crisis.[15] Then there is the vast body of work by Professor Hans Eysenck and his colleagues on extroversion and introversion (terms used earlier by Jung). Extroverts and introverts, according to Eysenck, are born that way, with extroverts needing a certain amount of external stimulation to keep their nervous system functioning efficiently, while introverts need to keep external stimulation at a low level so as not to overload an already active system. These neurological differences show very clearly in the way people behave and can be measured by tests as simple at Eysenck's famous EPI.

Of course, none of these various theories gives a complete explanation of the complex ways in which people, be they extroverts or introverts, behave, but what these theories do is to testify to the existence of the phenomena – that people tend to have a preference for attending to one reality rather than the other – and to demonstrate that any phenomenon can be described and evaluated in a multitude of ways.

It seems that we discover very early in life whether we are an extrovert or an introvert, although we may never hear these words or apply them to ourselves. What we discover very early is how we experience ourselves, how we know our own identity.

The poet Elizabeth Bishop described how, three days before her seventh birthday, she was sitting in a dentist's waiting room.

There were others waiting, two men and a plump middle-aged lady, all bundled up. I looked at the magazine cover – I could read most of the words – shiny, glazed, yellow and white. The black letters said FEBRUARY 1918. A feeling of absolute and utter desolation came over me. I felt . . . myself. In a few days it would be my seventh birthday. I felt I,I,I, and looked at the three strangers in panic. I was one of them too, inside my scabby body and wheezing lungs. 'You're for it now,' something said. How had I got tricked into such a false position? I would be like that woman opposite me who smiled at me so falsely once in a while. The awful sensation passed, then it came back again. 'You are you,' something said. 'How strange you are, inside looking out. You are not Beppo, or the chestnut tree, or Emma, you are you forever. It was like coasting downhill, this thought, only much worse, and it quickly smashed into a tree. Why was I a human being?[16]

I had a similar experience and wrote about it,

I recall that one day when I was six or seven I was walking home from school along a hot, dusty road, and, just at the point where the road divided, the realization came to me that I was I. I stood there in the heat and dust and marvelled at my discovery. I told no one – I was already aware of the necessity of shielding myself from adult laughter – but the knowledge and certainty of me as me became my central core which was often troubled but never shaken or destroyed by the turbulence and uncertainty that my later life was to bring. Nowadays, when somebody says to me 'I don't know who I am', or 'I

*am empty – I only exist in other people's eyes', or 'I don't
know whether I'm angry or not', I can accept such
statements as another person's truth, but I wonder to
myself, 'How can you not know yourself?'*[17]

When my sister Myra read this she wrote to me,

*Where you said how you discovered that you were you, I
remember something like that happening to me when I
was a child. I would have been 8 or 9 because I was
wandering home, alone, from Glebe School, and I was
thinking, 'What am I? What exists beyond this world?'
and I felt more alone than I could ever imagine it was
possible to feel. I didn't know who I was. I felt inside me
an emptiness bigger than the universe. It was so
overpowering. I could take you to the spot where I was
standing. Of course the feelings cannot be recalled, but
the occasion I have never forgotten.*[18]

The difference in how my sister and I each experience our
existence is easily seen in the ways we have lived our lives. I
have been engaged in a search for greater clarity while my
sister has created and kept around her a large family.

Along with our discovery of our existence comes our discovery of death. Children discover this quite early through the
deaths of pets or grandparents, or just through the unspoken
implications of parental injunctions like, 'Don't ride your bike
on the road'. When we discover death we have to give it a
meaning, and only two meanings are possible. Either it is the
end of my identity or it is a doorway to another life. Of course,
'another life' can be interpreted in a multitude of ways, but
the question remains, 'Does death mean the end of my existence?' We each give an answer, yes or no, to this question, and
then we have to find a way of living comfortably with our
answer. If we believe that our identity ends in death we have
to come to see our life as in some way satisfactory. If we
believe that we continue in our existence after death in some
other world (or return to this one in another form) we see this
future life as setting certain standards for this life and so we
have to live this life in terms of the next.

Whether we are extroverts or introverts we can interpret

our death in ways which make us feel secure or terrified. Introverts who see death as the end of their identity, who feel that they have achieved much of what they set out to achieve, who, holding their identity securely, are not constantly frightened of losing it, come to accept their own death. Extroverts who see death as the end of their identity, who know themselves to be a secure and loved member of a group to which they have made a lasting contribution can face death with equanimity. Both extroverts and introverts who see death as the end of their identity can accept their death if they can see something of themselves continuing in the world, through love of others, through children and through their work. But believing that death is the end of identity can be terrifying to both introverts and extroverts. An introvert can feel bitter and resentful at the swift passing of time when nothing has been achieved and no clarity gained but chaos increased. Death can be seen as the ultimate chaos. An extrovert who feels empty, barely knowing who 'I' is, fears death as the wiping out of this tenuous hold on the self.

Similarly, believing in some sort of life after death can mean courage or despair for both extroverts and introverts. An introvert who feels that he is living this life in accordance with the precepts of the next can feel confident that after death he will move to higher planes of achievement, authenticity and personal clarity. An extrovert who knows himself to be a secure member of a group can look forward to death as a reunion with loved ones. But equally an introvert can fear the afterlife as the chaos of Hell and an extrovert as the separation from loved ones.

And this marks yet another horror which a nuclear war will bring. *Physical survival after a nuclear war will be accompanied by the annihilation of the personal sense of existence.* For introverts the chaos of the post-nuclear world will mean the loss of all the careful planning and control built up over a lifetime (however brief) of trying to develop clarity and authenticity of themselves and understanding of the world about them. A nuclear war will destroy all that. For extroverts it will be separation from the group, the destruction of most, if not all, of the people through whom extroverts experience and create their own existence. A nuclear war will take away from the survivors of that war those elements of life which create and maintain a sense of our own existence. Survival will be a living death, an annihilation of the self. (This will apply equally to our leaders, safe in their nuclear bunkers, and the rest of us, taking our chance above.)

We all know this, though we may not admit that we know it, so when we come to deny that we are threatened by a nuclear war we make a double denial – a denial that we fear death, ordinary bodily death, and a denial that we fear annihilation of our identity in chaos or isolation. Such a double denial is more than doubly dangerous.

An example of just how dangerous it is was given by Patricia who came to see me about the panic she felt whenever she had an ache or pain. She immediately imagined the worst – that this was the start of cancer or some other fatal disease. These morbid thoughts remained with her night and day, preventing her from living an ordinary life. Nothing her doctor could say to her would reassure her.

Yet, terrible though these fears were, they concerned only undiagnosed illness. Once an illness was diagnosed, she believed, it could be cured. 'They cure cancer nowadays, don't they?' she said. It was the unknown illness which terrified her.

Venturing to use a word which she wished to avoid, I asked her whether she saw her death as the end of her identity or as a doorway to another life. She said she wasn't sure. She hoped there might be a heaven but she lacked the faith that it was so. Perhaps death was simply and terrifyingly the swallowing up of her identity.

I asked her whether she worried about a nuclear war. 'I never think about it,' she said, 'I never read a newspaper article about it or anything to do with politics. I think it's boring. Politics are boring. When people talk about it I don't know what they're talking about.'

It was not that she did not read. She read fiction, biography, magazines and the daily paper. Our local paper frequently carried stories to do with nuclear issues, both political and scientific, written by a journalist much concerned with the threat of nuclear war, and, as Lincolnshire is dotted with air bases, the paper reported a good deal of social news from these. So to read this paper and avoid all stories which have any connection with the threat of nuclear war required some skilled selective attention.

Panic at the thought of the possibility of a fatal illness is fairly common – or at least many such people come my way. As we talk I try to find out what meaning these panics and morbid fears carry. The implication which the person is often reluctant to put into words is that the undiagnosed illness will lead to death. For Patricia, as it is to all the people I have met with these kinds of fears, death meant leaving her family behind. This would be terrible, not only because she would be alone, but because her family would be upset by her death, and if there is one thing she could not bear it was the thought that she might have upset someone. If she upset people they would reject her and then she would be alone, and, being alone, would disappear. Of course, if her family loved her they would be upset at her death. If they were not upset it would mean that they did not love her and that she was alone and facing annihilation. If there was an afterlife and she looked back on the family she had left behind, she would see that either she had upset them by dying, or that they, not loving her, were not missing her at all. Either eventuality meant for her annihilation. And, of course, if death meant the end of her identity then that too would be the annihilation she feared.

Another implication of the panics Patricia felt was that she did not really trust her doctor. She would go to see him to tell him of her fears, and even as he assured her that her fears were groundless she knew that either he had missed some vital clue to a correct diagnosis or that he knew that she had a fatal illness but he was not telling her.

Patricia, experiencing her existence as being part of a group, fears isolation more than the threat of ordinary bodily death. She fears death in a nuclear war, and she fears surviv- al for she knows that it is unlikely that all the members of her family, husband, children, parents, parents-in-law, her sisters and their husbands and children, would survive in a targeted area where bunkers are provided for only the military and certain government officials. To ward off the fear of death she imagines surviving, and with that comes the terror of isola- tion. Moreover, she knows, as we all do, that the threat of nuclear war implies that those experts who should be looking after us are, like her doctor, either ignoring the danger signs or know the worst and are not telling us. That is, they are either fools or liars. It is terrifying to think that our lives are in their hands. Much better, then, to concentrate on the possibility of cancer or heart attack than on the threat of a nuclear annihilation, even though such a concentration of thought and energy on imaginary illnesses means endless anguish and the destruction of ordinary family life.

What Patricia's story shows is that denial costs. We can purchase some kind of peace by denying that we are in danger, but the price we pay far exceeds the value of what we get. Denial means the denial of reality, and that way madness lies. We may be denying what goes on around us – that our parents rejected us, or that our firm is going bankrupt, or that the airfield next to our home is a base for cruise missiles – or denying what is going on inside us – that we have never forgiven our parents for what they did, or that we resent the way our firm has used and will discard us, or that we are terrified of dying – and each act of denial, day by day, pushes us further and further away from reality, both our external and internal reality. Because we do not allow ourselves to see our external reality clearly we make stupid mistakes in dealing with it. Because we do not see our internal reality clearly we soon lose touch with who we are and we find ourselves being invaded by strange experiences – sleeplessness, nightmares, fatigue, physical pains and illnesses, sudden rages, devouring jealousy, inexplicable fears, obsessions, compulsions and addictions – all of which seem alien and uncontrollable. In the battle to keep from our consciousness all the unacceptable feelings and knowledge we can become very busy, taking on all kinds of extra work, making major issues out of minor problems, all busy, busy, too busy to be aware. When I read about the Newbury Ratepayers or the Women and Families for Defence, or the Survivalists I wonder how many of their members are engaged in a battle not so much against the untidiness of the Greenham Common women and the dangers of the Russian Menace as against their own despairing selves.

But then, not all of those who acknowledge the perils of nuclear war are uninvolved in denial. There is, so the psychoanalysts tell us, the process of unconscious denial, 'a split in the ego,' according to Fenichel,[19] 'into a superficial part that knows the truth and a deeper part that denies it.' This is the kind of thing that Liam Hudson meant when he was talking to me about how he denied to himself that he was in danger. He said, 'I just block it off. I think it's going to happen but not in my lifetime. I try not to think about it. My children think it's going to happen. They think all this business of joining the CND and going on marches is a waste of time. But I think that when they say it's going to happen they're just talking from their heads. Deep down they feel that they're going to be all right.'

Children who have never had to question the security of their family, whose experience of trouble and threat has always been that the family supported, protected and comforted them, can make a realistic assessment of their chances of living to old age, decide that the chances are slim, feel afraid, and yet not be overwhelmed by despair and terror, because they have the hope that the protection they have had in the past will continue into the future. Security gives them courage. But children who, like adults, know what it is to be in danger and alone, to be weak and helpless in the face of powerful terrors, know that the world is not to be trusted and that when destruction is threatened no help is at hand. Denial then becomes unconscious 'denial in fantasy'.

That we can have fantasies of which we are unaware, something that psychoanalysts talk about a great deal, seems to be a ridiculous idea. Yet we often show that we do by the way that we behave. One of the unconscious fantasies we all have is that we shall always go on existing. As Freud said, we cannot imagine ourselves not existing. We may consciously know that we shall die but unconsciously we deny it. We fantasise the world going on after our death and we are there, observing it. References to such fantasies can emerge in our conversation. I often find this in the workshops I run for health professionals on depression. I ask them how they see their death – is it the end of their identity or a doorway to another life. In such groups in England most of the people will say that they see death as the end of their identity. (The same question put to similar groups in America shows that belief in an afterlife is more common among American health professionals than among English health professionals.) We spend some time discussing what each person feels about this, and excellent reasons are advanced to support the view that a person's existence ends in death. Then I move on to another question. I ask, 'When you die, do you want to be buried or cremated?' Some people reply, 'It doesn't matter to me. I won't be there to know what's going on,' but others, people who were so sure that death meant the end, get into arguments about whether cremation is preferable to burial. They say things like, 'I wouldn't want to see myself buried. Graves have to be looked after, they look terrible all overgrown, and it's a big imposition to expect my family to keep it tidy the way I want', or 'I don't want to be cremated – what if you weren't dead and you were banging on the lid, trying to get out as the coffin went into the fire.' Such arguments reflect the fantasies that have been created to deny death – fantasies about approving or disapproving of the arrangements made for the funeral, about continuing relationships with relatives involving obligations and responsibilities, fantasies that the supposition of death is a mistake – the actor shot in the play rises to take the curtain call, the report of my death was an exaggeration, a mistake – but can I trust my family to find out in time? Fantasies, whether conscious or unconscious, do not always end happily. They do not always make us feel more secure and comforted. Sometimes fantasies can cause us to see greater, even more terrible terrors. Consciously we may accept the knowledge that we face extinction in a nuclear war, but unconsciously we may deny it just as consciously we may deny our own death, and to do this we create fantasies about our own superior power or of some external superior power which will protect and support us. Sometimes we give expression to these fantasies in a passionate interest in science fiction, or stories about huge disasters where we can identify with the powerful heroes and saviours and with the people who are saved. Sometimes we give expression to these fantasies by developing religious or mystical beliefs which promise perfect happiness and security.

Comforting though these stories and beliefs may be, reality is different and may force itself upon us to remind us that it is so. Disasters do occur, but Charlton Heston is not always there to drag us back from the earthquake's brink or to seize the controls of the damaged plane. Reminders of death, our death and the death of our loved ones, are around us every day. Simple denial, saying, and believing, that something isn't so, can only be effective when the processes of perception and memory are little developed, as in a small child. Once we have developed to any extent the ego functions of perception and memory ('I see and hear, and I remember') we have to create more complex forms of denial.

All the mechanisms of defence which Freud described (repression, isolation, projection, reaction formation, suppression, undoing) are all forms of denial, different ways of insisting that something that is isn't so. To some extent we all use, at some time or other, all the mechanisms of defence, but we each have our favourite mechanisms. Some people favour repression, a forgetting of painful feelings and events. Whole stretches of a person's life can disappear into the blackness of forgetting, leaving the person with a sense of a briefer life than that which has actually been lived. When a client says to me, at our first or second meeting, 'I had a perfectly happy childhood. I don't remember much about it,' I know that we have a long hard slog ahead of us to retrieve, face, accept and re-assess the painful events of childhood. Alternatively, isolated events, or the feelings belonging to an event, can be forgotten, so that what is remembered seems patchy and illogical. But repression, like all the mechanisms of defence, is never more than partially successful at keeping at bay what is painful and unacceptable. What is repressed can break through as itself or in disguise.

I was reminded of this when Kitty came to see me recently. Some four years before we had talked together for several months, and I wrote of her then,

> Kitty came to see me because she was so very anxious. It became apparent that she had much to worry about.
> Not only did she fear all the ordinary hazards of life, but every hazard was viewed in its extremity – every

journey would end in disaster, every illness would prove fatal. She said, 'When things are going smoothly, when things go right, I always worry that they're going to go wrong. Why am I so special that it wouldn't happen to me? I always think these things could happen to me. For as long as I can remember I've always expected things to go wrong. If you look forward to something, it's often a let-down.' Moreover, for Kitty, everything had to be perfect. Curtains must hang in exact folds, every garment must be flawless, children should behave themselves. As life is more full of potential danger than it is of actual perfection, Kitty lived in a constant state of fear and anger. Such a state is not conducive to good health, and so she suffered from frequent ailments, all of which she interpreted as leading to some terrible illness and death. 'I'm frightened of dying,' she said, 'I don't want to be left on my own.'[20]

Since that time Kitty had managed very well, including a difficult period when she had to look after her three young sons and baby daughter while her Air Force husband was in the South Atlantic during the Falklands war. Now she wanted to talk to me because, having survived all that, she was suddenly reduced to a state of extreme anxiety by an impending move of their home to another Air Force base. She thought that one talk with me would help sort this out.

It was not just the anxiety which troubled her. It was her temper, the violent rages which would come upon her, triggered by some trivial misdemeanour by one of the children. As we talked I wondered how much she worried about the possibility of a nuclear war. The first cruise missiles had been delivered to Greenham Common USAF base only two weeks before. I asked her what she felt about this. She said, 'I watched them arriving on television and it didn't mean anything to me. It just doesn't seem to have anything to do with me.' For someone whose vivid imagination could create a terror out of the most benign situation to contemplate the implications of basing the cruise missiles in England and not feel fear, if not for herself then for her children, a massive work of repression would have to take place. But for Kitty such repression was not entirely successful. She described, with much shame and guilt, her violent and irrational rages when some aspect of her neat and orderly home was disturbed. The subjects of her rage were her young sons who let danger into her house by failing to keep their bedrooms tidy. Poor boys. Poor Kitty.

But what could Kitty do if she allowed her fear of a nuclear war to become conscious? All the other fears she expresses she knows her doctor, her down-to-earth husband and her friends will be able to limit, if not abolish, with their sensible comments. They can say, with absolute certainty, 'Of course you haven't got cancer', but they can't say with similar certainty, 'There won't be a nuclear war'. Indeed, her husband's work is a statement about the necessity for preparing for a nuclear war. Of course he does not show any fear. As a member of the Armed Forces he has learned to deal with his anxieties by using the defence of isolation.

In the defence of isolation the emotions which are aroused by a certain situation are detached from the event and not experienced. This is a defence which is essential for survival. When we have to deal with a crisis or to carry out some task where calmness and efficiency are needed, we have to be able to detach ourselves from the powerful emotions which, if expressed, would prevent us from dealing with our task efficiently. But this does not mean that the emotions have disappeared forever. They have simply been held in abeyance, and their effects will be felt one way or another. I am a masterful exponent of the defence of isolation. In a crisis I am tremendously calm, sensible and efficient. No running around like a headless chook or flying into a violent temper. But afterwards, when the crisis has abated and I am alone, I am overcome by feelings of exhaustion, anger, anxiety and despair in proportion to the seriousness of the crisis with which I had dealt so well. If I am wise I link these feelings to the crisis, but sometimes I don't want to face the implications of the crisis, and so I attach these painful feelings to something else and lead myself astray in trying to understand myself and my world. Thus a prolonged use of the defence of isolation can put a person increasingly out of touch with reality.

We often see this in doctors who during their training have had to learn to isolate certain feelings so they can carry out their medical and surgical procedures. Not allowing themselves to empathise with their patients, they lose their ability to empathise with their fellow human beings, but do not recognise this, and instead act with imperious disregard for the needs and feelings of the people around them. (Fortunately, some doctors recognise this danger and work hard to undo the effects of their training.) The prolonged use of the defence of isolation means the death of that part of the imagination which makes us human – our capacity to live not just inside ourselves but to imagine what it is to be another person from the inside looking out. It is this act of the imagination which stops us from killing one another. That is why soldiers have to be trained to ignore or to eradicate this capacity to imagine and to be human.

Giving up the ability to join with fellow human beings by empathising with them can have the compensation that one gains power over people. There are many people who prefer power to love. If there were not, where would we find our dictators and politicians, our soldiers and our police?

But, denial or not, what most people feel in the face of nuclear threat is helplessness. Phillip Hodson, a counsellor and broadcaster working in London, wrote to me to say,

As for your question about the bomb, a few people raise it with me, fewer than you might expect; many people express anxiety, but an even more alarming proportion express absolute resignation to what they feel is to be an abrupt and inevitable extinction within a matter of years.
They may be correct, but I deplore their apathy.[21]

Robert Lifton, who has done more than anyone to make us aware of the damage that nuclear war and the threat of nuclear war can do to us, pointed out that many people have retreated

to a position of apathy and numbness, a state I call 'waiting for the bomb'. The guilt in that stance is fended off in the form of resignation, 'If it happens then so be it. What could I do?' I think these apathetic people increase

their sense of helplessness to justify their inaction. The
ineffectual but safe position of resignation is less
threatening than the decision to act.[22]

But apathy is a denial of pain and helplessness is itself a
form of power, a way of forcing others to accept one's wishes.
For many of the people who feel helpless and apathetic the
wish is for death.

Chapter 3

'THERE'S NOTHING I CAN DO'

Death – your finger beckons to me
Your gentle voice whispers constantly in my ear,
Like a siren call from the deep you beguile me.
'Come to me, come to me,' you murmur.
Irresistibly I am drawn to your soft, nebulous shape,
Tempted to lay my head on your shoulder,
To surrender to your embrace.[1]

When I was visiting the University of Lincoln, Nebraska, recently I talked with an undergraduate class about how they saw the nuclear issues which confront them. Most of the students spoke rather diffidently of feeling frightened and helpless, but one girl spoke out strongly. 'I'm very angry,' she said, 'because this has been done to me. No generation makes the world it comes into, and this is what we've been given. I'm really angry that I'm threatened like this – that I mightn't have a future – I can't do anything about it right now but as soon as I can I will.'

Later I sat round a table with Professor Al Landfield and five graduate students and I asked them the same question. Margot, who had already had to face a life-threatening illness, spoke of the need to come to terms with death and of how she hoped her faith would help her deal with the fear that a nuclear war would make the human race extinct. She believed that there was something which could not be destroyed, even by a nuclear holocaust. John, an Episcopalian minister, spoke of how he had avoided the implications of the arms race by finding diversions which stopped him from thinking about it and how he had devised only short-term goals. But now he had two small children he had to plan an extended future which might not eventuate, and so he had to learn to live with the pain of this. Gerrard said, 'Our generation has always had the shadow of a nuclear holocaust over our heads.' He went on to say that he seemed to think of the future as if it wasn't there. Steve spoke of a fate he might not be able to avoid and Deanne of her feelings in a situation which was quite out of her control. Al, who had previously said to me, 'I think we'll survive by the skin of our teeth', now talked of his experience as a soldier in World War Two and said, 'I was angry with Hitler. I was able to kill others because I could find a target to get up my anger.' He contrasted his inability to be angry now with the anger expressed by the undergraduate who was angry with her elders for creating such a perilous world in which she had to live. Then Gerrard said, 'You know, what we're all expressing is despair. We're not facing this situation with anger. We've retreated into depression.'

Perhaps 'depression' was too strong a word to describe what we were feeling. I don't think that any of us gathered around that table had retreated into that painful isolation which distinguishes depression from unhappiness, but we were certainly not showing the anger which is the appropriate human response to threat. However, from the opinions expressed I could see that each person there could, if pressed, move to that set of interlocking attitudes which comprise the prison of depression.

The essence of the experience of depression is a sense of isolation, a peculiar and painful solitude where the person knows, intellectually, that he is in the company of other people but experiences himself as completely alone, trapped in some kind of prison. A person who is repressed can describe this prison in an image which is a metaphor (not a simile) of what the person is experiencing. One person might say, 'I am at the bottom of a black pit.' Another, 'I am immobilised by a heavy weight,' or, 'I am alone in an open boat on an empty ocean', or 'I'm in a maze of corridors. Each one ends in a door, and when I open it there's nothing there.'

The human race's history of torture shows that while some brave people can withstand the extremes of physical pain, the one form of torture which eventually destroys the strongest is isolation, a separation from all contact with other human beings for an indefinite period. To maintain our existence we need relationships with other people as much as we need air, food, water and shelter. Whether we are imprisoned by others or whether we imprison ourselves in depression, isolation tortures and eventually destroys us.

The isolation of depression is very common, found in all cultures and races. Literature from past centuries shows that depression is probably as old as the human race. Just how many people are depressed at any one time is hard to determine since many people do not reveal their suffering to others, but figures like one adult in five are given in research literature. A World Health Organisation study on 'depressive disorders in different cultures' has recently been completed.

> The prevention and treatment of depression was the aim of workers involved in this research, its *raison d'être* the realization that increasing numbers of people throughout the world are developing clinically recognisable depression, (in 1983 it is stated that 100 million will do so) because, the authors claim, more people are being exposed to stressful life events, there is an increasing morbidity from chronic organic disorders leading to somatogenic depressive reactions, and depression is on the increase due to the consumption of alcohol and certain drugs. Some of the increase is iatrogenic since the drugs responsible include sedatives and tranquillisers, most anti-hypertensives and various hormone preparations.'[2]

So it is that the drugs which are used to treat depression themselves add to the problem. When the anti-depressant drugs were first discovered in the late 1950s and early 1960s it was hoped that the incidence of depression would decrease dramatically in the way that the discovery of antibiotics reduced the incidence of infectious diseases. But this has not happened. What we have found is that the anti-depressant drugs, properly used, can work like aspirin helping to control the pain so that the person can go on with living and sort out what is causing the pain. The repeated application of large amounts of anti-depressants simply makes the person taking them too lethargic and confused to make any progress in understanding what has gone wrong so that the drugs themselves become part of the problem. The diazepam-based sedatives and tranquillisers can produce somnolence and a calming of anxiety for three or four weeks, but after that they create a powerful addiction which is extremely difficult to overcome. The withdrawal symptoms from these drugs can be more unpleasant and disturbing than the original symptoms for which the drugs were prescribed. Unfortunately, some doctors, having rung the changes on combinations of anti-depressants, sedatives, and the minor tranquillisers and having produced no change in their depressed patients, then prescribe the major tranquillisers, the chlorpromazines and phenothiazines. These drugs are quite effective in reducing the fear and the bizarre thoughts which the person is experiencing and so bringing the person somewhat close to reality, but in the long term they produce side-effects of considerable seriousness which have to be controlled by further drugs, and in the even longer term serious organic damage can occur. A person who is not psychotic and who takes any of the major tranquillisers undergoes a horrible experience. Immediately the drugs produce an inability to think clearly, a feeling of cotton wool in the head. Continued ingestion of these drugs produce a somnolent stupidity, difficulties in movement, and, with large or prolonged dosages specific and serious cognitive dysfunctions. Depressed people who are given major tranquillisers are thus prevented from dealing with the stress which has played such a large part in creating their depression and with reassessing themselves and their way of life.

The relationship between stressful events and depression has been demonstrated in what is now a large body of research literature.[3] Nevertheless, there are still psychiatrists who insist that depression is a physical illness caused by some metabolic changes themselves triggered off by some genetic predisposition. Some of the metabolic changes which take place while a person is depressed have been identified but no metabolic change or brain abnormality has been found which invariably precedes the onset of depression. It is not surprising that metabolic changes take place while a person is depressed. Being depressed is a very emotional experience, and all emotions are accompanied by metabolic changes. Psychiatrists who claim that the predisposition to depression is inherited can show a lack of that imaginative ability which enables us to understand other people. They draw family trees, mark the individuals who were depressed or committed suicide, and claim that the familial tendency to depression has been inherited, without considering how family members may have learnt to share certain attitudes and how, in the history of unhappy families, 'the sins of the fathers are visited on the children'. Professor George Winokur of the University of Iowa, in his book *Depression: the Facts*, gives as support for his view that depression is genetically inherited the families of Tolstoy, Mary Wollstonecraft and Ernest Hemingway! To see these families as ordinary, happy families where depression and suicide occur like diabetes requires a very limited empathetic imagination. But then Winokur does not claim anything different. As he said,

> I do not believe that I understand the mind any better than I did before going into psychiatry. What's more I do not believe my colleagues in psychiatry, no matter what they say, really understand motivation, or what makes a person behave or think as he does. Most of them say that they do but I do not believe them.[4]

No doubt there are psychiatrists like Professor Winokur who are informing our governments that all that is required to deal with cases of depression after a nuclear war is a supply of psychotropic drugs, and no doubt boxes of these drugs are being stored in the nuclear bunkers. However, pills do not take away the pain of perils and loss in this present world. They will certainly not reconcile the survivors of a nuclear holocaust to the loss of all they valued in their life.

Depression is, as Phillip Hodson said, *a vital learning mechanism, allowing feelings to catch up with events, a time when you realise with painful consciousness the vital discrepancy between the facts of life and your pretence about them.*[5] In ordinary life coming to face the facts of our lives – old age, death, loss, the breakdown of important relationships,

the failure or end of a career, disappointment and unappreci-
ated sacrifices – accepting their existence and becoming reconciled to them is extremely difficult and often only achieved
because there is someone to help – a friend, a therapist, a
priest – who is able to help only because he or she has the
courage to face the present and has hope and optimism for the
future. How many people will there be like this after a nuclear
holocaust? As a therapist now I can help a person deal with
the discrepancy between his pretences and the facts of this life
because I see the facts as, on the whole, bearable and capable
of hopeful change. But in a post-nuclear-war world I could
never see as bearable the fact that stupid men had destroyed
the world I loved. I have no store of wisdom which I could use
to deal with a post-nuclear-war world and neither has any
other therapist. Nor has any other person. No one has encountered and survived a post-nuclear-war world.

The pretences of which Hodson speaks are the ideas and
fantasies which we create to bolster up and protect ourselves
from a harsh reality which we feel threatens to destroy us. For
people who become depressed these ideas and fantasies are
based upon six beliefs which are held as axiomatic truths
which are rarely brought to consciousness and never ques-
tioned. They are:

1 No matter how good I appear to be, I am bad, evil, unacceptable to myself and to other people.
2 Other people are such that I must fear, hate and envy
   them.
3 Life is terrible and death is worse.
4 I am unreconciled to the past and hopeless about the
   future.
5 Anger is evil.
6 Never forgive.

Each belief has implications for how we deal with the
nuclear issue. The first belief, experiencing oneself as bad and
valueless rather than good and valuable is not only the
cornerstone of the prison of depression but also determines
how the person responds to the threat of extinction.

An American woman who has been very active in the
anti-nuclear movement for many years and who is now

teaching at an English university told me how angry she got with her students who believe that they are doomed to die in a nuclear war but who will do nothing to prevent this. Their reasons for this despondency she regards as illogical and inadequate. She said, 'I say to them, "If you saw someone you loved in danger of dying, wouldn't you do something to help them?"'

But what if you don't love anyone else? And what if you don't love yourself? Then you won't do anything to save yourself. You think that you don't deserve to be saved. Indeed, you may think that being destroyed is what you deserve, because no matter how hard you strive to be good, you are never good enough. You deserve punishment and death. There are many people who feel like this. They expect of life nothing but doom and disaster, and the nuclear threat serves only to confirm this. There is no point, they feel, in trying to avert an inevitable nemesis.

Felicity, one of the most delightful people I have ever met, was sent to me by her doctor because in her efforts to do her job perfectly (she excelled at her work) and to always meet the needs of all her relatives and friends (an impossible task) she had developed ulcers and migraine. Her doctor thought that I might be able to teach her to relax. As we explored why she had to meet these excessively high standards she spoke of how she knew herself to be such a bad person. She said,

'I feel soiled, dirty – I always feel I'm going to be punished. At work, if a police car arrives, I feel frightened. I think they're coming to arrest me. I know – intellectually – that I haven't done anything, but I want to hide in a cupboard until they're gone. If there's a letter and I don't know from the envelope whom it's from I think, "now I've been found out". I've always been unhappy. I expect that's what I'll always be – unhappy.'

There are many people who feel, like Felicity, that their essential being is irredeemably filthy. Many more experience themselves as invariably inadequate and unacceptable. Experiences of rejection, chaos, loss of control and helplessness can create in even the most assured and self-accepting person a sense of being soiled and disgusting, of little or no value. We do not cherish and strive to protect something which we perceive as soiled, disgusting and valueless.

A baby comes into the world feeling, unreflectively, quite pleased with itself. How is it that a baby, so many babies, lose this sense of worth and come instead to hate themselves so much that they will not strive to save themselves from destruction and, indeed, may actively participate in their own destruction and the destruction of others?

When we were children learning to define our world through the language we were learning we were also finding out how the people around us defined us – not just as 'little boy' or 'little girl' but as, if we were lucky, that we were loved, wanted, cared for, strong, beautiful and capable. If we were unlucky we found that we were unacceptable, of no value and no importance. If we had a mother who declared when her friends remonstrated with her for punishing her little daughter for a childish error, 'She's my daughter and I can do what I want with her,' then we might never learn to define ourselves as a person but only as an object to be used.

Sometimes well-meaning, loving parents make mistakes in how they define their children because they cannot see what conclusions a child can draw from what goes on around him. Elizabeth Kubler-Ross, talking on the BBC, told this story,

'The biggest problem when you work with dying children are the siblings. That is a terrible problem and it is hard to solve it. I had a couple in San Francisco who had a little boy with cancer and I made a house call. (We see all our patients in house calls.) A little brother sitting in the corner of the room was totally ignored. Nobody introduced him, nobody acknowledged him, nobody talked to him. There was one big fuss about this very adorable boy who had cancer, but the little brother was the only one who was in really bad shape internally. When I finished the house call I said: "I want you to walk me to the car." And his first reaction was, "Who me?" I said: "Yes, you. I want you to walk me to the car alone. I want to be alone with you". He was very proud. I mean, he really stood up and came to the door and the moment we were at the door he closed the door behind him. He got the message that this was his chance to be somebody, or to talk to somebody. And no sooner was the door closed than he said: "Dr Ross, I guess you know that I have asthma." He held my hand very tightly and looked at me sadly and said: "I guess that's not good enough." "Good enough for what? Tell me what's happening. How can I help you?" I asked. He said, "My brother gets absolutely everything. He was taken to Disneyland, he gets baseball stars signing baseball bats for him, he gets electric train sets, he gets absolutely everything. Anything he asks for he gets." And the previous day this little boy had asked his father for a football and the father was very angry with him and said: "You can't have it." The child dared to say: "How come?" and the father got mad at him and said: "Would you rather have cancer?"

'Do you understand that if we don't hear him now, this boy will become a typical hypochondriac, he will develop symptom after symptom each time he wants something; he knew that the sicker you are the bigger the toys and the bigger the gift and the bigger the need of the parents to buy things. You have to talk to the parents and make them see what damage they do to a sibling, that by the time the brother dies, he resents him so much that he will be left with more grief, with more guilt, with more shame and with more fear. And this boy already believes that he's only lovable if he gets a horrible illness like cancer.'[6]

A small child knows that he is dependent upon adults for his care and protection. To feel secure he needs to see these adults as good. If they behave in ways which suggest that they are not good then the child finds himself in a double jeopardy. Only a child who has confidence in himself can bear the threat of seeing that the people who should be caring for him are not good people, that they have deceived, humiliated, abandoned, unfairly punished him. Most children in this situation deal with it in the way that Feiffer's little girl did.[7]

Felicity is an example of Feiffer's little girl. She experiences herself as very bad. Her essential being she feels, so she told me, is soiled, ingrained with dirt which is inseparable from every part of her being. She works very hard and efficiently, but always has the feeling that at any moment someone will come and say, 'You have failed to do something very important.' She spends no more money on herself than she needs to keep herself decently clothed, housed and fed, but she always buys her friends and family lavish presents. She will have a good holiday each year, but only because after a year's hard work she feels that she has earned it. She would not buy herself something simply because she wanted it nor does she allow herself to do something simply for enjoyment. Even when she is working as hard as her conscience dictates she feels guilty. She is always guilty of sins of commission and omission.

One day she said to me, 'I don't sleep well. I find it hard to get off to sleep, and sometimes I wake up screaming. Sometimes it's justs a scream and sometimes I'm screaming for my sister. My husband says it's very loud. It scared him the first time he heard it. I don't know I'm screaming. I think I'm dead. I'm closed in and I'm terrified. It's a horrible feeling. My sister's not there. I'm calling her. I dream a lot about death.'

We talked about being locked in. Felicity could not remember being locked in by herself, but she could remember how her father would lock her and her sister in the house while he went to work. This was after her mother had left the family and he was looking after his daughters. Then Felicity remembered how when her youngest sister was born he had taken the older sister with him to visit his wife and new baby and had left Felicity alone, locked in the house.

'I was terrified,' she said. I talked about how frequently small children get locked up – sometimes as a punishment by adults and sometimes in a teasing game by older children. The fact that in her dream she was calling her sister for help suggested that perhaps it wasn't her sister who had locked her in. 'If anyone did any locking in,' she said, 'it would be that I had locked my sister in.' She then remarked that both her parents were strong disciplinarians.

Being locked in an enclosed space – a room or a cupboard – could be that profound experience which forces a small child to construe herself as bad. Imagine a little girl, no more than four or five, who suddenly finds that her mother is very angry with her. Perhaps she has broken a cup, or left some clothes lying on the floor, and this has made her mother very angry, or perhaps her mother is very angry and the little girl does not know why. Then suddenly she finds her mother grabbing her and pushing her into a dark cupboard. The door is closed and the key turned. The little girl is alone in the dark.

The mother knows that the little girl will come to no harm in the cupboard. Perhaps she put the little girl in the cupboard because she thought that was better than hitting the child. Perhaps she prided herself on never hitting her children, or perhaps she was afraid of hitting the child and, being unable to control her rage, of killing her. Whatever the reason, from her adult point of view, the cupboard was safe and the child would be there for a limited time.

But the little girl does not know this. She does not know whether she will ever be released. Perhaps her mother has gone away and left her. Perhaps she will never get out. Perhaps she will be left alone in the dark forever. What hope has she got that her mother will open the door and let her out?

Up to this point the little girl could feel angry with her

mother for getting angry with her. She could feel the immediate hate we all feel when someone inflicts pain on us. She could hate her wicked mother and wish to harm her. But suddenly the hate turns to fear. If her mother is wicked then she may never open the door. Worse, perhaps her wishes to hurt her mother have worked and her mother is dead or vanished. How can the little girl retain the hope of being saved and not fall into despair?

There is one way. She changes how she sees herself. Instead of seeing herself as an innocent person being unjustly punished by a wicked mother she changes to seeing herself as a wicked person being justly punished by her good mother. Now she can hope that her good mother will open the door. She sacrifices herself for her mother and embarks on a lifetime of self-deception, sacrifice and self-punishment.

I have put this account of what could happen to a small child in words, but of course very little of such an event is experienced in words. Profound experiences occur to us as images and bodily feelings. Afterwards, reflecting upon them, we may, if we are lucky, have the mental tools to fashion these experiences into words and so, through thought and discussion, come to understand and master them. Small children do not have such tools, and thus these profound experiences of childhood remain with us as images and bodily feelings. If these images and bodily feelings give us a feeling of warmth, comfort, security and strength then they provide a life-sustaining and life-enhancing resource which maintains and protects us in times of trouble, which enables us to perceive goodness inside ourselves and in the world, and to develop a profound love of nature and a faith based on love and trust. But if these images and bodily feelings give us feelings of danger, hunger, cold and helplessness, then they starve and deprive us, they undermine our attempts to deal with our problems with courage and mastery, they create and maintain the expectancy that nothing of value can be found inside ourselves or outside in the world, and they lead us to despise and hate nature and to develop a faith based on justice and punishment.

We know our sense of essential self very much in images and bodily feelings. Some people know their essential self only in this way and never put their knowledge into words, not even to themselves. They are the kind of people who are confused when I ask them, 'Do you experience yourself as good or bad?' They are the people who live harmoniously with themselves, who know that while they are not perfect, they have within themselves something of value. Their sense of essential self is not in conflict with what they see as society's demands upon them and is not greatly different from their sense of what they ought to be (their ideal self) and so they have no pressing need to translate their experience of their essential self into words. But there are many people who know precisely what I mean when I ask. 'Do you experience yourself as good or bad?' They are the people who do not live harmoniously with themselves who experience themselves as damaged, soiled, containing something so vile that it must be hidden from the sight of others, something which, if let loose, will contaminate and kill. Their sense of essential self is always in conflict with what they see as society's demands upon them, and they respond with excessive compliance with its concomitant resentment or with an absolute refusal to comply with its concomitant aggression and sense of grievance and injustice. The sense of essential badness is experienced in powerful images and bodily feelings, in physical illnesses and complaints, in verbal thoughts in the continuous internal dialogue, the discussions we have with ourselves, and, in talking with other people, in statements about anxiety, guilt, shame, worthlessness, inadequacy and helplessness.

It is impossible to estimate the number of people who carry within themselves a pervading sense of badness. Most of these people, because they experience themselves as bad, strive to be good, to earn the right to exist, to deserve to be a member of society. They seek perfection, they maintain high standards, they are conscientious, reliable and hard-working. Often they try to overcome their sense of worthlessness by devoting themselves to a cause or to a leader whom they see as embodying everything that is virtuous and true. Such people will sacrifice themselves for their cause and their leader, and will violently resist any attempt to reveal the limitations of their cause and their leader.

People who experience themselves as bad shoulder impossible burdens and sacrifice themselves again and again for their family, their work, their country. Such efforts keep at bay the sense of unworthiness and impending doom, but as they get older they find it harder to maintain such standards and responsibilities. They may have sustained their efforts towards virtue with the beliefs that if you are good God will protect you, but the passing years bring increasing evidence that while God may be aware of every fallen sparrow He is not particularly efficient in providing succour for life's casualties, no matter how good such people might have been. An increasing sense of failure and disillusion links with a sense of essential badness and locks many middle-aged and elderly people into the prison of depression.

It is impossible to estimate how many children are in the process of acquiring those images of badness which will sour their lives and disarm them in the struggle to maintain life on earth. There is nothing to suggest that their numbers are decreasing. For a child to carry inside itself a sense of worth and safety it needs to have caring for it people who are themselves secure, warm, loving and patient. Parents who are struggling with poverty and loneliness, with the effects of war and natural disasters, no matter how much they love their children, find it impossible to be always loving, patient and unafraid. When the parents themselves disappear the child is filled with a sense of abandonment which shows him, in every fibre of his being, that the world is nothing but a phantasmagoria, a flimsy, ever-changing passing parade of insubstantial beings who are unreliable, untrustworthy, cruel and dangerous. The orphans of Belfast and Beirut, the refugees in Africa and Vietnam are not acquiring those experiences which create good, life-enhancing images and a strong, coherent sense of self.

It is not easy to describe those images and bodily feelings which we acquire so early in life and the ways we can experience our sense of self. Many of the images and feelings have to do with being held, of being given a boundary, a perimeter of being, before the baby can construct such a boundary himself. There is the opposite of being held, of being exposed, vulnerable, of falling without hope of being caught. Children whose early experiences have been of cruelty and abandonment sometimes express these experiences in games of falling. 'Either toys are dropped or the patient himself perches or jumps or falls perilously. One could see this kind of behaviour as expressing a feeling of being unheld by a caring person.' So wrote Mary Boston in the study of *Psychotherapy with Deprived Children*.[8] Such children can be left with a sense of chaos, the dread of falling to pieces or being burned up by a nameless feeling. Sometimes the child is left with the fear of being abandoned forever, no matter how caring and reliable the people looking after her later in life may be. Games that involve considerable risk or persistent bad behaviour may be attempts by the child to define the limits of safety and to master the terrible feelings of danger and abandonment. But early experiences so immediate and new, have a tremendous hold and power over us because we had no other experience with which we could compare them. Experiences of being held by a caring person of feeling contained, secure and loved, are just as strong and can provide a person with a fund of irrational optimism and courage quite at variance with the facts of that person's life.

We talk of a baby's experience but, as Donald Winnicot observed, 'there is no such thing as a baby – meaning that if you set out to describe a baby, you will find that you are describing a *baby and someone*. A baby cannot exist alone, but is essentially part of a relationship.'[9] *From the moment of conception we must be part of a group in order to survive*. A baby has to be part of a relationship to survive physically. A baby who is adequately fed and clothed but never held and cuddled will fall into a decline called *anaclitic depression* and die. A baby needs to be part of a group. Members of this group, usually the mother, set the boundary of the group by containing and holding the baby. 'Holding', as Winnicot defined it, means keeping the baby safe from unpredictable events which, by the nature of their unpredictability, are traumatic for the baby, and looking after the physiological needs of the baby, not just by knowing what most babies need but by understanding what this particular baby needs – the imaginative leap of *empathy*.

In describing the group of mother and baby Winnicot used the concept of 'dependence'. Had he been writing in Japanese he could have used the word *amae* to describe what goes on in this relationship. 'Dependence' has connotations of passivity on the part of the dependent person who, in the literal meaning of the word, 'hangs from' the more powerful superior. 'Amae' refers to a symmetrical relationship where the dependent person makes active and usually welcome claims upon the senior in the relationship. 'To amaeru' means 'to presume upon the affections of someone close to you'. This indeed is what loved and understood babies and toddlers do. Such babies protest about hunger pangs and cold, wet nappies and expect to be fed and warmed. Such toddlers demand a biscuit and climb upon friendly knees for a cuddle. Teenagers who securely demand a clean shirt or a loan of mum's lipstick 'amaeru'. The wife who in bed warms her cold feet against her husband or the husband who expects, and gets, a hot meal no matter what time he arrives home from golf 'amaerus'. We have no word for 'amae' in English, perhaps because in Western Europe we have been so concerned with the development of the individual, the person who can stand alone and have no need to 'amaeru'. The fact that no such persons exist is ignored by a culture which is so devoted to dividing the world up into discrete bits.

It is only through dependence and holding that the baby is able to develop gradually a sense of self. In this stage of *amae* or dependence the baby is both totally dependent and totally powerful. If the mother is reasonably skilful in understanding what the baby needs – does this cry mean he is hungry or is he simply lonely and in need of a cuddle ? – then the baby gains the idea that he himself has created the satisfaction that appears – he has created the nipple and the milk, the warmth and firmness of being held. He has fantasised satisfaction and the satisfaction has appeared. Fantasy and reality are one. This sense of omnipotence must give to the baby images which create enormous confidence.

It is only in the context of the group, the dependence on being held and understood, that the young baby can experience the first stages of the sense of self, what Winnicot called the I AM moments. Such moments probably occur first in states of the excitement of being fed or the greed and rage at feeling hungry or cold. As the mother accepts, contains and satisfied these states the moments of I AM become more frequent and gradually the baby acquires a sense of space and time, a sense of process, and a relationship with his environment.

The sense of I AM, the sense of space and time, the sense of process, of one thing following another, the sense of a relationship with people and things are all structures which we learn to create, provided, as a baby, we had the kinds of experiences which form the necessary learning environment. We learn to create these structures so early in our lives and we rely on them so constantly in our waking lives (in dreams these structures, especially those of time, space and process, often fall apart) that we take them for solid reality. When something happens which demonstrates how we structure what we see and hear we often label this as a trick or magic and go on imposing depth and distance on a photograph or calling one sound a noise and another a human voice. But when we were small babies our hold on these structures was weak and easily broken. When something traumatic happened – when we were gripped by hunger pangs and were not fed, when the pattern of our day was broken, when something warm and familiar disappeared and we were handled by strange and uncaring hands – then we were overwhelmed by an agonising and limitless anxiety which we experienced, as Winnicot described it, as a going to pieces, a falling forever, a having of no relation to the body, a having of no orientation, a complete isolation because of there being no means of communication.[10] Having experienced however briefly the sense of I AM we now discovered *annihilation*, the threat that the chaos or isolation would always carry for us for the rest of our lives.

For some of us, the lucky ones, such experiences of overwhelming anxiety were relatively few and we were able to build a coherent sense of self. If we were even luckier we were surrounded by loving and accepting people and so we were able to retain a sense of self-worth, to gather images of warmth, love and security, and strength and to develop and be ourselves. If we were less lucky the demands and inconsistencies of the people caring for us damaged our sense of self-worth, created images of danger, hunger, cold and helplessness, and forced a compliance which necessitated the giving up of the right to be ourselves. If we were very unlucky, if we were born to an environment which provided only erratic or inappropriate holding and containing then the I AM moments never cohered into a strong and continuing sense of self and we never developed that 'internal space' which Bion[11] called the capacity for dealing with lived experience which a baby develops provided the mother is sufficiently able to accept, mirror and contain the baby's emotions of need, rage and fear which suffuse his entire being. Such containment allows the baby to develop the space within where later he can turn bodily feelings into images and finally language, and to house the internal objects which will provide company, comfort and guidance through the rest of his life. But the child who is presented with many devastating events cannot cope with the pain such events arouse and so may never develop this space, or, having once developed it, lose it as a defence against this pain.

This sense of shrivelling to a 'two-dimensional shallowness', as a piece of cling film paper will, when treated harshly, 'shrivel into nothing',[12] is hard to describe because children who experience such a lack of care that forces them to this defence do not then go through the appropriate stages of development which allow them later to give an account of this experience. A few of these children – very few – might meet a psychotherapist who can understand and interpret the child's play and drawings, but most of these children by adulthood are living lives of uncomprehending misery, drifting on the edge of human life or incarcerated in a prison or an asylum. They may not understand the world they live in, but they often add to its problems by becoming uncaring parents. Famine must produce many such people.

Some children develop an inner space to contain what psychoanalysts call 'good objects', internal representations of kindly, loving parents who guide and support the child, but then the children, punished, abandoned, humiliated, suffer such pain and fear that the 'good objects' vanish and are replaced by objects which attack and persecute. 'Their internal world is a graveyard milling with frightened ghosts. When alone they are not really alone but in the company of internal persecutors.'[13]

One such child, now thirty-five, is John. I met John because I was asked to help to decide John's future – whether he should spend the rest of his life in a hospital for the criminally insane. John told me about his internal objects, a man and a woman, who talked to him constantly. They told him to mutilate cats and dogs and to follow and sexually accost young woman and then slit their throats. I asked John where these people had come from. 'They're part of me,' he said. He went on to tell me that he could answer the man and woman back and then they would be quiet for a while, but soon they would start up again. The only way he could quieten the voices was to do what they told him. In hospital he dutifully took the massive doses of tranquillisers prescribed for him. These, he told me, reduced the voices to a mumble, but they did not go away.

John lives in a society which regards cats, dogs and young women as valuable, and so he is confined by drugs and locks. Had he chosen things to attack which his society also attacked then he could have become, not a psychiatric patient, but a hero. Then society would have given him more destructive weapons than his collection of kitchen knives and taught him how to use them. Had he been physically bigger and stronger, had he had the opportunity to discover how military organization and discipline can comfortably house the irretrievably lonely and lost and give meaning and purpose to an empty life, then he would have made an excellent soldier. Untroubled by empathy, he could have killed on demand. If Britain's efficient army had allowed him too little expression of his hate he could have joined one of those multitude of armies that infest our world and killed to his heart's content. He could have been a Leader as well as a Hero. But wherever he lives, he will find it impossible to live without enemies.

Many of us carry within ourselves objects which, at times, urge us to damage and to kill. We can, if we are lucky, learn how to contain such rage and hate by refusing to accept these urges as compulsions which cannot be denied. We expend our rage in words, saying things like, 'I'll kill that bastard', knowing full well that we won't. We turn our urges into fantasy and do in fantasy what we would never do in real life. Unfortunately, many of us have accepted the biblical injunction that thought is as sinful as action and so feel enormous guilt at expending rage and hate in fantasy. Some people give to thought the power that only action can have, and worry that wishing someone dead is the same as killing him. Such people rarely make the mistake of believing that thought alone will carry out beneficial actions – they don't attempt to clear the snow off the path merely by thinking about it – but they see evil thoughts as having such a power. Frightening though this may be, it gives them a sense of secret power over their enemies which they are reluctant to relinquish. For such people enemies are necessary.

All of us carry around objects which criticise and punish. We each have an inner voice which says things like, 'You've made a mess of that', 'What a fool you are', 'Why don't you do something about the way you look?', 'Don't be weak with your children', 'Don't forgive such an injury'. If we are lucky our inner voice can praise and encourage us. If we are unlucky our inner voice only carps, criticises and punishes. It tells us how bad we are.

If we are parents our inner voice often tells us that we are not doing the job well enough. Our inner voice, and the endless array of child experts, can create the anxiety that bringing up children is an impossible task. Winnicot recognised this and spoke, not of 'the good mother', but of 'the good enough' mother. Children, he said, did not need perfect parents. In fact, perfect parents, totally empathetic parents who were always there, would inhibit the growth of the child as an individual. What a baby needed were parents who presented the baby with difficulties which the baby had the capacity to surmount – absences which were not too long, hunger not immediately satisfied. The baby manages to cope with a degree of loneliness and frustration, succeeds, and is comforted and made secure once the mother returns and the food supplied. Moreover, the good enough parents accept the baby's anger and do not retaliate. The mother knows that the baby is consumed with rage against her because she is neglecting him but she does not punish him for this. Instead she lifts him up and cuddles him, talks to him gently, contains and accepts his rage and, belatedly, satisfies his need. Such acts of tolerance and reparation teach the child about forgiveness, how to live together we have to accept that we often fail one another but that such failures can serve to increase our understanding and love.

Of course good enough parents do not say to the child, 'I forgive you.' (Statements like that always sound like threats.) They *show* their forgiveness by touch, by holding the child securely. Holding calms the angry or frightened child. Holding conveys love, acceptance, courage and forgiveness. Holding is reciprocal. The person being held, who wants to be held, takes part in the holding. When a person does not want to be held and is held there is a gap between the holder and the held, even though their bodies may be touching. What is conveyed then is a combination of coldness, fear, rejection and conflict about power. Touching is a vital part of communication.

Not all people like this form of communication. A touch can be an intrusion, and our society sets many limits to such intrusion. But there are many people who cannot tolerate even the touches which society allows. A touch is seen as dangerous, as an attack or as a threat to their essential being. A touch might reveal their intrinsic badness or contaminate the person who touched them. Such people usually come from families where there was no touching, except in anger. As children they were hit but never cuddled. They had to cope with fear and anger on their own, with no one to hold and comfort them. Such people find forgiveness difficult.

A child who is not forgiven for his transgressions does not come to understand that his actions are under his control. He cannot choose to do better next time. Instead, he learns that he himself is intrinsically bad. There is nothing he can do to change his badness. Believing this, he can never live at peace with his fellows.

Experiencing yourself as bad means that you always feel yourself to be weak and in danger. One way of building up your self-esteem is to vow never to forgive. Some people experience themselves as so weak and insubstantial that they fear to forgive lest such forgiveness robs them of what strength and substance they have. Others, wanting to be strong, see forgiveness as a weakness. They never forgive an injury and they never admit a mistake. They never say,

'Sorry'. Feeling impotent, they look to having power in the future and vow revenge.

Experiencing yourself as bad can mean disbelieving in the possibility that some other person might be concerned about your welfare. A sense of one's essential badness means that every other person in the world must be feared and never trusted.

Experiencing yourself as bad means that you always fear rejection. One way to avoid rejection is never to love completely, never expect to be loved. Always believe that, 'If anyone says they like me I know that person is either a fool or a liar.'

Such attitudes do not engender good relationships with other people. The child who acquires such attitudes does not develop through the stages of coming to understand other people. So the child stays fixated at the primitive level of assessing other people solely in terms of the way they can meet his own needs, that is, whether they satisfy or deprive. Or the child may reach and stay at the slightly more advanced level of seeing people solely in terms of the roles they fill, and so in adult life he bases his relationships on judgments like 'A woman's place is in the home', 'All Americans are imperialists', 'All Communists are bad', 'I don't know what the youth of today are coming to'. Anyone who in adult life judges other people solely in terms of what roles they fill or what needs they meet soon has difficulty in relationships simply because other people fail to fulfil expectations. Wives fail to be all-nurturing mothers, while Americans, Communists and the youth of today and all other types of people fail to function in the way their role demands. Such a person may deal with relationships by becoming totally unaware of the activities or even the existence of people around him except for those activities which actually impinge upon him. When such impinging does occur the person reacts with fear and anger. Some people, equally handicapped but not in sufficient control of their lives to reduce them to banal and predictable regularity, go through their lives in a state of anxious confusion and fearful impotence. I spend a great deal of my working life with these two types of people. The former is the spouse, usually the husband. The latter is the depressed client, usually the wife. I try to teach them both ways of observing and assessing other people's behaviour which will enable them to understand other people and react more appropriately to them, but I often feel that I would have greater success in teaching them the language of nuclear physics than the language of human behaviour, since while they may be able to create the internal images necessary to imagine the actions of nuclear particles they seem quite unable to create the internal images necessary to imagine the actions and feelings of other human beings. It is like trying to explain colour to the innately blind.

Not being able to understand other people, they must always fear them, and when we fear anyone for long enough we come to hate that person. Even when we are reasonably good at understanding other people, if we fear someone we don't allow ourselves to get close enough to that person to understand him. When we don't understand another person it is very easy to come to envy that person, simply because we do not see the difficulties which that person is facing. Not understanding, it is easy to look at another person and see that person going about his business without a care in the world and so come to envy that person while feeling great pity for ourselves. Envy is bad enough, but with it comes its bitter twin of jealousy, where we see someone else enjoying the advantages and pleasures which we feel are rightly ours.

Thus, people who experience themselves as bad can never live at ease with other people. Their world is always full of enemies. Neither can they live at ease with themselves.

The person who experiences himself as bad and must therefore strive to be good is in a constant state of guilt for he sees the emotions of anger, envy, jealousy and desire for gratification as evidence of his badness. He holds what Alice Miller calls 'the absurd belief that a person can have nothing but kind, good and meek thoughts and at the same time be honest and authentic.'[14] The person who experiences himself as good knows that these emotions are part of being human and as such are best limited by understanding and acceptance rather than by denial and rigid control.

To fight for your own survival you have to feel that you are worth saving. If not, you can say, as one depressed woman said to me, 'I'm a fatalist. If it's going to happen, it'll happen. I can't do anything about it.' If we are to change the way we organise and protect ourselves so that there will not be any disaster which destroys our species and our planet we have to have a concerted will to survive. We have to feel that we are all worth saving.

Widespread unemployment has made many young people feel quite worthless and rejected by the adult world. In the 1960s when there were plenty of jobs, teenagers could create a space for themselves before they entered the adult world of work and marriage. There was a unified youth culture then. Now teenagers might still wish to outrage their elders by their dress and music but there is no sense of belonging to a large and powerful group. Our young people are divided and despondent. In the US where, among white people at least, unemployment is not as great a problem as in the UK, adolescents who wish to protest against having to live under the threat of extinction are made to feel that it is unpatriotic to protest. It is sad that in those countries who pride themselves on their freedom of expression many young people feel that it is not worth the trouble of taking advantage of that freedom. So many young people, I find, construe their future in 'as if' terms. 'If I am still alive next year or the year after, then I might be finishing college.' Their future has a conditional, unreal quality which my future never has. I thought this was very sad until I realised that such a way of thinking about the future was a defence against depression. If the future is not real then you won't feel resentful about being robbed of it.

But even worse than unemployment is the sapping of selfworth which occurs when a person becomes a refugee. One such refugee, Melkamu Adisu, an Ethiopian who found himself unable to return home after several years' training in social sciences in the USA, said,

'There is a stage in being a refugee when you suddenly realise that it is not going to go away, like a bad dream. You're going to be a refugee for a long time, perhaps the rest of your life, you may never go home. Particularly if you're young, 16, 18 or 20, you've got to have something to do. It is the same in Africa as it is in the West, and when you don't have anything to do, you can't be productive in any way, you have no control over your future, your own life. Then, all of a sudden, you realise that tomorrow is going to be just like today, except that you will be older and probably sicker, and these things you had dreams of – education, a good job, home, family – all of these are not for you; you are a refugee. It is easy then to become bitter, to become angry – angry with the situation that made you a refugee, angry because you know you have only one life and you do not want to spend it like this. Somehow, you are no longer part of the living world, you are somehow outside it, your life has stopped, perhaps it is over.'[15]

All the survivors of a nuclear war will be refugees. The world will have changed completely and no one will have a home to go to.

A depressed person might react to this statement with a sense of despondency and helplessness. But depressed people are not merely despondent, unwilling to take any positive action. The state of depression is an attempt to find security and to deny the possibility of change. Better the devil you know than the devil you don't know. Preferring secure misery to insecure happiness, the depressed person resists change, and this resistance can be quite powerful. There is a theory that depression is a form of learned helplessness which derives from not being in control of one's life. This theory accounts only for the feelings of helplessness which depressed people feel and express. It does not account for something which depressed people feel and do but rarely speak about. It is that by being depressed a person can successfully control others while at the same time denying the responsibility for this. Many depressed people have retreated to this position of covert power because they live in families where discord is never expressed or, if expressed, can invoke severe sanctions. Many depressed people are engaged in a desperate battle not so much as to survive as to impose their will on the world.

One woman, Jane, spoke to me often of how her husband was so powerful that she feared that he would destroy her. Certainly he was always saying that he was strong and his decisions and actions were always right. He would tell me this whenever we met but I remained sceptical. Jane insisted that he was powerful and not merely bluffing as many wives know their husbands to be.

During our discussions Jane and I slowly elucidated the beliefs on which she built her life. We found that she had built herself the following trap –

Jim is stronger and more powerful than me.
I am in danger of being destroyed by him.
I have to battle him to survive.
I never fight people who are weaker than me.
If I do I shall hurt them.
If I know another person is hurt I feel hurt.
I cannot bear any more pain.
I can fight Jim because he is stronger than me.

This seems like a terrible trap, but then depression is, in one way, an act of submission performed in order to win. Jane, at the end of a long discussion about how her husband made her feel so weak and helpless, said, in the closing stages of our talk, 'I'll win in the end.'

I did not ignore this remark. 'What will you win?' I asked.

She seemed to be considering the possibility of convincing me that her remark had meant nothing, a throwaway farewell remark, but she decided to answer truthfully. 'I'll get my own way.'

'Even if it kills you?'

'Yes.'

Here Jane was admitting to the attitude which underlies the depressive experience – that it is preferable to be right and miserable than to allow that you might be wrong and consequently happy, and that no price is too high to pay to impose your truth upon the world. Stubbornness and implacability are seen as the highest virtues.

We should never underestimate the power which a depressed person can wield. Similarly, we should never underestimate the cruelty which a depressed person can inflict in the name of virtue, be it the virtue of revenge or the virtue of recognising one's badness – 'All people are evil but I am better than others because I know how evil I am.' A disgust with oneself can be coterminous with disgust with the human race.

Believing in the essential badness of human beings, many depressed people feel not only that they should not survive but that all other people should perish with them. As one woman said to me, 'I want to get a hammer and smash everything – all my beautiful vases – everything – so my family will get nothing. I wouldn't mind if there was a war and everything – the whole world – was smashed up. I wouldn't care.' Sometimes the disgust with the world is expressed and justified by a religious belief.

Chapter 4

'THERE IS SOMETHING BEYOND THIS LIFE'

When we strain to picture what the scene would be like after a holocaust we tend to forget that for most people, and perhaps for all, it wouldn't be like anything because they would all be dead. To depict the scene as it would appear to the living is to that extent a falsification. The right vantage point from which to view the holocaust is that of a corpse, but from that vantage point, of course, there is nothing to report.

Jonathan Schell[1]

Not everyone would accept Schell's statement that there could be no report on the end of the earth. Many people would say that a dead body could make no report, but the spirit which once inhabited that body could. Such a belief brings comfort and protection.

We can protect ourselves from the fear of extinction by believing that life in some form or other will continue. Such a belief can assist us in going on living day by day, but it can also undermine our determination to fight against forces which threatened to destroy us. One woman, a member of CND said to me,

'I think there is something more than this – beyond this – when I die part of me, my humanity, something – goes – joins this, whatever it is – it's greater, more than, what's here, and it'll go on existing no matter what happens to the earth. Everything here could be destroyed, blown apart, but the Supreme Being – call it God, if you like, will go on, and that part of me that goes on will go on. I think it would be stupid to have a nuclear

war. It's not necessary – we could avoid it and I'd do
whatever I could to stop it, but in the end it doesn't
matter. It's not important.'

This woman felt that some effort could be made to avert a
nuclear war, even if in the long run the annihilation of the
earth was not important. She saw herself as having some
power and choice to play her part in averting an unnecessary
catastrophe. A young man, Atul, a Hindu, believed in a Power
beyond all earthly things, but saw himself unable to contend
in any way with this Power. He said to me,

'As far as the nuclear thing is concerned, I have not
thought about it. I don't even read about it. It doesn't
really interest me because I find that my life is taken
over by so many things. What I want to do is to live my
life. I want to do so many things. It could be because of
my Hindu beliefs, I am sure, but I think also that I am
going to die one day, my biological destiny, and I have to
make it worth while. I just have to live. I don't know
what death is like. All I know is what life is like and I
want to concentrate on living. Sometimes I think about
starting an action group, but I don't think that I can
personally bring about any change, or I can bring about
change only in a very small, limited way. I think it
would be improper to stand up and say I know how to
get peace for all. Before you can do this you have to
weigh many things up – only some people are privy to
such information – politicians must know what they are
doing – I hope, anyway, and sometimes I think it is all a
joke, I don't think it's there, this nuclear arsenal – I
think it's purely a contrick – but then I know that
couldn't be also. These kinds of things come through as
fleeting thoughts but I never sit down and do anything
about them. In Oxford I think I must be the only person
who hasn't made up their mind. I wouldn't do anything
to stop it because the moment I do that I miss out on my
own life. My work with leprosy is very dear to my heart.
I want to be free to do what I want to do.'

I asked Atul what implications Hindu religion had for the nuclear issue. He said,

'It doesn't have, because it's like "The Lord giveth and the Lord taketh away". Nuclear things are never talked about in our house at all. There was a programme about it on TV recently. We all watched it, but after we didn't discuss it. We just turned the television off and went on with our lives. So I asked my father and he said, "There's nothing you can do about it. It's all written. If it is written then it is going to happen. Neither you nor anyone can change it." I don't think we should spend money on nuclear weapons. But when I think why do we have such mistrust of the Russians, I find it inherent in people. We all mistrust one another. It's not just the Russians – we mistrust one another, even in one university department. How can anyone bring about trust? Mistrust is inherited, it is there. You can change it in one setting – like in a therapeutic relationship – but I don't think I can bring about change in the massive way it is required. I don't think there'll ever be peace. I remember my mother saying once people were like utensils in a bag, they always rattle. Yes, the world is full of utensils and they'll always rattle. I don't think I can change what is written because I didn't write it. I think that at the end of the day I have to be content with myself and the few people dear to me. There are many different kinds of peace – different levels of peace. There's been much emphasis placed on peace and nuclear war and not on other kinds of peace – like inner peace which is very important for me – that is what drives me on, this inner peace of mind.'

The inner peace of which Atul spoke is *moksha*, liberation from the endless round of death and rebirth. Whenever my friend Usha hears me say anything about the threat of nuclear war she turns impatiently away or smiles at me as at an ignorant child. The world whose destruction I fear is for her an illusion and will continue as an illusion, part of the cycle of death and rebirth for those people who are failing to follow their *swadharma*, their life task, adequately and so obtaining *moksha*. Anxiety about the increasing population is clearly felt, for the inconveniences and dangers of that are present every day, but anxiety about a nuclear holocaust or the devastation being caused by the destruction of the Himalayan forests is anxiety about an illusion and an example of being bound to the wheel of death and rebirth. Usha and Atul are not exceptional in their faith. There are many millions who share their beliefs and live in the world of their faith in a way quite different from the way Christians live in their world which contains the Christian religion. For instance, a book review in *The Times of India* began with the following paragraph,

> Hinduism is a living, sprawling religion which continues to pulsate through the literate, illiterate, urban and rural sectors of India. It is kept alive mainly by elaborate ritualism – domestic, community and institutional. Worship through puja seems to be a compulsive Indian exercise. The variety of gods, goddesses, temples, festivals and even superstitions, the various levels for comprehending the Ultimate Truth; the 'guides' through literature and song, the plastic and visual arts, chiefly iconography – all these make religion an all-pervading influence. Body, mind and spirit are compelled into attention and we are led to strike stances which hopefully become attitudes and gradually progress into states of mind and being. Hinduism has a religious culture that is deep rooted and survives because it is flexible and inclusive – it is, in a very real sense, the sociology and economics, the poetry and philosophy of daily living.[2]

A similar description might have been given of medieval Christian Europe when everything in the world was seen and dealt with as part of the Chain of Being which stretched from the rocks and plants and meanest insects through a hierarchy of animals to man, the angels and finally to God. But with the Renaissance and the extension of the scientific mode of thought over greater and greater areas of life the vision of the Chain of Being vanished and the world took on a solidity and reality which is quite foreign to the Hindu experience. The result is that those of us who live in a Christian world can conceive of the end of life on earth as a possible reality whereas those who live in a Hindu world cannot. An illusion does not die. It merely disappears or changes.

Hinduism distinguishes between *reincarnation*, which only the gods can experience, where a personality enters a new body and *rebirth* where only the *jiva*, the living essence, is reborn. The cycle of rebirth and death is seen as a burden and liberation as the losing of all sense of self and becoming one with One. A belief in reincarnation is held by many people who live in a Christian culture. When I was researching for my book *The Construction of Life and Death* I was surprised to find just how many people believed in reincarnation. Those people with whom I had opportunity to explore their beliefs in detail revealed a set of beliefs much affected by the Christian concepts of sin and redemption. They saw reincarnation as an opportunity to improve oneself in subsequent lives, to make reparation for past sins, and, finally, remaining the person one has always been, though now near-perfect, to join God in heaven.

One such person was Philip who, when I asked him how he lived with the detailed knowledge he had of the consequences of a nuclear war said,

'It's like everything else. I drive a car. I could have a fatal crash. I just hope it won't happen. Organisations like the CND has limited success. I don't think there's much people like me can do. Politicians and scientists should take responsibility. Scientists should make it more public. The more that is known the more chance there is of getting rid of these weapons. In terms of reincarnation and spiritual evolution, if nuclear war made life impossible we would have to wait somewhere until we were able to return. If life was possible but hard, the worst karma would be reincarnation into that world. Better people would come later. I'm not evil but I'm not particularly enlightened, so I'd be somewhere in the middle. The nuclear issue is not an issue on its own but the phase that the human race has reached. We can make a conscious decision to change, to create or to destroy. We can decide to get together and live as the human race should live or we'll have a mighty conflict and get it over. I suppose my greatest worry is that politicians on all sides will agree not to use nuclear weapons but to fight their wars with conventional weapons. People don't realise how destructive conventional weapons are now. . . . I'm hoping that I'll live till I'm ninety. Choice is not a possibility. It is an obligation. The earth has a karma and it is our duty to look after it. . . . I have this image – it's like a cartoon picture – of us all being blown up in a nuclear war and then going up somewhere and meeting these higher spirits, like angels, I suppose, and having our knuckles rapped and being told to go back to earth and do better next time.'

What Philip is describing here is his own version of the story often told in mythologies of the end of the earth. In all these stories the cycle starts again. The orthodox Muslim and Christian myths do not take this cyclical form. Death, be it the death of a person or the death of the world, is followed by entry into Paradise or Heaven. A firm belief in the promise of Paradise allows many Muslims to sacrifice themselves in a *jihad*, a holy war.

Many Christians see war as far from holy – '*a sin against God and a degradation of man . . . an institution incompatible with the teaching of our Lord Jesus Christ*', according to the World Council of Churches in 1948. The British Council of Churches in 1983 issued a statement on *The Making of Peace in a Nuclear World* where they stated firmly,

God the Creator calls us to choose life. The love of God sets us free from fear, free to work for the times when, in the words of Jewish prophecy, the nations will 'beat their swords into ploughshares . . . and teach war no more.' We believe that life in peace is more than a dream. We believe that God's will, if it becomes our will, is capable of fulfilment. In the power of the Spirit, against all odds, the disciples of Jesus are called to love their enemies and to 'overcome evil with good'.[3]

Christians might become impatient for this vision to become reality, but as the Catholic Bishops of the United States reminded Christians in their pastoral letter on war and peace,

Christians are called to live the tension between the vision of the reign of God and its concrete realization in history. The tension is often described in terms of 'already but not yet': i.e., we already live in the grace of the kingdom. Hence, we are a pilgrim people in a world marked by conflict and injustice. Christ's grace is at work in the world; his command of love and his call to reconciliation are not purely future ideals but call us to obedience today.[4]

In his appeal for peace at the Peace Memorial in Hiroshima the Pope said,

'To remember the past is to commit oneself to the future. To remember Hiroshima is to commit oneself to peace. To remember what the people of this city suffered is to renew our faith in man, in his capacity to do what is good, in his freedom to choose what is right, in his determination to turn disaster into a new beginning. In the face of the man-made calamity that every war is, one must affirm and reaffirm, again and again, that *the waging of war is not inevitable or unchangeable*. Humanity is not destined to self-destruction. Clashes of ideologies, aspirations and needs can and must be settled and resolved by means other than war and violence.'[5]

The American evangelical theologians Ronald J. Sider and Richard K. Taylor, in their book *Nuclear Holocaust and Christian Hope*, remind all Christians that they are

Members of Christ's body. 'For by one spirit we were all baptised into one body – Jews or Greeks, slaves or free' (1 Cor. 12:13). The same verse might be applied to Germans and Ethiopians, British and Chinese, North Americans and Russians. Unless we deny our Lord, our loyalty to Christ's worldwide body of brothers and sisters must far exceed any loyalty to nation or country.

'If one member suffers, all suffer together; if one member is honoured, all rejoice together' (1 Cor. 12:26).

Unfortunately St Paul's advice has not always been followed by Christians.

Has not the long tragic history of European wars made a mockery of this biblical belief in the unity of Christ's body? German Christians have destroyed French and Dutch Christians. English Christians have obliterated German and Italian Christians. Over the centuries, European Christians have slaughtered their brothers and sisters in Christ by the millions.

Now we have plans to do it by tens of millions. A higher percentage of the total population attends church in the USSR each Sunday than in Western Europe. Atheistic Communism has not been able to halt the expansion of Christianity in the Soviet Union. If Christianity perishes there, it will not be due to atheistic Communism. It will happen because European and American Christians approved of a nuclear policy that culminated in a holocaust destroying 70 million Soviet Christians.

Do we not crucify Christ anew when we kill other members of his body? If Paul's doctrine of the church is valid, should not our loyalty to Soviet members of Christ's body exceed our loyalty to any secular nation?[6]

The early Christian Church was strictly pacifist, but once the Emperor Constantine in AD 313 adopted Christianity as the state religion the church found excuses for not condemning war. Many reasons have been advanced over the centuries to explain why it was permissible for Christians to kill other Christians, let alone people of other faiths, and why God supported a particular side in a war. He was especially busy at this in the First World War when both German and British theologians claimed that He was supporting their side. Why God should support the killing of so many men is quite beyond me to understand. The pusillanimous response by many Anglican theologians, described in Scully's cartoon, can be understood only in terms of the commitments the Church of

"Funny, he managed to put Transubstantiation into a nutshell. With the bomb he's completely at sixes and sevens."

PUNCH April 20 1983[7]

England as the state religion, has made to maintaining its position and power. Jesus' teaching on the importance of non-violence, forgiveness, love and reconciliation is quite unambiguous.

Each of the world's great religions teaches in its own way the wisdom of love, trust, forgiveness and a simplicity of living, and each religion has adherents who follow these teachings faithfully. But each religion has its adherents who ignore these basic teachings or interpret them in ways to suit their own ends. Jesus taught the wisdom of poverty; and Christian churches became some of the wealthiest institutions in the world. Mohammed taught the peace and unity of the Muslim faith; and now the Sunni and Shi'ites and the Iranians and the Iraqis fight one another as fiercely as the Protestants and Catholics once did and still do in Northern Ireland. Buddha and Lao-Tsu taught the wisdom of simple living, trusting nature, paying careful attention to the reality of daily life and the futility of agonizing over metaphysical questions and seeking solutions to problems of life in this way; and now multitudes of Buddhists and Taoists put their faith in gold leaf and magic.

All the world's religions teach that in the world and beyond is a great power which is often conceived of as Universal Love. Unfortunately, the belief in Universal Love can become a refusal to love oneself and fellow human beings not just for their virtues but also for all the faults and infirmities of character to which human beings are prone. The belief in Universal Love can become a consolation for hating humanity and for being unable to live in the present. I found this when I was talking with a woman acquaintance whom I had always regarded as a warm, gentle, concerned and loving person. We were talking about the dangers of a nuclear war when Sally suddenly shocked me by bursting out with, 'Why not tell them to press the button – get it over – wipe the slate clean and start again.'

Sally believed that the arms race had gone on past the point of no return – not only with the stockpiling of nuclear weapons but also the creation of satellite weapons. She felt sure that something worse than nuclear weapons were already circling above us – probably the weapons of germ warfare. But the thought of worldwide devastation did not appal her because she believed in reincarnation and a spiritual being. Life on earth, she believed, had existed many times before and would exist many times again. Thus death held no fear for her. Indeed, she welcomed it. Within everyone, she believed, was a spiritual being which does not perish and through which we can reach a universal spiritual love which is the source of strength and healing. This spiritual benefi-cence with the promise of eternal life was a great comfort to her. The comfort and assurance she received from these beliefs counteracted the profound distaste she had for the human race and its petty, self-seeking, materialistic activi-ties. She longed for a Golden Age, where everyone had defined roles and lived in tune with Nature. She believed in heroes and heroines and looked to superior people like Gandhi and Mother Teresa to inspire and protect her. When she found that someone she had worshipped from afar was simply human she felt profound disgust and, despairing, she wanted to shut everything about that person out of her life. 'Wipe it out, get rid of it.'

Holding a set of beliefs which offers a universal panacea prevents the person from actually seeing what is there in reality and asking questions about it. The simplicity of the fundamentalist Christian beliefs can be disarmingly charming. One married couple who had come to consult me about the wife's depression explained to me that they were Jehovah's Witnesses and that they knew from what God had said in the Bible that what was good in the world would not be destroyed but that evil would be punished and destroyed. They were sure that there would be no nuclear holocaust which would destroy both the good people and the bad. But, they assured me, there would be a Day of Judgment, after which life on earth would be perfect and the lamb and the lion lie down together. I wanted to ask them whether, after the Day of Judgment, the lion would become a vegetarian, but I would not risk any remark which might seem to question their gentle faith, any more than I would show them this irreverent cartoon from Punch.

"I thought perhaps we ought to have a co-ordinated crowd control plan in case deterrence doesn't work."
PUNCH June 22 1983[8]

The Jehovah's Witnesses who see God's goodness protecting us from a nuclear holocaust do nothing themselves to prevent the holocaust. They rely solely on God. Thus they are of no use themselves in combating the forces which may lead to our destruction, but at least they are not as dangerous as those fundamentalists who seem not only to view a nuclear holocaust as inevitable but to positively welcome such an event. Billy Graham, when he was in London recently and interviewed by Colin Morris on the BBC, said,

'I think the prophecies are quite clear, that there is a possibility of one-fourth of the human race being destroyed at some point in history under the judgment of God, and God may allow man to have his atomic war, but, in the midst of it, before man has destroyed himself, because that would be Armageddon, then God is going to intervene, Christ is going to return and set up His kingdom, and that to me is a glorious hope.'[9]

But even more frightening is the possibility that a world leader like President Reagan could hold these fundamentalist beliefs. Ronnie Dugger, writing in the *Washington Post*, reported that,

'On at least five occasions in the last four years Ronald Reagan has referred to his beliefs that Armageddon may well occur during the present generation and could come in the Middle East. He associates Amageddon with 'the end of the world'. As authorities for this premonition he cites Bible prophecies and unnamed theologians. . . .

At Armageddon, in Bible stories, God takes charge of human history. He descends from heaven and defeats the wicked. On the Day of Judgment, He damns the wicked, admits good people into eternal life and ushers in the millennium – a thousand years of peace and happiness during which Satan is chained up. Then eternity begins.

For Christians who believe the prophecies literally, Armageddon thus signifies not only terror and incalculable bloodshed, but also the Second Coming of Christ, the Day of Judgment, the Millennium and eternity.

During the campaign for the 1980 presidential nomination, in the course of an interview with TV preacher Jim Bakker of PLT Television Network, Reagan was discussing the need for a 'spiritual revival' when he suddenly said, 'We may be the generation that sees Armageddon.'

Speaking before a group of Jewish leaders in New York City during the same campaign Reagan cryptically disclosed a connection in his mind between Armageddon and the Middle East. As quoted by William Safire, the candidate said, 'Israel is the only stable democracy we can rely on in a spot where Armageddon could come.' . . .

At an interview on December 6, Reagan was asked, 'Do you consider yourself lucky?'

'. . . In the long run,' he replied, 'it goes back to what we were discussing before. The point of reading the Bible is to realise that this world and our lives don't really belong to us. What the Good Lord wants from each of us, and from this world, is up to Him, not you and me.' . . .

When Caspar Weinberger, the Secretary of Defence, was asked by a Harvard student, 'Do you believe the world is going to end, and if you do, do you think it will be by an act of God or an act of man?'

'I have read the Book of Revelation,' Weinberger replied, 'and yes, I believe the world is going to end – by an act of God, I hope – but every day I think the time is running out.' . . .

William Martin, a sociology professor at Rice University who writes on religious subjects, asked in an article in the June 1982 *Atlantic* on end-of-the-world evangelical theology: 'If a president were to appoint one or more premillenialists to key foreign policy posts (who at the confirmation hearings think to probe for beliefs about the Second Coming?), what incentive would they have to work for lasting peace in the Middle East, since they would regard a Russian-led attack on Israel as a necessary precursor of the Millennium . . . ?'[10]

Fundamentalist groups of different religious persuasions often fight one another, but sometimes they join together against a common enemy. *The Sunday Times* (UK) carried a story which began with a quotation from the Old Testament.

And I looked, and, behold, a whirlwind came out of the north, a great cloud, and a fire unfolding itself, and a brightness was about it . . . Ezekiel 1:iv

Ezekiel's vision of God's apocalyptic prophecies are ominously relevant in Jerusalem this weekend: in the

biggest trial of Jewish terrorists in the history of the
state of Israel, 20 men are accused of attempting to
assassinate Arabs, of blowing up two West Bank Arab
mayors, of the illegal possession of huge arms caches.
But perhaps the most serious charge, and the one for
which evidence has been presented in camera, is that
they plotted to blow up the Dome of the Rock mosque in
Jerusalem.

Some of the accused believe, on the strength of biblical
interpretation, that the mosque is an 'abomination' and
that its destruction will usher in Armageddon and the
coming of the Messiah.

What disturbs many Israelis is that the men on trial
are not part of a lunatic fringe, but are leaders of the
Jewish establishment on the West Bank, businessmen,
Israeli Defence officers and a former fighter pilot.

Their messianic fervour, if not the violent means they
employ, is shared by millions of Christian
fundamentalists; since 1981 an odd alliance has been
forged between American fundamentalists and
orthodox Israeli Jews.
'The Dome of the Rock is one of the best-known of
Jerusalem's sights. It was built in AD691 and is the
place where three religions – Christianity, Judaism and
Islam – meet. For Muslims it is the third holiest place,
after Mecca and Medina; they believe that Muhammad
leapt to heaven from the rock on a white horse.
Christians believe the rock is where Abraham came to
sacrifice Isaac and where Jesus taught.'

It is the site of the ancient centre of Jewish religious
life. Solomon's temple, built there in 950BC was
destroyed in 586BC; a second temple was destroyed by
the Romans. A convoluted interpretation of the Bible
leads some to believe that after the destruction of the
Mosque construction of a third temple may begin and
this will herald the Second Coming.

The Dome has been the target of fanatics for years,
but the pace has quickened (since 1968). . . .

Not all orthodox Jews believe the mosque should be
destroyed; one who condemns the violence is Stanley

Goldfoot, a South African Jew, who founded 'The Faithful of the Temple Mount' in Jerusalem. Goldfoot maintains strong links with Christian fundamentalists in America which he tours on the evangelical circuit. He went down so well at the Rev Chuck Smith's Calvary Chapel in Costa Mesa in California, that every night, before he goes to bed, Goldfoot replays the tape of his speech 'just to hear the applause'. . . .

The reason for the increasing support for Israel among the 43m US fundamentalists is the growing belief that the end is imminent. 'The world is ready for the final curtain,' said Smith. His interpretation of Ezekiel chapter 39 is that the Russians will suffer an overwhelming defeat and five-sixths of their army will be destroyed.

'We are living in the last days,' said Smith. 'At any moment the Middle East could erupt into a conflict that will be the war of annihilation – this time of Russia and her allies by the Israelis. Then the Lord will take us out of the whole, mad scene and into the heavenly glories of the Father.'

'This alliance is proving useful for Israel. The Israeli prime minister's adviser on the evangelicals, Harry Hurwitz, told the *Jerusalem Post*: 'To go up the hill (Capitol Hill in Washington) with these Christians to lobby for Israel is better because the fundamentalists are the most powerful element in America.'

Just in case any fanatical Jews or Christians try to hasten Armageddon by blowing up the Dome of the Rock, the Israel government has increased security: closed-circuit television and searchlights have been installed on the Old City walls, metal detectors fitted at the entrance to the Dome compound and a 120-man guard placed on round-the-clock duty.[11]

Such protective devices are not enough. The belief in the inevitability of any event itself becomes a force to bring that event into being. Those people who believe that Armageddon is inevitable are themselves in the process of causing Armageddon and the extinction of the human race. And, of course, a belief in the imminent end of the world means that nothing need be done to solve the world's problems of famine, debt and an increasing population.

Certainly a belief in the inevitability of God's will saves many people, not just politicians, from accepting responsibility for their actions. As Margaret Ballard wrote to me,

> The acceptance of God's will preached by almost all religions must be a great asset, because, after all, if this whole cruel mess is God's will then there's nothing we can do about it and we needn't trouble ourselves with it – an excellent cop-out and denial of responsibility, but I suppose it helps the wretched, starving millions whose children die in infancy to survive and bear their dreadful lives. It also stops them blaming greedy and incompetent governments for their plight and thus prevents revolution; all very handy for governments.[12]

Religious belief can be very useful for governments to control people and keep themselves in power. But religious beliefs have more use and purpose than that. We all have some kind of religious or metaphysical beliefs. They are part of the structure we create to explain the world to ourselves and to predict and control events. Part of the structure we create relates to observable and controllable events, those kind of events which we can understand by using methods of rational and scientific thought. When the car won't start or the gravy is lumpy we can solve these problems by thinking about them in a rational and scientific way. Of course, even as we do this we can be thinking about them in a metaphysical way. We can pray that God will use His mechanical or culinary skills to help us, or we can blame Him or a malign Fate for cursing us and bringing our efforts to naught, or we can cringe under the pain of these disasters, knowing them to be just punishments for our evil deeds. A belief in the usefulness of prayers for divine help can assist in the solution of practical problems, because it can promote confidence and reduce tension and nervousness, but a belief in divine punishment can prevent the simplest practical problem from being solved. However, a belief in divine punishment, like most metaphysical beliefs, has one great advantage. It promotes a sense of security.

All human beings, be they small children, or people living in primitive Stone Age communities, or uneducated, illiterate people, or educated, rational scientists, use both rational and metaphysical thought. The earliest human beings used rational thought to devise tools and to create and control fire. The progress of the human race has been the extension of those areas of life about which we can think rationally and scientifically. But no matter how far our own scientific knowledge and expertise extends there still remains an area of human experience which cannot be understood by science. Science helps us understand *how* things happen. It does not help us understand *why*. Physicists can explain *how*, possibly, the universe came into existence and *how* the human race evolved. They cannot explain *why*. Yet these are the questions which all of us, from the simplest and uneducated to the cleverest and most knowledgeable must answer. Why is there a universe? Why am I here? We all puzzle over these questions and we all arrive at an answer, often a very vague, unspelled-out answer, but an answer nevertheless, which we can never prove, scientifically, is right, but which gives us an explanation and with that a sense of security.

The sense of security which our metaphysical beliefs give us derives from the fact that our explanation of *why* there is a universe and why we have a part in it imposes a pattern on what otherwise appears to be chaos. Whether our explanation is in terms of a Divine Plan, or a battle between the forces of Good and the forces of Evil, or the inevitable working out of karma, or the handing down of life and wisdom from ancestors to heirs, or the orderly progression of cause and effect (all scientific thought is underpinned by the metaphysical belief in events being determined by temporally preceding events) our explanation brings order out of chaos. Because our religious and metaphysical beliefs make us feel more secure we resist anyone who tries to make us change them. The more insecure we are in ourselves, the more fiercely we cling to our metaphysical beliefs. Admitting doubt opens an abyss beneath our feet. Those people who say that our belief is wrong and those people who hold different beliefs about the nature of the universe and the purpose of life threaten our security. That is why we scorn, hate, and, when feeling sufficiently endangered, seek to kill them. To be secure we must feel that our metaphysical beliefs are not our constructions and are in need of no proof. They are the Truth, Fixed, Real and Immutable. Many people find the thought of discovering that the truth may be something other than what they believe more terrifying than the thought of a nuclear holocaust. That is why they believe in Armageddon or Paradise or 'the Lord giveth and the Lord taketh away'. Security is preferred to change.

Our metaphysical beliefs do more than impose order on chaos. They give us a special sustenance which we fear may disappear if we change our beliefs. They give us a sense of meaning and purpose, and help us overcome our fear of death by providing a structure of continuity which overcomes the discontinuity of death. We may fear death, but at the same time be reassured by our beliefs that we have fulfilled our part in the Divine Plan or that we shall be reborn to a better life or that though we may end our life in death, some part of us continues on in our children or in the love of our friends or in the value of our work. We imagine our death and its aftermath not just in these general terms but in its particulars. We imagine a deathbed scene, or grieving friends, or a joyous reunion with loved ones in heaven. In thinking like this we may confuse ordinary death with what death in a nuclear holocaust will be. For instance, I see my death as the end of me and an afterlife as a purgatory of work which I wish to avoid, just as I wish to avoid senility and a lingering, painful death. Incineration in a nuclear fireball, I think, will avoid those aspects of death which I fear. I must be careful not to impose my ideas of what ordinary death will be on my picture of a nuclear holocaust in case, subtly and even slightly, I connive at my death in a nuclear holocaust.

More than simply sustaining us through life our metaphysical beliefs can give us a sense of having access to great power, be it the power of God, of magic, or of scientific knowledge. Science and technology developed in predominantly Christian and Hebrew cultures, and in the Hebrew and Christian tradition teaches that God gave man the world for his own use.

> *Then God said, 'Let us make man in our image, after our likeness; and let them have dominion over the fish of the sea, and over the birds of the air, and over the cattle, and over all the earth, and over every creeping thing that creeps upon the earth.'*[13]

This tradition has served to empty the Western world of all sense of the sacred. The world is there to be used, not to be preserved, communed with, experienced as joined inextricably to human life in the way that it is seen by the American Indians, the Australian Aborigines and all people who love nature. Thus the Hebrew and Christian tradition allows that the world can be, with impunity, consumed, devoured and destroyed. The forests are cut down to provide hamburger meat and wrapping paper and the nuclear arsenal grows, all justified by some people as part of God's will.

Belief in God's will also has the advantage of maintaining the belief that this is a just world. When Melvin J. Lerner reported his studies of the lengths to which people will go to preserve their beliefs that, somehow or other, in this world or in the next justice prevails, he called his book *The Belief in a Just World. A Fundamental Delusion.*[14] We all like to see the world as possessing some kind of orderly pattern. That way we don't feel overwhelmed by events. We want to be able to predict the future and prepare for it with some degree of success. One orderly pattern which many of us see is that we live in a just world, that even though terrible things happen in this world, somehow people get what they deserve, or that in the end truth, justice, or God's wisdom and goodness will triumph. Lerner, who, as a Jew, has had to come to terms with the Jewish Holocaust, calls this belief a delusion, and, as a social psychologist, has carried out a great deal of research into what people do 'when they discover they are not living "in a rose garden".'

The greatest threat to the belief in a just world is the suffering of innocent victims. What Lerner's research shows is that rather than admit injustice people will devalue the victim (i.e. 'not really suffering', or, 'brought it on himself', or, 'those people don't feel pain like we do'), run away from the victim, or resort to primitive magical thinking to explain the events. Where people are prepared to help the victim, the extent of the help is limited by the observer's perception of himself in a just world. Thus the starving and debt-ridden people of the Third World can be seen to have brought these disasters upon themselves by their incompetence and wickedness, or to lack the ability to suffer because they are sub-human (i.e. animals do not feel pain as we do). Famine or the possibility of a nuclear holocaust can be construed as a means of ridding the world of inferior people and ensuring the survival of superior, virtuous and powerful people. A belief in the Master Race did not die with Hitler. Such beliefs are a desperate defence against the realization that being good does not protect you from disaster and suffering.

We all have to face the question of suffering. We may be oblivious to the sufferings of the starving people of Ethiopia, or the boy soldiers of Iran and their mothers, or the unemployed and hopeless young people in the industrialized West, or the exploited women in the sweatshops and brothels of Bangkok and Hong Kong, but sooner or later suffering enters our own lives. We are forced to ask questions like, 'Why should my child be killed by a drunken driver?', 'Why should my husband lose his job when he has worked hard all his life?', 'Why should I get cancer when I have always tried to be so good?'

In such circumstances those of us who have no religious beliefs turn to the metaphysics of science and talk in terms of chance and probability. Those of us who have religious belief have to ask, 'Am I being punished for past sins? Am I being treated for some Divine purpose? Is this all part of the Lord's plan?' Sometimes the suffering can be seen in these terms and so endured. But sometimes the suffering is too enormous, too disproportionate to the capacity of those who have to bear it, and then the question has to be asked, 'Is God Himself evil?'

Job struggled with this question, and many men and women before and after him, Job's answer, that we have to trust God even though we may never understand Him, was taken up and elaborated by Jung who saw within God the Shadow which we have to learn to trust and accept, just as we have to learn to trust and accept our own Shadow, or else be torn by conflict and uncomprehending misery all our lives. The American theologian Jim Garrison extended Jung's understanding to the problem of God and the nuclear holocaust and wrote,

> *The paradox Hiroshima confronts us with, therefore, is this: On the one hand we must accept the message and person of Christ with an intensity we have never had to before, for if we fail to integrate the darkness Hiroshima represents into a deeply lived Christian consciousness we face our own annihilation. On the other hand, Hiroshima demands that we recognise the darkness of God and come to grips with the antinominal character of a God who creates both good and evil. In this sense, Hiroshima is the gateway to Christ crucified even as key to understanding Hiroshima. This paradox can be a path to wisdom if we realise that the action of God in Hiroshima, like the action of God in Christ crucified, points not to our destruction but to a deeper commitment and experience of the resurrection. The goal is not annihilation but wholeness.*[15]

But understanding and accepting the darkness of God is no easier than understanding and accepting the darkness within ourselves and other people.

Chapter 5

'WE NEED THE BOMB'

---

*'These wise guys need having some fear put into them.
These Russians think they can roam around the world
and take whatever they want. No way. Atom bombs? I'm
more scared of crossing the street. Ronnie – he's
seventythree years old and he stands up for America.
You've got to get tough in this world. You can't be easy
with people. If you're nice and polite nothing happens.
Those Libyans – your Margaret Thatcher should blow
them off the face of the earth. This nuclear fear is just a
big joke.'*

a Boston taxi driver

When this taxi driver discovered that I was Australian he
was delighted. He had fought alongside Australian troops in
the South Pacific during the Second World War. We talked
about where he had fought, and I could understand how, as a
young man, he had had to develop such aggressive attitudes
in order to cope with the danger and the deaths of his
companions. The trouble was, he had simply carried over
these attitudes to other situations without considering
whether such attitudes could be wisely applied there.

We do not always see that attitudes which might be suitable
for one situation ought not be generalised to cover all situations – like the Air Force officer who flew bombers which
carried nuclear warheads and who said to me, 'You put a
fence around your home, don't you? That's what we do – put a
fence around our country.' The image of putting a fence
around a piece of land is thousands of years old, ever since

various tribes of human beings gave up wandering as nomads and settled in one place to grow their crops and herd their cattle, and since that time many fences have been put up, fallen down, and been replaced. Such an image could remain with us forever. But this is not an appropriate image for describing the present relationship between the superpowers today. Charles E. Osgood observed that,

> Surely no sane man can envisage our planet spinning on into eternity, divided into two armed camps poised to destroy each other, and call it peace and security! *The point is that the policy of mutual deterrence includes no provision for its own resolution.*[1]

Such a policy of mutual deterrence cannot contain a provision for its own resolution because what is being maintained and defended is something more profound and felt as more precious than the mere possession of territory. It has to do with the way in which all men and women see themselves and the way in which they live their lives.

The arguments for deterrence rest on the assumption that we must defend ourselves and our possessions from attack. In the speeches of those who see nuclear weapons as essential to defence we are told that it is 'our way of life' which is being defended. Little mention is made of possessions. It may be no more than a co-incidence that the middle-aged, who tend to have more possessions than the young and the old, are more likely to favour nuclear weapons, or at least are not so likely to bestir themselves in protesting against nuclear weapons.

GUARDIAN WOMEN Tuesday May 1 1984[2]

While one of the figures in Sophie's cartoon bears a resemblance to the kind of woman who in England supports nuclear defence (middle-aged and middle-class) the cartoon is not fair to women generally. Opinion polls show that more women than men are against the possession of nuclear weapons, But it is men who do the defining and defending of territory. So we need to look at how men define and defend themselves.

BBC Radio 4 holds regular phone-ins on serious subjects each Tuesday morning. Recently the topic was 'Space' and two scientists, Dr David Whitehouse and Dr Gary Hunt, with the presenter Judith Chalmers were there to answer listeners' questions.[3] One caller queried the cost of space exploration when there were so many problems on Earth needing solutions. The two scientists, so Judith Chalmers told the listeners, shook their heads in disagreement all through this caller's exposition. They were quite sure that space exploration was worth every penny. They talked about the various technological advances which had already improved life on Earth, how certain processes, such as the relatively cheap method for purifying certain drugs in space, could not be carried out on Earth, and how, in the very far distant future, the Earth will become uninhabitable and so by then people will have to move on to another planet. Perhaps Titan, which should be warm enough by then, would be a likely home. Further, while they hoped it would never happen, but if there were a nuclear war then at least some people would be able to escape and establish colonies in space where they might survive until the Earth was habitable again. The caller thanked the scientists, and we all felt ourselves suffused in pleasure and gratitude to science.

The next caller was a nine-year-old boy. He asked, 'What kind of lasers are used as weapons in space?'

This boy brought us back to reality. He showed us that science, an almost totally masculine activity, is as much concerned with death as it is with life.

Perhaps it is not surprising that so many nuclear weapons look like phalluses, built to penetrate and destroy. Brian Easlea, a nuclear physicist turned philosopher, argued in his book *Fathering the Unthinkable* that nuclear weapons represent 'the pregnant phallus', a desire for the omnipotence to give birth and to destroy. He examined the language of those involved in the building and using of nuclear weapons during the Second World war and showed how images of pregnancy and birth recur. For instance, he recounted how

Two days after the (first) test President Truman's Secretary of War, Henry Stimson, attending a meeting of the 'Big Three' at Potsdam, was delighted to receive a cable from Washington which, after decoding, read: *Doctor has just returned most enthusiastic and confident that the little boy is as husky as his big brother. The light in his eyes discernible from here to Highhold and I could have heard his screams from here to my farm.*[4]

Just how many men envy women their ability to give birth I could not possibly say, but I have certainly met many men who have so closely identified themselves, their penis and their car that they find it hard to distinguish one from the other. It seems to me quite likely that there are other men who make a complete identification of themselves, their penis and their weapons of destruction. A threat to one means a threat to the others.

Brian Easlea describes how since the early nineteenth century the metaphors for nature as used by scientists have been of a woman to be sexually penetrated – Mother Nature, not as a bountiful giver, but as a woman to be uncovered, overcome and used. Along with this were the metaphors for science as a source of omnipotent power. Many scientists believe that they should not be restrained from exercising this power. As Edward Teller said, 'We would be unfaithful to the tradition of Western civilization if we shied away from exploring what man can accomplish.'[5]

If the biographers of Edward Teller and the making of the atom and hydrogen bombs are to be believed, then his words 'what men can accomplish' refer to accomplishments in terms of competition – not just making but winning. Edward Teller seems to be the kind of person Phillip Hodson had in mind when he wrote,

Boys are instructed from birth that you can only be somebody if you make external achievements which

credit your power, financial or social. The corollary of
this is that you cannot amount to anything in yourself,
indeed you are not a person unless you have influence
over some portion of the world at large. Life is presented
as a competitive contest, with you set against the rest
. . . (Boys) learn the happy knack of making themselves
feel better by making others feel worse.[6]

One of the problems I always have at work is that so many
of the men I work with believe that I must be as competitive as
they are and that, not content to be in charge of a department
of ten psychologists, I want to extend my power to being in
charge of the hospital. Whenever I make some suggestion
about how our health service might be improved, or when I
ask for more staff because ten psychologists cannot meet the
demands made on us, my suggestions and requests are heard
by some of the men as a devious ploy on my part to take over.
They are competing to build their own empires and to extend
their power and influence, or at least to protect those parts of
themselves which they identify with power. So in their eyes I
must be too. Denials by me are not believed. Composition for
them is a way of life like breathing. I hesitate to say what I
really think – running a psychiatric hospital or a district of
the National Health Service appeals to me as much as having
the job of scrubbing the stairs in the Empire State Building –
because that would denigrate the goals which they prize so
dearly. When my clients reveal attitudes like 'everybody is
competitive' or 'it's always better to expect the worst' or
'everybody hates me' I can subject them to the kind of inquiry
which shows how partial their Absolute Truth is, that not
everybody competes, that sometimes it is a good idea to be
optimistic, that no one is universally hated. But committees
and discussions over coffee do not lend themselves to such
inquiries, and, moreover, I lack the courage to try. Men who
have built their entire life on being competitive don't want the
basis of their existence to be swept away, and we all get
aggressive when the structure of our world is threatened.

Moreover, competing and feeling aggressive go together.
Arnold Palmer, describing how he became such a successful
golfer said, 'I decided to treat all 18 holes as foes to be

conquered.'[7] Dean Lukin, after winning the Gold Medal for weightlifting in the 1984 Olympics, said in a television interview that he saw the weights as something he hated and had to defeat. Tony Wilkinson, writing about *Marathon Mentality – the risks sportsmen run*, told how 'A recent poll of 100 runners in the States showed that 50 would take a drug which would kill them within a year if it could also win them a gold medal at the Olympics.'[8]

When I first read Phillip Hodson's book on men I thought it was excellent. Then I wondered if perhaps I liked it because it confirmed my prejudices about men. So I asked my son to read it and give me his opinion. Ordinarily Edward does not read such books – he doesn't think much of 'soul-searching' – but this one he read in a day and returned it to me with, 'Every word of it is true.'

For a man, Phillip Hodson wrote,

Life is presented as a competitive contest, with you set against the rest. It may be prudent from time to time to form alliances to advance your interests, thus engaging in team work, but in the last analysis a successful 'winner' plays his emotional cards very close to his chest. First he is told that emotions are unimportant, since only the world outside is real. Secondly, he is taught to keep them to himself since one of the prudential rules of the adult game of work is to give no person a hold over you . . thus it is that little boys who learn the value of working together evolve into taciturn men who apply these teamwork lessons only in order to get the other guy fired first. If women are good at picking up psychological cues at home, men are brilliant at sensing the nuances which determine the fate of their careers in relation to other men at work.[9]

Women, despite the efforts of the Women's Movement, have made little headway in the man's world of work. Judi Marshall, in her book *Women Managers: Travellers in a Male World*[10] shows that in 1975 one in ten managers in Brtiain was a woman. Now it is only one in twelve. In America only one chief executive of a top company is a woman, while a survey of European companies showed that 74 per cent of companies which had no women executives said that they had no intention of appointing any women to these posts.

It is the same in the National Health Service in Britain. While women fill the lowly ranks in nursing, medicine, administration, catering and cleaning, few women reach the most senior positions. So it is that much of the administrative work I do is with men only. What I find there is most disturbing.

Sometimes I see something on television, or read something in a newspaper, something to do with the issues which face the world today, that makes me feel terribly sad. But the only time I get really frightened and angry and despair that the human race will survive is when I see in the course of my work what men – competitive men who want their own way, no matter who gets hurt – will do. These are some of the men who run the Health Service, doctors, nurses and administrators. I have known administrators who, rather than compromise, will obstruct in various petty ways those they see as competing with and challenging them, and when these tactics fail they will use violent abuse – and all this over matters of little importance such as modest sums of National Health Service money. I have seen doctors abuse and belittle nurses; and nurses in senior positions confound and obstruct the doctors. I have seen doctors fight one another over the number of beds each has in a hospital, and give no regard at all to the patients who might need to use those beds. Small boys squabbling over marbles behave with more dignity than these men. And even more undignified are the doctors who fall into screaming tantrums when the reality of hospital life fails to conform to the doctor's wishes.

Of course I work with many good men who deplore this behaviour in their colleagues. But little is done about it. For two reasons, I think. First is the difficulty some good men – and women – have in actually understanding the reality of evil, of the hate and destructiveness which some people carry within themselves. Sometimes this is simple ignorance. People who have grown up in sheltered homes with gentle, loving parents, have simply not had enough experience of the world to understand that out there and right beside us terrible things can and do happen. More often, I fear, it is cowardice, a refusal to contemplate evil and take on the responsibility to do something about it. Acknowledging the presence of the forces of hate and destruction means losing one's sense of security and discovering that the world is a dangerous place where no one is safe. It also means either embarking on a dangerous venture to counteract the forces of hate and destructiveness or feeling oneself to be helpless. It is much easier to say, 'Oh, no, nothing happened. It's not serious. It's not really a problem.'

The other reason that good men do not recognise and deal with the destructive competitiveness of their colleagues is because, despite their goodness and understanding, they see competition among men as an Absolute Reality, a First Principle of Being. They might deplore the way some men compete, but they do not deplore or even question that for men life *is* competition. Providing a National Health Service is just as competitive an activity as running IBM or winning the America Cup.

The sad thing is that when men are not competing they can be very wise and clever, but when they are competing, they may solve problems brilliantly and develop some creative ideas in oneupmanship but in matters of importance – like the love of their family, or the continuation of life on earth – they became quite stupid. Like the men in the Punch cartoon.

"The thing is, the Communists are dumb. Otherwise, why would they be Communists? So they probably wouldn't even know they were destroyed unless we did it about eighty times."
PUNCH February 1 1984[11]

Why are so many men competitive and aggressive? Is it

some inborn characteristic carried by their genes? Or has it something to do with the way little boys are taught to be men?

Alistair Mant, in his study of *The Leaders We Deserve* divided people into 'raiders' and 'builders'. Raiders are those people who have a single purpose, acquisitive survival, while builders have an awareness of something more than personal survival and acquisition, something Mant called 'the third corner'. The raider is somewhat similar to Adorno's 'authoritarian personality'.

> The binary obsession with the Other and the projection of badness on to scapegoats and outgroups is a crucial element in the make-up of the authoritarian personality, according to Adorno and his colleagues. In the binary mode you may be intolerant of the Other for what you take him to *be* rather than finding out what he does or what he states to be his purpose. Finding out about the latter calls for hard work, sympathy and a real curiosity about what on earth other people are thinking.[12]

Mant called his book 'a sexist book'. He explained,

> It is not that all men are authoritarians with stunted intellect, but that a startling number of those who rise to high positions are. Any possessor of a womb has an intellectual short cut, potentially at least, to the notion of the 'third corner'.[13]

The difference between the raiders (usually boys) and the builders (usually girls) begins, so Mant said, at school where

> the boys specialize in rational/logical serial relations between symbols and begin to develop special graphical skills; the girls begin to think systematically about people in networks or, as many men would have it, 'illogically' or 'emotionally'. Anyway, playing with dolls demands a conceptualisation not just of relations between dolls but also the relationship between all the dolls and the family or household they belong to. If little boys play with the idea of institution, the institution will probably be the army, locked in mortal (and binary) combat with a detestable enemy.[14]

Mant went on,

> It follows, of course, that more women ought to rise to
> high office. Unfortunately, the first to do so will,
> inevitably, rise via the virtual *absence* of the useful
> feminine logic so much needed in high places. It is very
> much in the interests of men (in their largely
> unconscious defence of male privilege) to ensure that
> those women who are permitted to rise will provide us
> with a chilling example of all the most disagreeable male
> traits.[15]

We get the leaders we deserve, the ambitious raiders,
because we prefer as leaders those people who will fail to see
the complexities and ambiguities of life and instead present
us with simple answers to complex problems, answers which
promise us a security which we do not have to question.
Thinking of ourselves as living in our own country with a
fence around it with all the baddies outside is a much simpler
idea than trying to comprehend the size of the planet and the
multitudes of people on it, all with their different needs and
different ways of living. It is much easier to explain the
endless wars and fighting in terms of an aggressive instinct
than to try to understand how we feel under threat and why
we fight. As one man said, 'You look at nature. The head cow
in the herd gets more food because it bullies the other ones.
We've got to bully Russia in the same way. "You hit me, I'll hit
you".'[16]

But this is not the opinion of Professor Michael Howard who
has spent much time considering the causes of wars. He
concluded that,

> in general men have fought in the past two hundred
> years neither because they are aggressive nor because
> they are acquisitive animals, but because they are
> reasoning ones; because they discern, or believe they
> can discern, dangers before they become immediate, the
> possibility of threats before they are made.[17]

What Michael Howard is describing here are the structures
that we create and the way we react when these structures
are threatened.

I spoke earlier of how the newborn baby begins to impose structure on his world and how out of these first structures there develops, if the child has adequate mothering, a coherent sense of self. Along with this gradual creation of self goes the feeling of greed which, as Winnicot described it, is the basis of aggression – aggression before hate sets in. A baby must have a sense of greed or else it will fail to thrive and so will die. In the excited states of hunger, greed and satisfaction the moments of self occur, the I AM states out of which come what Winnicot called the most aggressive and therefore the most dangerous words in the world – I am.

To create the structure I AM is not enough. We have to impose this structure on the world and try to get the world to respond in a suitable way. We impose the structure 'I am hungry. Feed me' and, if we are lucky, the world does. A warm breast appears, or bread and jam, or money, a job and the chance to feed oneself. But if the world does not respond, if the mother is absent or starving, if the world yields no money and no job, we become angry and try to force the world to conform to our structures and to yield to our wishes. Sometimes it does. Our aggression succeeds. Our structures are safe. But sometimes the world does not conform to our structures. Then we have to change our structures, or else fall into confusion and despair. Rather than do this we can go on and on being aggressive, until we exhaust our body's resources and die, or we are destroyed by other people who want to impose their structures on us. Aggression is the means by which we can live; it is also the means by which we can die.

When we structure our world we stake out an area which we regard as our territory and the rest we define in vague and general terms – 'not my concern', 'not worth bothering about, not our sort of people'. We want our territory to be clearly structured, controlled and predictable. When it threatens to be not so structured, controlled and predictable we become aggressive. That is why men go to war and women give their families hell.

Any child who has been at the receiving end of a mother's determination that her house will be perfectly clean and tidy *all the time* and that her family will do *exactly* what she wants has no doubt that women are just as aggressive as men.

Indeed, we all know this, for no matter how kind and gentle a mother we had, at one time we were totally in her power. She could refuse to acknowledge our structures ('You're not hungry. You're tired') and impose her structures on us ('If you're not in bed in two minutes you'll be in trouble'). Childhood is the period when parents and children compete over whose structures should prevail. Some parents acknowledge the child's structures and try to find suitable compromises. Some parents refuse to acknowledge the child's structures and insist on imposing their own. But whichever kind of parents children have, they know that until they are old enough to look after themselves they are always in danger of having their structures destroyed, of being annihilated by the powerful woman who held, contained and fed them when they were babies. This is why we all have, one way or another, trouble with our mothers.

In societies where women have more to do than be just wives and mothers and where fathers take part in caring for young children, the amount of time when a child is totally in the power of the mother is limited. But in societies where the role of the woman is defined as only that of wife and mother, the woman remains dangerous and powerful in the eyes of her children for a very long time, and in societies where a woman's value is assessed solely in terms of the sons she has borne, she must create and maintain a hold over her son for all of his life. (In traditional Hindu and Japanese families a woman's closest relationship is with her son, not her husband). Daughters can try and deal with their (often unconscious) fear of their mother by identifying with her, by growing up to be 'just like mother', by incorporating both her tenderness and love and her power and strength. This avenue is not available for a boy growing up in a society which labels as 'feminine' and despises the qualities of tenderness and love and labels as 'masculine' and admires the qualities of power and strength. He has to find ways not just of separating from his mother but also of denying part of himself.

The importance of power and strength are realised by a young boy when he discovers that he must separate himself from his mother and establish an identity which is different from her. He must break free of his dependence on her. This

can happen without too much distress if the adults around
him make it easy for him to do this by stages, but some boys
are suddenly wrenched away and made to feel unacceptable
and inferior if they show any distress ('Big boys don't cry').
Moreover, if the boy has been made to feel humiliated and
helpless by his mother he has to deal with his anger and
resentment as well. I recall a scene in a supermarket. A
three-year-old boy was lying on the floor, screaming and
kicking. His mother, tired and exasperated, picked him up by
the walking reins he was wearing and held him, dangling face
down, as they went up the elevator. For her, no doubt, it was
the quickest way to get out of the store and into the privacy of
her car, out of sight of staring, censorious shoppers. For him it
was an experience of total helplessness and total rage.
Perhaps later his mother was able to help him contain his
rage and fear but if she did not manage to do this then he had
within him devastating images of fear and impotence against
which he would have to defend for the rest of his life. It would
not be surprising if, when he grew up, he treated the women
in his life very badly.

The helplessness which a small boy feels in the power of his
mother and the pressure put on him by both males and
females in his environment to 'become a man' force the boy to
develop an image of what a man is and then to try to conform
to it. Images of Man as Hero are all around him in myth and
story. Man as Hero is strong, brave, direct and logical, and
(here is the reward for becoming a Hero) can overcome Doubt
and Death. All a boy has to do is to prove that he is a man.

The myth of Man as Hero has to be retold every generation
in images the child can understand. Once Man as Hero was a
knight in shining armour. In the 1970s he became an astro-
naut who had that mysterious and wonderful quality, what
Tom Wolfe called *the Right Stuff*.

A young man might go into military training believing
that he was entering some sort of technical school in
which he was going to acquire a certain set of skills.
Instead, he found himself all at once enclosed in a
fraternity. And in this fraternity, even though it was
military, men were not rated by their outward rank as

ensigns, lieutenants, commanders, or whatsoever. No, herein the world was divided into those who had it and those who did not. This quality, this *it*, was never named, however, nor was it talked about in any way.

As to just what this ineffable quality was . . . well, it obviously involved bravery. But it was not bravery in the simple sense of being willing to risk your life. The idea seemed to be that any fool could do that, if that was all that was required, just as any fool could throw away his life in the process. No, the idea here (in the all-enclosing fraternity) seemed to be that a man should have the ability to go up in a hurtling piece of machinery and put his hide on the line and then have the moxie, the reflexes, the experience, the coolness, to pull it back in the last yawning moment – and then go up again *the next day*, and the next day, and every next day, even if the series should prove infinite – and, ultimately, in its best expression, do so in a cause that means something to thousands, to a people, a nation, to humanity, to God. Nor was there *a test* to show whether or not a pilot had this righteous quality. There was, instead, a seemingly infinite series of tests. A career in flying was like climbing one of those ancient Babylonian pyramids made up of a dizzy progression of steps and ledges, a ziggurat, a pyramid extraordinarily high and steep; and the idea was to prove at every foot of the way up that pyramid that you were one of the elected and anointed ones who had *the right stuff* and could move higher and higher and even – ultimately, God willing, one day – that you might be able to join that special few at the very top, that elite who had the capacity to bring tears to men's eyes, the very Brotherhood of the Right Stuff itself.

(If a pilot could not achieve this) in what test had he been found wanting? Why it seemed to be nothing less than *manhood* itself. Naturally, this was never mentioned, either. Yet there it was. *Manliness, manhood, manly courage* . . . there was something ancient, primordial, irresistible about the challenge of this stuff, no matter what sophisticated and rational age one might think he lived in.

To prove that he had the Right Stuff a man had to confront every day

'the binary problem . . . Right Stuff/Death'.[18]

'If you are a Hero you will never die.' What a wonderful promise! At least you'll get your name on a war memorial. (But who'll be there to read it after a nuclear war?) Of course not all boys make this myth the point and purpose of their lives, but many do, and either die trying to prove the myth, or spend their lives trying to deny that it was a myth (hence the popularity and vociferousness of returned servicemen's organizations).

Ian Moffitt's novel *The Retreat of Radiance* tells the story of an ageing Australian man, brought up on the images of the Australian Hero, trying to complete his working out of the myth and finding that

> His life, he was beginning to suspect, was a process of
> discovering what he was not – as his mother had
> sensibly warned him. And yet the juvenile dream of
> courage persisted like sexuality; the need to prove
> himself, as his father had done, remained dominant.
> Doubt, surely, was weakness.[19]

The myth of the Hero is, I find, one of the greatest hurdles to overcome in therapy where my client is a middle-aged or elderly man who is depressed and anxious. Sometimes the man has every good reason to mourn – family tragedies, loss of loved ones, inadequate reward after a lifetime of hard work – but the myth of a Hero says that a man must not cry, and so the tears which would express and relieve his sorrow are not allowed to come. Sometimes the tears rise unbidden when he is watching some simple tale on television, and he feels nothing but shame. He knows so little about feelings that he does not realise that the stories we find the most interesting are the ones which in some way symbolise our life, either what it was or what we would like it to be, and the function of drama, be it *King Lear* or *Dallas*, is catharsis, the recognition, expression and resolution of our emotions.

Not merely not understanding their emotions these men do not understand their bodies. Their muscles ache from tension, and they fear a heart attack. Their eyes ache with unshed tears, and they fear a brain tumour. At a conference of therapists recently we were told of a man who, having worked with great commitment for thirty years as a foundryman, lost his job when the steel mill closed; instead of enjoying an early retirement devoted to racing pigeons and fishing he became prey to all kinds of physical illnesses, the causes of which his doctor could not find. He collected pills and potions, but none made him well. He withdrew into himself, sold his pigeons, and became a fearful, desolate old man. Finally, to his wife's great distress, he threw himself into a canal and drowned.[20] We talked about what had happened to this man, and the psychologist and writer Don Bannister, himself no stranger to hard physical work, suggested that what had happened was that he had never listened to his body until unemployment had been suddenly forced upon him. As a foundryman renowned for his strength and endurance this man had trained himself not to be aware of pain. He had 'tuned out' all those messages we get all the time about how our body is functioning. But when he no longer had to do this he suddenly became aware of all sorts of things going on in his body – a faster heartbeat as he hurried for the bus, quicker breathing as he went upstairs, twinges in his gullet as food went down, surging in the ears as he bent and straightened. Having paid no attention to these matters for thirty years he had lost the knack of being able to tell whether the signal was one of danger or one of the body making appropriate adjustments. The anger he would have felt at the steel works being closed could not be vented on something so indeterminate as government policy; probably he did not realise how much of his self-esteem was bound up in the work he did; and these inchoate feelings would have produced that kind of misery which leads us to interpret everything that happens to us as a portent of danger. He died not of illness but of ignorance.

Even more deleterious than leaving the man ignorant about what is going on inside him, the myth of the Hero creates the belief that no man is of value just as himself. To be of value he must achieve. This means that when he fails to achieve or reaches a point in his life where achievements in sex, sport and work are no longer possible the man is left with the feeling that he has no right to exist. He may describe this

as 'I've lost confidence in myself' but what he feels is something akin to the fear and guilt of the hunted fugitive who has
no home to go to, but far, far worse.

Proving yourself to be a man can be the positive activity of
learning, exploring and discovering who you are, or it can be
the meagre, self-destroying activity of trying to hide what is
experienced as essential worthlessness. In the former the
achievement desired is creative and the goals are flexible. In
the latter the man is always at the mercy of what he sees as
other people's demands on him, or else he seeks to deny and to
avoid these demands by gaining power for himself. Of course
the obedient male needs the power-seeking male to tell him
what to do and to take responsibility, and the power-seeking
male needs obedient minions. How can you be Chief without
any Indians?

The myth of the Hero calls for great courage, and many
times the followers of that myth have had such courage. But
courage is only courage when there is fear. Sometimes the
fear of fear is greater than the fear arising from a realistic
assessment of the danger. Then the fear itself is not faced but
buried under the reaction formation of 'I am never afraid'
which makes what Fenichel called 'a "once-and-for-all"
definite change of the personality'. That most devastating
form of fear, guilt, can be combated by the acquisition of
power, for the simple reason that

> the more power a person has, the less he needs to justify
> his acts. . . . 'I alone decide what is good and what is evil.'
> However, this process may fail because the superego is a
> part of one's own personality. Thus the struggle against
> guilt feelings through power starts a vicious circle,
> necessitating the acquisition of more and more power
> and even the commitment of more and more crimes out
> of guilt feelings in order to assert power. These crimes
> may then be commited in an attempt to prove to oneself
> that one may commit them without being punished,
> that is, in an attempt to repress guilt feelings.[21]

What Fenichel is describing here is a pattern many men
follow in the acquisition of and holding on to power. To gain
power the man may commit certain crimes, he may be devious

and lying; he may use and betray his colleagues and friends; he may threaten and blackmail his competitors or even murder them or have them murdered by his followers, thus binding his followers to him in a compounding of guilt. Such a process is like riding the tiger. He fears that if he attempts to dismount or if he is thrown off he will be in danger of being destroyed either by his guilt or by his enemies.

JULES FEIFFER 'MARRIAGE IS AN INVASION OF PRIVACY, & other dangerous views'.[22]

The man who turns to the gaining of power, either for himself or for his leader, as a way of denying his sense of essential badness has been subject as a child to much shame and humiliation when he knew himself to be completely helpless. A defence against the breakthrough of these feelings of helplessness is feeling contempt for those who are weaker and smaller than ourselves. This is a defence much used by boys and men. As the psychoanalyst Alice Miller wrote,

> So long as one despises the other person and overvalues one's own achievements (he can't do what I can do) one does not have to mourn the fact that love is not forthcoming with the achievement. Nevertheless, avoiding this mourning means that one remains at bottom the one who is despised. For I have to despise everything in myself that is not wonderful, good, and clever. Thus I perpetuate intrapsychically the loneliness of childhood: I despise weakness, impotence, uncertainty – in short, the child in myself and in others.[23]

Weakness, impotence, uncertainty, so the myth goes, are the attributes of the feminine, and a Real Man, a Hero, is All Man. Nothing feminine about him. So contempt for the feminine inside onself becomes contempt for women and women's affairs. Such a denial of an important part of oneself and estrangement from half the human race has profoundly deleterious effects. As an army psychiatrist said to me,

> The army is a difficult ethos in which to practise for many reasons and over the past three years an attempt has been made to identify these difficulties. One which recurs is the crippling need to maintain a macho image with a deep rooted fear of release of feminine attributes (as they are so regarded). Tenderness, sensitivity, aesthetic ecstasy and, of course, the denigration of 'love' and need. Pain is weakness and unacceptable. The whole ethos is infantilising.[24]

The process whereby a boy learns to deny his 'feminine' attributes relies heavily on the defences of intellectualism and isolation.

To achieve a goal we have in some measure to narrow our perception and ignore much of what goes on around us. We can, for a short period, ignore the emotional and the ambiguous aspects of our life. But if we do this for a long time, if we feel that we must do this because we want to feel in control of our lives and to force the rest of reality to conform to our wishes then we start to lose touch with reality and to make some terrible mistakes in the conduct of our lives.

To avoid the emotional and the ambiguous we can resort to the defence mechanisms of intellectualism, a mechanism, as Alice Miller said, of great reliability. Become logical and objective and despise intuition and uncertainty – male commonsense as against female nonsense. Any woman who wishes to compete in a male world has to become skilled in the use of intellectualism as a defence. It is the key to doing well at university, even in subjects like psychology where the naive observer might think that some understanding of emotions, ambiguity, uncertainty and intuition would be useful. Such topics are rarely the subject matter of psychology.

All of us who have been through the educational mill have learned how to intellectualise. We know how, for instance, to assess the military might of America and Russia, to consider the outcome of various tactical manoeuvres, to calculate the probabilities of a nuclear war and the likelihood of certain events taking place after such a war. We know how to do this without reference to anything so immeasurable and ambiguous as human suffering. There are many people engaged right now on this kind of intellectual activity. Some of us, after we finish our education, never ever intellectualise again. Some of us do it now and then because it is a useful way of solving a practial problem or avoiding an emotional upheaval. But some of us, usually introverts, make intellectualism a way of life, and that way madness lies.

Intellectualism is akin to the more profound mechanism of defence which Freud called isolation. It is the mechanism much favoured by introverts since with it those aspects of experience which threaten to swamp the person can be controlled by dividing the experience up into its practical and emotional aspects. The emotional bits can be locked away and ignored – but not for ever. They come back inappropriately in outbursts of rage or disguised in strange and frightening dreams and fantasies or disabling obsessions. Or as the delusions of a psychosis. Sometimes the obsessions and delusions are so florid and bizarre that the person is seen by the people around him as clearly mad and dealt with accordingly. But sometimes the obsessions and delusions become part of a paranoid structure which the person has created to explain to himself why life is as it is and to defend himself against the dangers that he sees. Intellectualism and paranoia can be most effective as tools for gaining political or military power.

The defences of intellectualism and isolation are the enemies of the empathetic imagination. To be able to understand what another person is experiencing and so through that come to know that person, we have to be aware of the full complexity, ambiguity and paradoxes of our own experience and use that as a springboard for the leap of consciousness which takes us outside the lonely prison of our own skin and into the lived experience of another person. However, such a leap is fraught with danger. We may, in taking this leap, find ourselves sharing an experience in such a way that we feel nothing but immense joy and delight. But equally we may find ourselves sharing another person's pain and with that pain feeling our own confusion and helplessness to end that pain. Or we may find that by making the leap we are experiencing another person's world so different from our own that the comparison makes us doubt ourselves and the world we have created. The empathetic imagination is a dangerous talent. Moreover, it requires the ability to doubt, to hold at the same time several points of view about an event or a person, to feel pity for another person's weakness and acceptance of one's own weakness and helplessness. If these abilities have been labelled 'feminine' and so despised then the talent for empathetic imagination is unused, and an unused talent is soon lost. The lack of the empathetic imagination means that other people appear to you as objects to meet your needs and to do as you tell them. When these objects don't do as you want you hit them. This is how small children behave, and men who pride themselves on their machismo.

The macho man has bought the myth of the Hero wholesale, without any doubts or modifications and so has crippled himself in all his relationships with other people. He understands other people so little that he may not understand how little he understands and so claim to understand people extremely well. Or he may label women as a complete mystery, but a mystery not worth unravelling, and divide men into two groups, men like himself (direct, straight-forward, uncomplicated, able to stand up for himself, likes to know where he is, won't be put upon, won't let his mates down, able to get it up, a bit of a lad) and the others. Because he understands other people so little he is totally inept at persuading them to meet his needs and do as he tells them. When they fail to do what he wants he feels frustrated and angry and expresses these feelings violently. When abuse fails to produce the desired result he has to resort to bigger and more destructive weapons. It would be kind to pity the macho man, poor crippled being that he is, but he is such a danger to all of us that this is hard to do.

The empathetic imagination encompasses not just other people but the natural world in which we live. Through the empathetic imagination we can come to understand how we are all part of the delicate continuous network which we call the natural world, a network which we must maintain if we are to survive. In cultures where humans are seen as part of the network the Hero has to contend with natural disasters but he is not in contention with nature. But when the myth of the Hero combined with the Judeo-Christian belief that God gave man the earth for his own use, nature became one of the Hero's enemies to be conquered and used as a source of wealth and power. The myth of the Hero, in its Judeo-Christian form, changed the face of the earth.

For instance, in Australia, 'the Birdsville Track region sustained the aboriginal economy for some 1500–2000 generations. A *single* generation of European cattlemen converted the same region into desert.'[25]

But then being a cattleman is a very important activity. Walter T. Anderson is a political scientist specializing in environmental and biological issues. He wrote,

> If you fly over Central America in an airplane, you don't see CIA agents, death squads, guerrillas, multinational corporations, Communists, journalists, politicians or priests.
>
> You do see something so widespread that people tend to take it for granted: mile after mile of bare ground.

In many parts of Central America deforestation is a national pastime, performed with a rare unity by government and the private sector, Indian and Latino, rich and poor. . . .

Today population growth, new technology and the pressure for export earnings are making Central America's forests disappear at an unprecedented rate, even though it is clear to everyone that forests play an integral part in the economy of the region.

For example, deforestation has indirectly increased oil consumption. Oil is widely used in Central America as fuel for generating electricity, so the oil-price increases of the 1970s contributed sharply to the economic problems that are now facing most of the region.

One answer would be hydroelectric power. Central America has extensive river systems and heavy annual rainfall. But when you destroy a forest you destroy a watershed; heavy tropical rains now carry tons of silt from denuded hillsides into reservoirs. Siltation raises the cost of irrigation and of reservoirs to provide water needed in rapidly growing urban areas. Many dams will become useless without the expenditure of hundreds of millions of dollars. . . .

Most Central American countries should accurately be called 'hamburger republics', for the cattle business has become a reasonably profitable form of agriculture. It also confers charisma. In Guatemala and Honduras, as in Texas and Wyoming, there is a certain distinction attached to ranching, and many people who have never roped a calf wear cowboy boots anyway. There is strong evidence, however, that cattle-ranching is not as good for the land as it is for the cowboys.

Much of the grazing land is converted forests. Usually the process takes a while. First come the road builders, then the logging companies, then the people who clear the land and plant it for a year or two until its limited fertility is exhausted. Finally the ranchers come to graze their herds. Once the land is cleared it begins to erode. With grazing (or, more commonly, overgrazing) the stubble-covered hills are scored by cattle trails, and whatever topsoil remains is rapidly washed away.

Most of the beef thus produced is for export, and the prime customer is North America. . . . As a French agronomist put it, 'It is the animals of the developed countries that are starving the Third World.'

Despite agricultural economists' arguments in favor of grain crops, a more efficient protein producer, some land owners deliberately choose to raise cattle instead, even at a loss, simply because of the social prestige. 'You can get more status out of three sick cows than you do out of two healthy cornfields,' said Garrison Wilkes, a biologist and Central America expert at the University of Massachusetts. . . .

Ranching has political clout. The associations of *ganaderos* are powerful in every Central American country.

Many aid programmes, including those of the United States, actually encourage cattle-raising for sorely needed export earnings. In fact, it is not unfair to say that U.S. eating habits and U.S. policy are the most important forces behind the spread of cattle-grazing.[26]

And, of course, Real Men Eat Meat.

The process whereby a small boy who is aware of the diversity of feeling within him and of the infinite possibilities for the person he could become changes into a man who represses or isolates much of his emotional life, who argues 'logically' and 'intellectually', being unable to tolerate doubt, paradox and ambiguity, who sees women as strangers, either sexually enticing or of no value at all, and other men as competitors, and who reacts to frustration with violence which he regards as both justified and manly, is a process which inflicts much pain and fear on the boy. He is threatened, punished and humiliated by many, if not all, of the males he comes in contact with – his peers, his teachers, his male kin. There are only two ways that he can avoid this pain. He can separate himself as much as possible from male influence and become the odd one out who, while perhaps becoming the person he wishes to be, has to endure loneliness and contempt and continued attacks from other males. Or he can decide to join them, to accept their values and to behave as they do. The initiation period can be extremely painful and humiliating, but, once endured, means that the comfort and security of a men's group is now available. If the small boy has already learned to defend himself from annihilation by 'identification with the aggressor' then he has at hand the technique for accepting the cruelty of the group.

Identification with the aggressor is the name Anna Freud gave to one of the processes whereby a child can defend himself against the punishments an adult inflicts on him. When a child finds himself being punished by the very person who should care for him and on whom he depends he can deal with this perilous situation by making the transformation from

'I am being unfairly punished by my bad parent'
to
'I deserve to be punished by my good parent.'

As well as defining himself as bad the child can resolve to be just like the parent who is punishing him. He identifies himself with his parent's 'righteous' anger and justification in inflicting pain. Now he can endure pain and humiliation because he knows how to inflict pain and humiliation. Now he can chastise his own children and feel virtuous ('I was beaten as a boy and it never did me any harm'). Now he can become a soldier and kill Commies, gooks and the running dogs of Capitalism because they are not true and valuable people like the ones he is defending. And now, when the opportunity presents itself, he can indulge his sadistic fantasies on the people he has in his power.

During the Prisoner of Conscience Week in 1984 the *Guardian* carried the following report.

> Amnesty International estimates that some 20,000 political prisoners languish in gaols where torture is routine.
>   Nursal Yilmaz for instance was detained for membership of a left-wing organization. 'Once I was taken to the torture room and saw my fiancée suspended from the wall. His head was behind his arms. His body

should have been straight, but I think it was arched. His trousers were undone, and I realised he had been given electricity on his penis. This was more painful to me than my own torture.'. . .

Any form of sexual degradation one can imagine, and probably some one can't, has been perpetrated on women in detention. Rape is common and brutal. Seven Latin American countries have devised deviations that almost defy description. Adriana Borquez, now living in exile in Britain, was arrested in Chile for membership of the Committee for Peace (Comite para la Paz), a human rights group assisting torture victims. Of 881 confirmed 'disappearances', she says, she is one of only four alive today.

Although never formally charged, Adriana was confined for three months in what she describes as 'a hole' and then taken to a house in Santiago known as La Discotheque. Pop music was played at full volume to mask the screams of the tortured. Here, she says, (women have been) sexually assaulted by a dog specially trained for the task. Other Chilean ex-prisoners allege that mice and rats have been inserted in women's vaginas during torture sessions.

Nor are women spared any of the sufferings inflicted on men. Beating, flogging, *el telefono* – simultaneous blows to the sides of the head that frequently rupture the tympanic membrane; *pau de arara*, the parrot's perch, a Chilean specialty in which the victim is suspended upside down from a horizontal pole under the knees with the wrists tied to the ankles; *submarino*, in which the head is forced into water, vomit, or urine until the point of suffocation.

Electric shock, such as Nursal experienced, is universal. It is administered by cattle prods (known as shock batons) metal grids, or electrodes applied to sensitive parts of the body. In women this means the breasts and genitalia, including the vagina. The body is frequently wetted beforehand to ensure the maximum effect. . . .

Women's caring role and emotional ties with their

families are merely other levers to manipulate. At the notorious Evin Prison in Iran's capital, Teheran, women are arrested with their children 'When the mother is whipped,' one prisoner reported, 'the child is made to watch. One such mother screamed that she was ready to confess when she could no longer stand the mental agony of her three-year-old daughter.' Torturing the child itself may be considered more effective. In Iran, it is alleged, small children are placed in a sack with snakes or wild animals and their mothers forced to listen to their screams.

Political prisoners have usually committed no more heinous crime than belonging to a banned political organization, a human rights group, or even a religious denomination.[27]

When Jorge Valls Arango was presented with the International Poetry Prize in 1984 he had only just been freed from a Cuban jail where he had spent 20 years. He said that in prison

There's very little difference with hell. From hell you cannot get out, but from prison you may die and get out. All sorts of physical, psychical and moral violence is exerted upon us. We have never six weeks of peace: we have never one day of safety, or tranquillity. They are always teasing, provoking, doing something to disturb and to destroy. The most important thing is not the physical violence. That has been horrible many times. It is the risk you are always running of becoming mad or becoming an idiot – which has been the case with many of my companions. Some of them have even become idiots. After a time, a man doesn't know how to talk, and we live every minute defending our soul, our structure, our human identity.[28]

Not all men have been caught in the trap of childhood experiences and adult circumstances which lead them to become wife-batterers, muggers or torturers, but all, to some greater or lesser extent, have been taught to be wary of feelings. As Phillip Hodson said,

During infancy there is a change in the boy's

pleasurable consciousness towards a condition of wariness. He has learned not to trust his subjective feelings. They are not factual. He must be rational. He must be objective, like his father. He must be impersonal, unlike his mother. He must be competitive with fellow males in order to achieve power. Such potency must be hard, external, visible, measurable, or it is effeminate and does not count. Men must manoeuvre openly to make their mark upon the world. Inner power is a self-contradiction because it is not asserted over rivals. And the essence of masculine potency is that it robs another of status: I win, you lose. All of which is built on the original childhood misconception that it is an asset to be emotionally invulnerable. As the years go by, this causes the boy-child to reject physical touch from his parents and to cease to give voice to inner fears. If you don't use a skill you tend to lose it: already by the age of nine boys are poor at communicating with their peers. They prefer to talk about play, which is safe: girls tend to do the opposite.[29]

I saw a splendid example of this male inability to conceptualise what goes on inside him recently on BBC TV. It was just six months after the terrible car bombing at Harrods in London. Two of the policemen who had been very close to the car when the bomb went off were invited to the studio to reminisce about the experience. Each of them had suffered severe injuries and each was extremely lucky to be alive. Several of their colleagues had been killed along with some of the Saturday shoppers. The presenter, Sarah Kennedy, asked them how these events had changed them. They were nonplussed by this question. Each said that he had not changed at all. Neither said what many people say after a close brush with death, that he had a greater appreciation of life now, or that he was making sure that he did all the things that were important to him. As an afterthought one police-man remarked that his wife and his colleagues had said that he had changed. His wife said that he was much harder now, and his colleagues said that he was much more easygoing now. He had no idea why they should say these things. The other policeman said that he, too, had been told by others that he had changed, but he couldn't see it. Why should pain and suffering and a glimpse of death's dark door make any change in him? They could not even say that they were happy to be alive.

But happiness, as Phillip Hodson pointed out, is an emotion, so in effect it is impossible for many men to find happiness. Only tangible material and power rewards are valuable to them. *'Men,'* he said, *'couldn't pass an O-level in describing their emotions. That is why they so often become violent – it is the only way we can convey our passions while at the same time somehow denying the importance of them.'*[30]

Denying or hiding what one feels, eschewing doubt and ambiguity, wishing to appear 'logical' and 'objective' (I put these words in inverted commas because the logic and objectivity men use in everyday life rarely reaches the standard set by scientific method) have a profound effect on the way men use language, a way very different from the way women use language. Japanese has two distinct forms, men's Japanese and women's Japanese. Japanese mothers make sure that their small sons learn the masculine form. Students of the English language can perceive a man's English and a woman's English. Dale Spender, in her study of how men retain their power by having control over the language, stated firmly that 'the English language has been literally man-made and it is still primarily under male control'.[31] Bev Roberts, writing about Ockers and malespeak (an Ocker is an Australian Real Man who takes a special delight in being uncouth) wrote,

There has been much scholarly debate about what constitutes the distinctively Australian form of English, concentrating on national and regional colloquialisms and on styles of speech. But there has been virtually no recognition that most of the generalisations about Australian language are derived from the language and speech of men. Most distinctive Australian colloquialisms originate in male spheres of activity: from the pioneering settlers, the explorers, the miners, the bushmen, the sportsmen, and from the workplace, the battlefields, the pubs and the street corners. Australian women exist in a language environment that does not reflect their particular experiences and which largely denies their existence or portrays them as subsidiary or inferior. . . . Because of the gender differences in socialisation, women do not speak the same language as men; they are encouraged to adopt a more 'genteel' form of speech, and slang, invective and obscenity are considered (by men) inappropriate for use by women.[32]

Wittgenstein remarked that *the limits of my language are the limits of my world.* If your language is limited either by lack of education or by restrictions about what words are permissible to use (e.g. women mustn't talk directly about sex and men mustn't talk about feelings other than those of anger and hate) and about what forms of expression are appropriate (e.g. women must use forms expressing subservience and uncertainty and men must never use expressions of doubt, uncertainty and ambiguity) then your world is small and without variety and flexibility. The smaller your world the fewer people with whom you can share some communality. If you do not understand that each of us lives within an individual language world and that to communicate effectively we have to learn what is significant in another person's language world, then your attempts at communication always fail. This is why so many men and women fail to understand one another and why so many attempts to find an agreement and compromise in government and business end in failure.

Comprehending another person's language world is always hard work. It means thinking, and that is always hard work. It also means giving up the security of 'Anyone who doesn't think like me is either mad or bad' and living with the knowledge that your world is not solid Reality but merely structures which may or may not reflect an unknowable otherness. Comprehending another person's language world makes us realise how few of life's problems admit of a once-and-for-all solution. It is very disturbing to find that although America learnt, through much suffering, that a militarily powerful country cannot win a guerrilla war, many Americans still think that a once-and-for-all solution can be found for the fighting in Central America. They do not see that war breeds war and suffering suffering.

The desire for a simple, once-and-for-all solution is often the sign of a sense of great insecurity, and this, so my American friends tell me, is quite prevalent in the US today. I am always sceptical when people tell me that there is a sense of insecurity now, in contrast to some time when people felt secure. I don't doubt that people feel insecure now. I just think that people have always felt insecure. If people feel insecure inside themselves there is always something in the outside world that they can feel insecure about. And there has always been something in every age to feel insecure about. Inside us we must always feel some degree of insecurity, for no matter how wealthy we are, no matter how powerful we and our country may be, we still have to face old age, death, and the loss of our loved ones. If we can recognise these inner insecurities then we can talk about them to other people and find comfort and reassurance. But to do so means admitting weakness, and if that clashes with your macho image you can't do it. You have to find some other way of dealing with your insecurity, and one splendid way is to have real, identifiable enemies out there. There's nothing like paranoia for making you feel secure. Paranoia gives a purpose to life and makes you feel important. It adds drama to an otherwise dull life. Macho paranoia seems to have found an outlet for its strong feelings in the Survivalist movement, which, according to the *Survive* series on Channel 4[33] could have as many as two million members. When John Metzger took over as editor of the *Survive* magazine his editorial summed up the intellectualism, the power seeking and the paranoia of the macho man:

> He who adapts survives. Nature offers us an adverse challenge, and I believe in voluntarily taking on that challenge in order to be better prepared for what uncertain times the future may bring.
>
> But forces beyond nature have compromised our position of dealing with nature on her own terms. Nuclear war would be a horrible thing, but the

complexities of the arms race run amok compel us to deal with the problem on rational terms. Avoiding nuclear confrontation requires more than emotions and sensational descriptions of life after war. Life after 'The Bomb' will be difficult at best, BUT I believe that a nuclear war is survivable. And that's one reason why SURVIVE is here. This magazine will continue to be written for like-minded people who have the conviction that *they will survive*.

Our enemy is Russia, and I'll make no bones about it. But another enemy we are facing is words, words of our own countrymen advocating nuclear freeze and unilateral disarmament. Words from people who are convinced that nuclear war is *not* survivable. People who refuse to prepare for it, and refuse to accept the concept and value of civil defense. If our policy makers are eventually won over by the anti-nuclear movement's emotional ravings and pipe-dream solutions, war may become a reality sooner than we think. Nuclear war is not only survivable, it is avoidable – but avoidable only through carefully planned, rational approaches through diplomatic channels. We need to continue dialogue and careful negotiations. But let us fall behind in the arms race, or to follow the advice of the anti-nuclear people and trust the Russians. . . . Well, that course of action would amount to national suicide.

I'm going to make a commitment to you: You're going to get the best information possible to stay alive. Our nation has a vested interest in people like you. When everything falls in around us, you'll be the ones who will pick up the pieces. You will be the leaders, the movers – you will push on and get civilization back on its feet.[34]

When the *Observer* defence correspondent Ian Mather visited El Paso in Texas he finished his account of this missile town with a description of a ceremony at which Major General James P. Maloney, the base commander spoke.

'As Alexis de Tocqueville wrote in 1835, he intoned, "the principal instrument of the American is freedom, of the

Russian servitude". . . World affairs revolve around one key issue, the struggle between freedom and communism.'

On our way back from the ceremony I pointed out to an officer that in 1835 the Russians were living under the Tsar, that Marx had not written the Communist Manifesto, and the future of the world looked grim if it was perceived wisdom that the Russians and Americans were predetermined to hate each other for ever.

'Gee,' he said, 'I never thought of that. But I don't think anybody dare point that out to the general. It's his favourite quotation!'[35]

Three months later the *Observer* carried an article by its editor, Donald Trelford, where he told the story,

After the umpteenth vodka deployment, the Soviet general unbuttoned his tunic and leaned earnestly across the table. 'The distance from Berlin to Moscow,' he said, 'is only 2,000 kilometres. Yet 20 million Russians died to stop the Germans getting here. That is 10,000 dead Russians for every kilometre of road. You'll understand why those of us who remember the war are so concerned by Europe's failure to heed our warnings on cruise and Pershing missiles.'[36]

The history which each general quoted is correct, the question is whether they remain fixated in that history or whether they can move on to some new understanding. Not just these two men, but all men. There are some women who still adore John Wayne, but an increasing number of them are wishing that the boys would outgrow their deadly toys.

It does seem that men are men the world over. Phillip Hodson included men of all nationalities when he wrote,

In the battle of the sexes nowadays, it is men's behaviour that appears to be anachronistic. We are an old-fashioned conscript army ever eager to obey our leaders' orders and I daresay we could do a passable imitation of a goosestep on request. In our steel skulls we are enclosed. We are noisy. We always seek out prominence. We automatically hit those who hurt us as if that will make our hurt any the less. We don't hesitate to kill when we are challenged on our chosen ego-ground, be it philosophy, politics or economics. In the world at large screens beam at us daily pictures from fresh killing zones of young warriors in identical poses exulting in their male lethality. Some 50 millions have died at the hands of psychiatrically normal males since 1900. We are the death sex. Men say they fight for a cause, but that cause is their own identity, an external source of power, which they cannot find in themselves. The wars of virility are without end since those who have learned nothing from history's errors are doomed to repeat them in a cycle of tragedy and farce.[37]

Can men change? Phillip Hodson hopes that they can. He argues that over the last two decades women have reflected on the way they live their lives and have changed. Men can do the same. I certainly see a difference between my generation of men and that of my son. Many men in their twenties and thirties seem to be able to maintain their self-esteem without having to regard women as their inferiors, even though living with a woman who is your equal makes for a less comfortable life than that with a dutiful and industrious wife. (Anyone who comes home to a cooked meal, a tidy house and clean clothes to put on the next day doesn't know what hard work is.) But Yvonne Roberts who interviewed at great length some forty-five men in their thirties, compared her findings with other research, and concluded that,

Contemporary man can now enter what was once considered the exclusive domain of women, such as the care of children, but not to the extent where he shares the drawbacks as well as the advantages. At the same time, he sees no reason to concede any of his own power of privilege. He still regards the woman's role as secondary. A number of the men I interviewed, for instance, described great 'involvement' with their children in terms of the more pleasurable tasks – playing with them, putting them to bed, dropping them off at school. The mundane daily chores, the trips to the dentist, the ferrying to and fro, were still left to the wife.

In short, they have adjusted but not, in my opinion, *changed*.[38]

Researchers into the cause of heart disease (to which men are more prone than women) have found links between being a certain type of personality and developing coronary failure, but they are not optimistic that such men can change. As reported in *Newsweek*,

Cynics, Oscar Wilde once said, are those who know the price of everything and the value of nothing. Even the savviest cynic, however, has probably not calculated that cynicism itself may have a heavy cost: increased coronary disease. By the recent reckoning of psychiatrists at Duke University Medical Center, the untrusting heart is often unhealthy as well. While exploring the so-called Type A personality – supposedly more prone to heart attacks – the researchers identified one flaw as fatal. 'We suggest that "cynicism", better than any other single word, captures the toxic element in the Type A personality,' says Duke scientist Redford Williams. . . .

Williams and psychologist Paul Costa of the National Institute of Aging analysed the true-false questions (answered by the research subjects) – and found that most really were weighing mistrust. (Samples: 'Most people lie to get ahead', and 'It is safer to trust nobody.') People who score high 'are not angry,' concludes Costa. 'They are just cynical.'

The researchers argue that the link between cynicism and heart disease also makes sense physiologically. Laboratory experiments have shown that mistrustful people produce more 'fight or flight' hormones in a variety of situations than do less cynical folk. Since these hormones are believed to accelerate plaque buildup on artery walls – 'hardening' of the arteries – those who expect the worst from the world around them might find themselves leaving it sooner.

The Duke findings come on the heels of other revelations about Type A's from their coprogenitor, Meyer Friedman. In his most recent study Friedman reports that hard-driving behaviour is sometimes reversible – and that those who do slow down significantly lower their risk of suffering heart attacks. Williams hopes that the dangers of cynicism may also be reduced or even prevented. He suggests, however, that drugs to block the offending hormones may be a better bet than behavior modification. Those who have already made a career of disbelief, after all, will not be so easily persuaded to adopt a change of heart.[39]

There are many individuals who know that their behaviour – their hard-driving competitive cynicism, the ingestion of alcohol, nicotine, cocaine, heroin – will kill them, yet they do not choose to change. Many claim that they cannot, that this is their immutable personality, their inherited weakness, their working out of their dramatic fate, their revenge upon their parents or the world. Or simply, that it will never happen. If people will not change to save their own individual lives, they are not likely to change to help save the human race from extinction.

But what if men did change? What if they decided that all this murderous competition was nonsense and that they would rather co-operate with one another than fight? What would happen to the world economy which is so dependent upon the manufacture and sale of arms? War is not a matter of fighting over noble principles of nationality and justice. It is a matter of power and money, and those with power and money rarely suffer from war's effects. Gibbard's cartoon about the fighting in the Falklands between Britain and Argentina summed up what all wars are.

In the arguments about nuclear weapons the contrast is sometimes presented that nuclear weapons are bad but 'conventional' weapons are right and sensible, what all responsible governments would want to have, along with a fine body of men who would use such weapons only with the highest sense of justice and responsibility. What is overlooked here is that all weapons, whether nuclear or 'conventional' are made to kill and that the arms trade is the arms trade, whether it is in neutron bombs, nerve gas or tanks. The function of the arms trade is to sell weapons.

THE GUARDIAN Monday May 31 1982[40]

Ten or 15 years ago the Nigerian town of Yola, up near the Cameroun border and 500 miles from the sea, was an administrative backwater with not much more than a muzzle loading rifle for 100 miles around. Within the past two weeks 1,000 people are reported to have been killed there by Muslim fundamentalists armed with 'sophisticated weapons'. For as the current yearbook of the Stockholm International Peace Research Institute (Sipri) observes, no significant initiative towards restraint in the conventional arms trade has been made for a very long time, with the result that 69 per cent of Soviet arms exports and 56 per cent of American are now directed at the Third World. There was a steep drop during Carter's term at the White House when he imposed a unilateral curb. Under Reagan the traffic has picked up again, and Soviet trade has continued undisturbed.[41]

And it is not just 'sophisticated weapons' which are being manufactured and sold.

Third World Governments are currently importing nearly 25 billion dollars worth of armaments from the major industrialised nations. Until an internal memo leaked from the Crown Agents last year, the public were kept largely ignorant of the fact that the arms trade also includes technologies and weapons specifically designed for quelling internal dissent.

The memo, which emphasised the need to avoid ministerial embarrassment when handling sensitive items such as execution ropes and leg irons, spurred two journalists from the *Daily Mirror* to investigate a company in the West Midlands – Hiatt & Co. Hiatt offered the reporters who were posing as buyers for the South African Secret Police, leg shackles, gang chains and more specialised restraining equipment made to order if required. Perhaps even more shocking was the response of the Trade Minister, Norman Tebbit, 'if this country did not export them somebody else would.'

Such equipment is merely one of the cruder components in what Michael Klare, of the Institute for Policy Studies in Washington, terms the international trade in repression. Modern technologies of political control include riot weapons, e.g., shotguns, watercannon, stun rounds, plastic bullets and the chemical irritants CN, CS and CR; internal security vehicles used either to disperse or capture; area denial technologies such as the concertinas of razored tape used to seal off selected zones; computerised police communication, command and control intelligence networks and message switching systems, surveillance and telephone tapping equipment; intruder detection devices, helicopter – mounted crown monitoring equipment, human identity recognition systems; night vision sights and silenced assassination rifles; prison and torture technologies.

There are also numerous standard operating procedures or techniques of repression, which form the software components of the trade. For example, the riot and counterinsurgency training, the advisory support, technical assistance including the business of teaching, scientific methods of interrogation torture and the more brutal forms of human destruction supplied to the state security, intelligence, military and police agents of authoritarian regimes.

In any bureaucracy of repression, there are personnel schooled in the ideological attitudes necessary to keep such systems in operation. They include the various technical advisors, counter-insurgency strategists; paramilitary and police training officers, military intelligence personnel, the merchants who supply the equipment and the 'white collar mercenaries' who act as key technical operators in any repressive system.

The leading suppliers are the same countries primarily responsible for the arms trade as a whole – USA, USSR, France and the UK. However, it is generally agreed by researchers in this field that the United States, because of her extended global interests, is the biggest supplier of repressive technology, followed by Britain whose continuing war in Northern Ireland spawned a new generation of technologies to maintain internal political control.[42]

Nuclear weapons, 'conventional' weapons and the weapons of repression and torture are all part of the system whereby men compete with one another for power. Fear of the devastating effects of a war where nuclear weapons are used may restrain some men from actions which could lead to such a war, but meanwhile wars are being fought in countries where previously there was peace, and the number of terrorist attacks are increasing. Those of us who remember the Second World War will remember how comforting it was to know just who your enemies were. Now, if you get blown up by a bomb, you can't be sure who planted the bomb, and nine times out of ten it wasn't meant for you anyway.

There are many men and women who would tell me that I am being foolishly idealistic if I think that we can live without weapons to defend us. They would argue that we can never live without the bomb. The question, though, is *'Can we live without enemies?'*

Chapter 6

MUST WE ALWAYS FEAR THE STRANGER?

My saddest, guiltiest parishioners say that they sinned terribly by not taking some kind of personal action on behalf of peace between the United States and the Soviet Union. They say they should have demonstrated against this or in favour of that. But I tell them no, the sin was that we did not accept one another in our heart, neither side. Our leaders hardly even knew each other. The two greatest nations on earth, with almost total responsibility for the fate of the planet and the species, and they hardly even spoke! They should have made it their business to be close personal friends. And there should have been as much communality of policymaking and government as possible. Instead the two countries were separate islands, distant from, and mysterious to, each other. That was the sin of pride, doing that.[1]

Pride, so the Christian church teaches, is the deadliest of sins because it prevents us from recognising our faults and changing. This teaching is based on the Church's belief in free will which means that we are capable of change, that we are free to choose whether we shall change or not. The question is, are human beings capable of changing themselves so that they can all live in a world without enemies? Or do we need enemies the way we need air, food and water?

Many people say that human nature never changes. History certainly shows that people make the same mistakes, century after century, while, as any therapist can testify, one generation seems to be incapable of learning from another.

Our scientific knowledge of the real world is immense, our technology races from one triumph to another, yet our knowledge about ourselves remains the same. Psychologists and sociologists do research and discover what we already know. They have shown that we learn better by being rewarded for success than punished for failure (or 'You catch more flies with honey than you do with vinegar'), that babies who are loved and cuddled do better than those that aren't and that if a woman doesn't think much of herself and has no one to confide in she gets depressed. I wrote a book on how to escape from the prison of depression and many people told me how novel it was, but I knew that I was not saying anything that wise people have not known in every age and place. All I did was to try to put this wisdom in a language understandable for our time. As far back as written records exist we have accounts of how to live life wisely. All these accounts, though differing in particulars, are the same in general – love one another and treat life with respect – and all these accounts have had a limited effect on the people who heard such wisdom being taught. We have continued not loving one another and not treating life with respect. Is this just human wilfulness and stupidity, or is it something we cannot help doing because this is the way we are?

When some people talk of human nature they mean that there is a solid reality there which we all know and of which human nature is a part. But, in fact, while there is probably a reality there, we can never know what it is. Human beings are so constructed that we can never know reality directly but only the structures that we create. Our eyes create colour, space and distance, our ears create sound. The language we speak divides up the amorphous sensations we experience, labels and evaluates them. No two languages do this in the same way. Thus, *language creates reality and not reality language.* (This is why our leaders need around them advisers who have a good understanding of the language of other countries.) Each of us uses the language we speak in an individual way. Everyone knows this. We all know that different people see things differently. Because we created the structures of our world we can change them. This is why we are able to say, 'I used to think that so-and-so was so, but now I think differently.'

But what is fixed is how we perceive. We cannot perceive just anything. For us to become aware of something that thing has to have a contrast. Where there is only sameness we perceive nothing. If our light came not from the sun but from some unchanging, eternal source, if there were no shadows and no dark, then *we would not know there was light*. If everything and everybody lived for ever, if nothing died, then we would not know that we were alive. We know perfection only because there is imperfection; good because there is bad; hot because there is cold; height because there is depth; near because there is far; presence because there is absence; I because there is You.

A newborn baby does not know the extent of its being. It feels itself to be coterminous with all that exists. (We remember that time through images from that 'oceanic feeling' when we are suffused with bliss or in the grip of fantasies of omnipotence – peak experiences or the delusions of power.) But then some parts of this existence become detached. The baby discovers its toes as belonging and its mother as separate and so enters into the loneliness and insecurity of being. To counteract this loneliness the young child gladly sees itself as part of a group – the family – and takes on the characteristics of that group as its own. It is quite extraordinary how, no matter how old we grow and how far we travel from home, how much we think we have outgrown our family, this early identification with our family is in the marrow of our bones. Even if we didn't have a family, if our parents died or abandoned us, we still carry the memory of the fantasies we constructed about what our family would have been had we known them. Our family give us the first group identity. We knew the world to be them and us. 'Us' might remain just for the family or it might be extended to take in our country, our race or our religion.

We can define ourselves and the group we belong to in a multitude of ways, but whichever way we choose and whatever demands the group may make on us, we feel enormously reassured by being a member of that group.

Expulsion from the group is a fate to be feared, for none of us can live in isolation. Extroverts need other people to

"It's all right, Sophie, here comes ours now."

PUNCH June 8 1983[2]

stimulate them and to create the bonds which give them a sense of existence and prevent them from vanishing into nothingness, while introverts need other people to set standards, to give approval, and to anchor them in reality so that they do not disappear into their own inner world. If we have to live alone, we need to be able to carry images of our group inside us, or we need to turn the animals around us, our pets, into people, the members of our group. But being part of a group means giving up much of our individuality and with that comes the fear of being submerged, taken over by other members of the group. So every group, to some greater or lesser extent, is always involved in some struggle for power and influence. Sometimes this struggle causes groups to be split apart. Sometimes the group recognises that such a split is necessary and beneficial, as when parents help their adult children leave the family and set up their own groups. Sometimes members of the group feel unable to tolerate any weakening of the group. Then they will try to keep the group together by pointing to a dangerous enemy out there – the Stranger.

The characteristics of the Stranger are different from the characteristics of the group. If these characteristics were the same the Stranger would be a member of the group. If the characteristics are only slightly different from those of the group (e.g. the person lives in the next village, is Irish like my grandfather, comes from a country with a democratic government), then that person can be seen as a member of a wider group and labelled as slightly different but not dangerous. However, if the characteristics of the Stranger are seen as very different from those of the group, then those characteristics are the ones which the group dislikes and deplores and defines itself as being against. The sense of being for something and against something else binds the group together. The sense that out there is a dangerous Stranger threatening to attack us creates a group cohesion from which all members of the group draw comfort, security and a sense of self-esteem ('I mightn't be much myself but I'm a member of the greatest family/nation/race the world has ever seen). As the anthropologist Mary Douglas has shown, the stronger the group adherence, the more the Stranger is seen as 'impure'.[3]

This is the way human beings have defined themselves for as long as the species has existed. But now this way of perceiving and defining ourselves threatens our whole existence. As E.P. Thompson said in a lecture which the BBC refused to broadcast,

'There appears to be a universal need for "the Other" as a means of defining the identity of any group, and of the individuals within it. We cannot define who "we" are without also defining "them" – those who are not "us". If "they" can be seen as threatening, then our own bonding and self identity are all the stronger. Rome required barbarians. Christendom required pagans or heathens, Protestant and Catholic Europe required each other. The nation state bonded itself against other nations. The same process may be followed in the family, the community, and in sects; and also in class formation.

Technology, communications, and missiles are all shrinking the world. The Cold War, by dividing this world into two opposing parts, each of which is threatened by the Other, has become necessary to provide both bonding and a means of regulation within each part. But this is an immensely dangerous condition. In fact, unless this condition is somehow transcended, then civilization can have no perspectives longer than a few more decades. For it means that human culture carries within itself a principle of human bonding-by-exclusion which must (with our present armoury) lead to autodestruction.

'This perhaps will happen. We cannot expect our planet to have the good fortune to be threatened, in the 1990s, by invaders from outer space, who would unite humanity against an Outer Other. The only possible resource which could prevent self-destruction would be a renaissance of rationality and imagination: a lived perception, informing multitudes of the human ecological imperative. The "Other" would then have to be redefined as the very forces bringing destruction upon us – that is, not "Russia" or "America", but the military and political establishments of both blocks, and the mechanisms and structures of their ritual opposition.'

What Thompson is saying here is what I have said, that the only way we know ourselves as part of a group is because we perceive those people who are not part of the group – those we call the Dangerous Stranger. Thompson assumes that this is the *only* way in which we can define ourselves and the Stranger and he recommends that we redefine who is in our group and who outside it – instead of us, the good people, and the Russians, the bad people, there should be us, the members of the human race who want to go on living in this lovely world, and the dangerous Strangers, those militarists and politicians of all nationalities and political persuasions who are preparing for a nuclear war. Whether or not such a change is possible is another matter. What is important is what Thompson, an historian, is assuming – that human beings cannot live without an enemy.[4]

If this is so, if we can define ourselves only by defining the Stranger as different and dangerous, then we are doomed. We shall destroy ourselves, if not by nuclear war, then by the despoiling of our natural resources on which our lives depend.

In the changes which must come about if the nuclear holocaust is to be avoided and the resources of the earth replenished rather than exhausted a very large part must be played by Japan, since Japan as the second largest industrial nation devours the world's resources to extend its production and to maintain its standard of living. Every object, it seems, in Japan, if not made of plastic and paper, comes wrapped in layers of plastic and paper. Clyde Haberman, writing in *The New York Times*, said,

> Japan has succeeded through diplomacy in gaining
> stable markets and accessible sources of raw materials
> that it could not hold militarily. As before, it now taps
> the natural resources of those countries – paying
> handsomely, to be sure, but making its suppliers willing
> consumers for its products, a fact apparent from the
> ubiquitous billboards throughout Asia advertising Sony,
> Fuji, Casio, Toyota and others.[5]

A young Australian businessman told me, 'The Japanese have got at least fifty percent of Australian business. Anything we can't handle, they take over and make a success of.'

The Japanese have good reason to fear a nuclear war. Yet when I was in Japan I found that many Japanese, like many English and American people, say that they never think about nuclear war. But there are also active anti-nuclear movements, *Gensuikyo* and *Gensuikin*, and the members of the latter organisation whom I met were busily working for the abolition of nuclear weapons, although some of them expressed anxiety that their efforts were not proving successful.

But as much as the Japanese remember the horrors of Hiroshima and Nagasaki and strive to prevent their repetition, the way they organise their society demonstrates the great difficulty, perhaps impossibility, there is in making the changes necessary so that we do not need to fear the Stranger and wish to destroy him.

What I have to say now comes not from personal experience but from what I have read and what American, English and Japanese people have told me. In the brief time that I was in Japan I was treated with the greatest kindness, warmth and concern for my comfort and safety. Even the middle-aged Japanese woman who looked quite frightened when I sat down beside her in a bus understood and answered my question as to whether the bus went to Nijo Castle, made sure that I left at the right stop, and checked with a smile and a bow to see that I walked in the right direction. But that is the natural courtesy of a naturally courteous people. Had I announced my intention of staying in Japan permanently, of becoming a Japanese citizen then that would have been a different matter.

Of course I could not become a Japanese citizen. No *gaijin*, foreigner, can. The only way to become a Japanese is to be born one.

Self-evident truths need no explanation or acknowledgment. So to the Japanese their inherent superiority over all other races is not mentioned, much less explained and defended but simply acted upon. Inferiors are excluded. Koreans who have lived in Japan for several generations remain Koreans and carry identity cards. Those 40,000 Koreans who perished in Hiroshima and Nagasaki are not listed among the commemorated Japanese dead. It was not until September, 1984 that the first official visit by a South Korean leader was made by President Chun Doo Hwan who received Emperor Hirohito's very modest apology for what the Japanese had done in their occupation of Korea. These are hardly the kind of actions which will overcome the mutual antagonism between the Japanese and the Koreans. The *Eta* or *Burakumin*, a race of people native to Japan but not considered to be Japanese, are totally excluded from society and discriminated against in economic and social ways. And no foreigner, no matter how long he or she has lived in Japan, no matter how well he or she speaks the language and respects the culture, can become a naturalised Japanese citizen, much less take part in the way of life and so influence it in the way that immigrants have altered the pattern of life in the countries of Western Europe, the Americas and Australasia. There has been no influx of new people into Japan since the 8th century AD. When a Japanese speaks of his compatriots as brothers he is speaking the literal truth. Robert Christopher wrote,

> Racially and culturally Japan is the most homogeneous
> of the world's major nations. . . . (they are) members of a

single great tribe united not just by common citizenship
or common language but by common bloodlines,
common racial memory and common tribal codes, some
of which stretch back into pre-history.[6]

This was illustrated for me by Kitty and Bob, a newly
married couple whom I met in a Zen temple in Kyoto. Though
Kitty's parents were Japanese she did not speak Japanese as
well as Bob who had left Ohio to work and study in Japan for
some ten years. We spent the day exploring Kyoto together.
That evening we tried to put together some of our experiences
of Japan. Kitty said, 'My father might have lived a long time
in America but he didn't change much. He never judged
individuals as individuals but just as races. The Jews were
right up here,' she gestured with her hand above her head,
'almost as high as the Japanese, because they achieved so
much. The Africans were right down here because they had
achieved nothing.'

Bob said, 'When I talk to, say, an American, I feel that I
understand the meaning behind the words, but the longer I
stayed in Japan the more I felt I didn't understand. Often I
thought I understood and then I would find that I didn't, that
behind what I understood was something else, and behind
that something else and so on.' Bob looked very sad as he told
me this. Being excluded from a group of people whom you love
and want to be close to is a very painful experience. But
joining a group means being able to speak the language of
that group, and that is not always possible.

What comes to us as reality is, in fact, divided up and
evaluated differently by every language. Learning another
language so as to speak it with understanding and not merely
to make one's basic needs known is not a matter of learning
different sounds as names for common objects and activities
but means entering another world. Different languages
pursue different aims. Frank Gibney, in contrasting
Japanese and English, said that Japanese

is rooted in the here and now. It is interested in moods
rather than judgements. It is concerned more with
sensibility than sense. When you use English you are
using a language that constantly makes logical value

judgements and invites value judgements in return. In Japanese, on the contrary, you have a language that is shy of making logical, legal or philosophical judgements . . . English is a language intended strictly for communication, Japanese is primarily interested in feeling out the other person's mood in order to work out one's own course of action based on one's impression.[7]

In therapy I often have to resort to getting the person to describe their feelings in images ('If you could paint a picture of what you are feeling, what kind of picture would you paint?') because English words for emotions relate more to discrete feelings, like 'anger', 'hate', 'love', and not to the complexities of feelings which can so much trouble us. In Japan I came across two words which I would find most useful in my work. One is *kuyamu* which means 'regret for allowing oneself to fall into a situation where one was obliged to feel regret'. This appears to encompass the amalgum of guilt and self-pity which is part of the essence of depression. The other is *higaiteki ni* which means 'to take something (mistakenly) as an attack on or criticism of oneself'. This relates very much to the feelings of people who are depressed, anxious or perennially lonely.[8]

However, useful though these words may be, I would not find the way the Japanese, especially Japanese women, talk easy in therapy. The therapists whom I met in Japan tried to convey to me the polite vagueness of social discourse in Japan. In English the rules which define what is sensible discourse state that sensible discourse is made up of sentences. Words which do not belong in sentences are considered to be without sense. Every sentence must have a verb, and a verb must have a subject – 'I feel . . . ', 'You said . . . ', 'He did . . . ', 'We have . . . ', 'They went . . . '. Sometimes the subject is not stated but implied, as in '(You) come here!' In English we can try to hide behind the impersonal 'One does not do this sort of thing', or the general 'People care about these things', or the formal 'It is regretted that the service is cancelled', or the passive voice 'The work was not completed', but the listener is never deceived about who is actually doing these things and can bring this out into the open by a question or two. In

Japanese it is possible to talk without a subject, to mention feelings, hopes, desires, aspirations, actions without being specific about who owns these feelings, hopes, desires, aspirations or actions. It would be impolite to demand, 'Whom are you talking about?'

In English positive and negative statements are very clearly distinguished. 'You did it.' 'I did not.' 'Yes you did.' 'Never. Absolutely not.' In Japanese negatives and positives can be hidden in delicate circumlocutions or left indeterminate. It is possible in Japanese to begin upon a sentence, leave the subject of the sentence vague, and not indicate until the end of the sentence whether the statement is positive or negative. A Japanese woman is very skilled in discourse where she tries to sense as she progresses through a sentence how her listener is responding and then to alter the ending of her sentence so as to be in accord with her listener's sentiments. It is no wonder that native English speakers are often baffled by the Japanese.

Of course, every discourse, whether in Japanese, English or any other language, has many levels of meaning, only one of which is made explicit. When the discourse is between members of the same cohesive group most, if not all, of the levels of meaning are perceived and understood by the participants. The daughter who hears her mother say, 'Be a darling and do the washing up' can know that this means 'You had better do as you are told or I'll punish you' and 'I shall get angry with you if you disobey me because I am angry with your father for being late home' and perhaps may sense the meaning 'Your father has rejected me and I cannot cope with the terror of this'. Women who live in a society which expects them to know their place and to stay there and which defines anger and self-assertion as unfeminine become, in whatever language they speak, very skilled in discourse which implies far more than it says. Since they cannot bargain, fight, and attempt to control others openly in their group they become extremely skilled in unspoken threats, especially those which mean provoking shame and guilt in their listeners ('How could you do this to me who loves and cares for you?') It is only in a group where each person sees every other as an equal that discourse can be clear and open.

However, a group which allows plain speaking by all its members is always in danger of breaking up or suffering frequent changes in its composition. Plain speaking can mean great insecurity, and this many people cannot tolerate. Security with secrecy is much preferred. So it is in Japan where the aim of discourse is not the achieving of clarity but of creating and maintaining good relationships. It is the group which is of prime importance.

If I asked an American or a Briton or an Australian 'What group do you belong to?' the answer could contain a list of groups – family, work, student, sport, hobby, social, charity, political, religious. Some of the groups would be small and specific ('My cricket club') and some large and vague ('the middle-class'). If I asked which group was the most important then the person would put the groups into an hierarchy, like 'I always put my career before my family' or 'Family comes before friends'. If I asked, 'But which is *your* group?' meaning 'Which group totally encompasses your being? Which group do you totally identify with?' then the answer would be 'None'. In these societies we are expected to see ourselves as individuals who happen to be members of several groups. No matter how desperately we may need the closeness of our family or the respect and approval of our colleagues we are expected to be able, as adults, to operate as an independent individual. The aim of psychotherapy in the West is to strengthen the individual, even though this may mean that the individual might then have to choose to leave the family group or change the work group. (Takeo Doi has commented on 'the indifference towards the patient's sense of helplessness shown by most American psychiatrists influenced by psychoanalytic theory'.[9]) Thus when we in the West try to understand the Japanese we lack the necessary concept of the importance of the group in Japanese life.

When I was in Tokyo I met a delightful young woman, Manami, who had a responsible job and shared a small flat with a friend. She took me out to dinner and talked to me about her work and her hopes and plans. I saw her as being like the young women I meet and admire so much in the profession of psychology – independent, strong, sensitive, capable, vibrant, uncluttered by the rubbish which was taught to my generation (which was 'A woman is of value only as a wife and mother: feminine women never get angry, know nothing about sex, are always immaculately attired: unfeminine women are not loved'). Manami seemed to be like her English contemporaries whom I knew, but there was something else. When she was telling me about some of the problems in her work I asked her what she would do if she decided to leave her job. She replied immediately, 'I would join another group.' She smiled as she explained, 'You know, here in Japan everyone lives in a village.' This applies to all people, even if they live in Tokyo which, as Frank Gibney describes it, 'is not a city at all. It is a modular assembly of hundreds of villages clustering around and radiating out from the big transport centers.'[10] If events separate a person from the village then 'the sense of living in a village is supplemented, if not replaced by their business. The corporation becomes the village. Within it, as with the old villages, there are the departments and the divisions with their own inner sense of people who belong, the families with their sense of obligation.'[11]

Thus by 'village' Manami meant *kaisha* which Chie Nakene, in her study of Japanese society, defined as ' "my" or "our" company, the community to which one belongs primarily and which is all important in one's life ... The human relationships within this household group are thought of as more important than all other human relationships.'[12]

The community or group to which every Japanese belongs begins with the mother and child, that special union which the Japanese call *amae*, which, as Takeo Doi described it, 'is a key concept for the understanding not only of the psychological makeup of the individual Japanese but of the structure of the Japanese society as a whole.'[13] *Amae*

refers, initially, to the feeling that all normal infants at the breast harbor toward the mother – dependence, the desire to be passively loved, the unwillingness to be separated from the warm mother-child circle and cast into a world of objective 'reality'. It is Dr Doi's basic premise that in a Japanese these feelings are somehow prolonged into and diffused throughout his adult life, so that they come to shape, to a far greater extent than in adults in the West, his whole attitude to other people and to 'reality'.

On the personal level, this means that within his own intimate circle, and to diminishing degrees outside that circle, he seeks relationships that, however binding they may be in their outward aspects, allow him to presume, as it were, on familiarity. For him, the assurance of another person's good will permits a certain degree of self-indulgence, and a corresponding degree of indifference to the claims of the other person as a separate individual. Such a relationship implies a considerable blurring of the distinction between subject and object; as such, it is not necessarily governed by what might be considered strict rational or moral standards, and may often seem selfish to the outsider. Sometimes, even, the individual may deliberately act in a way that is 'childish' as a sign to the other that he (in fact, as Dr Doi points out, this is a license traditionally permitted among adults to women rather than men) wishes to be dependent and seeks the other's 'indulgence'.

It is the behavior of the child who desires spiritually to 'snuggle up' to the mother, to be enveloped in an indulgent love, that is referred to in Japanese as *amaeru* (the verb; *amae* is the noun). By extension, it refers to the same behavior, whether unconscious or deliberately adopted, in the adult. And by extension again, it refers to any situation in which a person assumes that he has another's good will, or takes an – possibly unjustified – optimistic view of a particular situation in order to gratify his need to feel at one with, or indulged by, his surroundings.[14]

But, of course, the desire to *amaeru* is not always fulfilled. Japanese, unlike English, has words

that relate to various states of mind brought about by the inability to *amaeru*. *Suneru* (to be sulky) occurs when one is not allowed to be straightforwardly self-indulgent, yet the attitude comprises in itself a certain degree of that same self-indulgence. *Futekusareru* and *yakekeuso ni naru* (indicating, respectively, the attitudes of defiance and irresponsibility in speech or behavior associated with 'a fit of the sulks',) are two phenomena that arise as a result of *suneru*. *Higamu* (to be suspicious or jaundiced in one's attitude), which involves laboring under the delusion that one is being treated unjustly, has its origins in the failure of one's desire for indulgence to find the expected response. *Hinekureru* (to behave in a distorted, perverse way) involves feigning indifference to others instead of showing *amae*. Under the surface one is, in fact, concerned with the other's reaction; although there appears to be no *amae*, it is there, basically, all the time. *Uramu* (to show resentment towards or hatred of) means that rejection of one's *amae* has aroused feelings of hostility; this hostility has a complexity not present in simple hatred, that shows how closely it is linked with the *amae* psychology. . . . (Michael Balint) was fascinated to hear that in Japanese there was not only an everyday word corresponding to his 'passive object love' but a word – *uramu* – expressing the special type of hostility arising from its frustration.[15]

Much of the hostility which people of all nations carry within themselves and project on to those they see as their enemy comes from the frustration of their desire to *amaeru*. This is one of the reasons for the popularity of seemingly benign (to their followers) grandfatherly figures like Reagan and Khomeni.

The fact that there is no equivalent word for the experience of *amae* in English shows that in the English-language world this relationship is not regarded as important. When Winnicott needed to talk about this relationship the best word he could find was 'dependence', but 'dependence' has the negative connotations of 'immature' and 'undesirable'. Such connotations do not pertain to *amae*. Indeed, the word and its verb *amaeru* are related to *amai*, meaning 'sweet'. And sweet *amae* needs to be, for it provides the form that all relationships take in Japan.

In the West no one is given respect simply because that person fills a position of authority. The position *by itself* is not considered to confer status and authority. It is the responsibility of the individual to bring to that position the necessary qualities which will enable him to be seen as deserving the status of the position and the respect of others. Thus parents have to strive to be good parents, teachers have to strive to be good teachers, judges must behave as judges are expected to behave. The President of the United States has to convey an image which shows that he is worthy to be President, while Britain's Royal Family have to work very hard to live up to the expectations of their subjects. They are always on trial by the media, and the threat of being forced to abdicate like Edward VIII is always there. (One of my earliest memories is of my mother greeting with great satisfaction the news that this, in her eyes, dissolute and hard-drinking man had been deposed.) However, in Middle Eastern and Eastern countries *the position itself* confers the status and respect on the individual filling that position, no matter how inadequate that person may be. (This is why overseas doctors who come to fill consultant posts in England and their English staff frequently misunderstand one another. The consultant expects to be respected automatically; the staff wait to see if he is worthy of their respect.)

In Japan, all senior posts are respected because they are senior and all relationships are cast in *oyabun – kobun*, parent – child terms, where the person in the *kobun* role looks to the person in the *oyabun* role with respect and with the expectation that the senior person will indulge his need for dependence. 'This dependence,' Takao Doi wrote, 'the *amae* of a child towards its parent, of a student toward his teacher, of a company employee towards his superiors, of a junior towards his senior is considered utterly natural in Japanese society. *Amae*, a Japanese would say, is surely something essentially innocent, something indispensable in cementing human relationships.'[16] Thus, according to Chie Nakene who called Japanese society the *Tate Shakai*, 'the vertical society', 'a group is organized vertically and keeps its solidarity and exclusiveness.'[17] This is shown clearly in the Japanese language where, in discussing a practical problem 'the Japanese may not be too specific about who is to handle the problem and what problem or problems are to be handled. The language is extremely precise, however, about the authority relationship between the speaker and the other ... person involved.'[18]

In relating every aspect of his or her life to the group, the Japanese looks to the group to set the standards of conduct and to define the norms by which a person is judged as good or bad. This means, as Robert Christopher described, that 'at the core of Japanese behaviour is the notion of reciprocity – the idea that people are not good or bad in any abstract sense but good or bad in light of their relationships with others.'[19] In contrast, the Judeo-Christian ethic sees good and bad as relating to absolute standards outside specific situations and demands that the individual consult his own conscience on questions of right and wrong and not be swayed by the expectations and orders of others. Thus when Eichmann pleaded that in carrying out his ghastly crimes he was only following the orders of his superiors his plea was dismissed and he was hanged. God represents the absolute standard of good, and those of us who are brought up in the Judeo-Christian ethic, even though we may not believe that we are forever under the watchful eye of God, know that we are forever under the watchful eye of our conscience. Away from home we may be able to misbehave without being shamed in the eyes of those who know us but we cannot misbehave without feeling guilt. However, in Japan where shame and guilt relate to the group there is an old proverb *tabi no haji wa kakisuti*, 'a man away from home need feel no shame'. Thus,

> a respectable business man who is a model of probity within his own neighbourhood will regularly carouse at bars and dubious 'Turkish baths' in the next ward. School children who scrupulously help to keep their own street clean turn into needless litterbugs when they enter an adjoining neighborhood. This spirit was epitomized in the so-called garbage war of 1972, when one Tokyo ward refused to accept the neighboring ward's refuse in their garbage dump. Citizens and ward officials joined to bar entrance to trucks from the outside.[20]

Thus people who are brought up to relate everything in their lives to the group in which they belong have little interest in matters outside the group. The Japanese have a word for outside the group – *tanin* – and consider that it is neither possible nor ever necessary to have a real relationship with a *tanin* person. *Tanin matters* are those matters which are of no concern of yours. Yet, if the human race is to survive we all have to look outside our groups and see the strangers in our world very differently. In the matter of survival there can be no tanin matters.

This is much easier said than done. None of us can live entirely outside of any group, for the groups that we belong to meet our basic needs in maintaining our existence. For extroverts the group provides that circle of relationships which confirms their existence, while introverts discover their authenticity and clarity by accepting and extending the ideals of the group and by receiving the approval of the group. However, the group can be dangerous for the extrovert by threatening expulsion and to the introvert by threatening chaos. So each of us, every day, has to find some optimal balance between being an individual and being a member of a group. The culture we belong to pushes us in one direction rather than another. The push in Western culture is to being an individual, and while this has produced many strong individuals it has also created many lonely ones. The push in Japan is to being part of the group, and while this has produced many caring and extremely efficient groups it has also created many people who feel that they do not exist apart from the group. Yoshiya Ariyoshi of Nippon Yusen Kaisha said, 'Being excluded from the group is the most appalling thing any Japanese can imagine.'[21] Manami said, 'When you get to university your parents, your teachers aren't there to tell you what to do. You feel empty.'

What Manami was describing there was the sense of imminent annihilation of identity which reawakens the overwhelming and primitive anxieties felt as a baby in the process of establishing a self and having these frail structures damaged or destroyed by unpredictable trauma. I would guess that many of the Japanese students who commit suicide do so because the shame they feel at not reaching the standards which they feel their family requires annihilates their insubstantial identity and they cannot live with the terror this provokes. Married women frequently suffer from what is called social phobia, when they dare not expose their fragile identity to the open spaces and unexpected dangers of the world outside the supportive structure of their homes. Similarly, many Japanese men find retirement, or even shorter working hours, intolerable because the work group is their whole existence and outside of it they do not feel that they exist or are worthy of existence.

Thus anyone who relies for his very existence as a person on the unchanging structure of the group will resist any attempts to change that group, either in its composition or in the way it defines itself. People who are sure of themselves as individuals can cope with such change. The only way groups can change without causing great pain to their members is for those members to develop individual identities which are not defined solely in terms of the group. This is not always an easy thing to do. Change is always risky, because by its very nature it is unpredictable. If one of us changes then all of us have to change, if only in how we see that person. The trouble with people who have a strong sense of their own identity is that they tend to argue and disagree. They each have a different point of view and each wishes to impose it on the others. A society which see itself as constantly threatened by outside dangers – in Japan the dangers are the frequent natural disasters of earthquakes, tidal waves and typhoons and the political dangers of China and the USSR – cannot afford to be torn by internal dissent. That is why the Japanese have to have what Robert Christopher called 'one absolutely immutable goal which is to ensure the survival and maximum well-being of the tribe.'[22]

Pride is an excellent way to defend yourself when you are facing great danger. Seiichiro Ishikawa of Seishin Shobo laughed when he said to me, 'Only the Japanese and the Jews will survive a nuclear war', but the pride was there. Of course, all races and nations of people claim for themselves superiority over all others in their intrinsic virtue and ability and in the way they are favoured by their gods. But, alas, whatever virtue, ability or favour a race or nation may see itself as enjoying, unless its members are impervious to radiation and can survive without a stable air supply and sunlight and can live in the very extremes of heat and cold, then they, like their inferiors, are doomed to perish – that is, they are doomed to perish unless they can redefine their superiority as being the ability to care for all human beings, whatever their nationality, race or creed, and to cherish our planet.

While in Japan the *kaisha* may be the family or the corporation, in traditional Hindu life the only group which matters is the family. In his psychoanalytic study of childhood and society in India Sudhir Kakar wrote,

> problems are resolved in the Indian family on the basis of the hierarchical principle; the difference is that the hierarchy of roles within the extended family is legitimated by the tradition and the social sanction not of generations but of centuries, so that for an Indian, superior and subordinate relationships have the character of eternal verity and moral imperative . . . regardless of personal talents or achievements, or of changes in the circumstances of his own or others' lives, an Indian's relative position in the hierarchy of the extended family, his obligations to those 'above' him and his expectations of those 'below' him are immutable, lifelong. Already in childhood he begins to learn that he must look after the welfare of those subordinate to him in the family hierarchy so that they do not suffer either through their own misjudgement or at the hands of outsiders, and that he is reciprocally entitled to obedience and respectful compliance with his wishes.
>
> The ordering principles of this hierarchical system are age and sex. Elders have more formal authority than younger persons – even a year's difference in age is sufficient to establish the fact of formal superiority – and men have greater authority than women. . . .
>
> Implicit in the organization of Indian society, in which each individual is a part of a complex, hierarchically ordered, and above all stable network of relationships throughout the course of his life, is a psychological model of man that emphasises human dependence and

vulnerability to feelings of estrangement and helplessness. The core of emotional life is anxiety and suffering, *dukha* as the Buddhists would call it. Thus Hindu social organization accentuates the continued existence of the child in the adult and elaborates the care-taking function of society to protect and provide for the security of its individual members. We might also view traditional Indian society as a therapeutic model of social organization in that it attempts to alleviate *dukha* by addressing itself to deep needs for connection and relationship to other human beings in an enduring and trustworthy fashion and for ongoing mentorship, guidance and help in getting through life and integrating current experience with whatever has gone before and with an anticipated future. In the relatively more activist and task-orientated social organization of western countries, these dependency needs of adults are generally seen as legitimate only in moments of acute crisis or circumstances of 'sickness'. . . . From the earliest years, the Indian child learns that the core of any social relationship, therapeutic, educational, organizational, is the process of caring and mutual involvement. What he should be sensitive to (and concerned with) are not goals of work and productivity that are external to the relationship, but the relationship itself, the unfolding of emotional affinity. . . .

The conflict between the rational criteria of specific tasks and institutional goals rooted in western societal values, and his own deeply held belief (however ambivalent) in the importance of honouring the family and *jati* (caste) bonds is typical among highly educated and prominently employed Indians. And among the vast majority of tradition-minded countrymen – whether it be a *bania* bending the law to facilitate the business transaction of a fellow *jati* member, or a *marwari* industrialist employing an insufficiently qualified but distantly related job applicant as a manager, or the clerk accepting bribes in order to put an orphaned niece through school – dishonesty, nepotism and corruption as they are understood in the West are merely abstract concepts. These negative constructions are irrelevant to Indian psycho-social experience, which, from childhood on, nurtures one standard of responsible adult action, and one only, namely, an individual's lifelong obligation to his kith and kin. . . .

Much of the individual behaviour and adaptation to the environment that in westerners is regulated or coerced by the demands of the superego, is taken care of in Indians by a *communal conscience*. This comprises, from the beginning, not exclusive parental injunctions but family and *jati* norms. In contrast to the western superego, the communal conscience is a social rather than an individual formation: it is not 'inside' the psyche. In other words, instead of having one internal sentinel an Indian relies on many external 'watchmen' to patrol his activities and especially his relationships in all the social hierarchies.

The greater authority of the codes of the communal conscience, as opposed to the internalized rules of the individual superego, creates a situation in which infringements of moral standards become likely in situations 'when no one is looking'. Such situations normally arise when the individual is away from the watchful discipline of his family, *jati* and village groups. Thus, although Indians publicly express a staunch commitment to traditional moral codes, privately, in relation to himself, an individual tends to consider the violation of these codes reprehensible when it displeases or saddens those elders who are the personal representatives of his communal conscience.[23]

When I was travelling in India I was accompanied by two disturbing feelings. One was the effort to keep at bay the horror and pain at the sight of such suffering and waste (I had prepared myself for the beggars but not for the barren and eroded Himalayas) and the other was the sense of having come from another planet which was of no interest at all to the people I was meeting. To the Japanese the rest of the world is quite real. Things and ideas outside Japan are examined with curiosity and, if they are interesting or useful, they are made over into Japanese things and ideas. To the Indians, so it seemed to me, the rest of the world was of interest only if it offered a source of increased wealth – a good job in America, a supply of objects unobtainable in India, or some coins in an outstretched hand. I can understand and accept this. The West seems so rich, compared to India. Indians do not always realise that not all Westerners are rich. Wherever I travelled in India I was met with great warmth and was looked after with great hospitality. People were delighted that I was there being interested in what was important to them. Because they were sharing their lives with me I would try to share my life with them. I would start to talk about my family and friends or how clinical psychology works in England, and suddenly I would sense a change in the people I was with. They simply weren't listening. I never waste my breath talking to people who aren't listening, so I would fall silent or go back to matters which interested my companions. This reaction contrasted very much with what I find in my travels in the US and Canada where people take a lively (though often misinformed) interest in Britain and Australia, while here in England I am forever explaining Australia to the English. The odd feeling I had in India was not that my Indian companions were not interested in my concerns (all my life I have been surrounded by people who find their own concerns more interesting and more important than mine) but that the world I came from didn't exist. I knew there were two worlds – their world and mine – and I was having difficulty finding my way around their world, but as far as they were concerned there was only one world and that was theirs – their India, and, inside India, their family groups.

It is understandable why the Indians need to form protective cohesive groups – they have always been at the mercy of natural disasters and foreign invasion – and now they are threatened by their burgeoning numbers (a family must have sons and heirs). The question is whether they can come to see the planet as sufficiently real to require cherishing and whether they can find a way of reconciliation with their Muslim neighbours.

For this latter task they are not likely to find much help in the Christian experience.

There are two matters which Jesus is reported as speaking about with great firmness and clarity. He praised and recommended both poverty and forgiveness. The Christian churches have repeated His praise and recommendations often in words and rarely in action.

Jesus apparently had no doubt that people were capable of coming to forgive and to love their enemies. In the Sermon of the Mount He said,

Ye have heard that it hath been said, An eye for an eye, and a tooth for a tooth:

But I say unto you, That ye resist not evil: but: whosoever shall smite thee on thy right cheek, turn to him the other also.

And if any man will sue thee at law, and take away thy coat, let him have thy cloke also.

And whosoever shall compel thee to go a mile, go with him twain.

Give to him that asketh, and from him that would borrow of thee turn not thou away.

Ye have heard that it hath been said, Thou shalt love thy neighbour, and hate thine enemy.

But I say unto you, Love your enemies, bless them that curse you, do good to them that hate you, and pray for them which despitefully use you, and persecute you.

That ye may be the children of your Father which is in heaven: for he maketh his sun to rise on the evil and the good, and sendeth the rain on the just and on the unjust.

For if ye love them which love you, what reward have you? do not even the publicans do the same?

And if ye salute your brethren only, what do ye more than others? do not even the publicans so?

Be ye therefore perfect, even as Your Father which is in heaven perfect.[24]

As the history of the Christian church shows, there have been many Christians who have not been able to reach this level of perfection, and, indeed, often those Christians who have tried to do so have been persecuted by other Christians. An example of this is given in a story published in the *Observer*.

A Presbyterian minister in Ulster, who has been threatened with dismissal for wishing Roman Catholics seasons greetings during Christmas Day Mass, said last night he remained unrepentant.

Rev David Armstrong, minister of the First Limavady Presbyterian Church in County Londonderry, sparked off a storm in the town when he crossed the street to bring greetings to worshippers in the Church of Christ the King.

Mr Armstrong said: 'I am opposed to bigotry and hatred and there will be no U-turn on my part. I was doing what any Christian should have done on Christmas morning, embracing all people.

Earlier on Christmas Day Catholic priest Father Kevin Mullan had entered the Presbyterian church bringing similar Christmas greetings. The congregation applauded as Father Mullan spoke and worshippers reached out to shake his hand.

The Roman Catholic church had only been reopened a year earlier after it had been bombed. Mr Armstrong spoke of his joy and reception when he entered the Christ the King Church on Christmas Day. 'The Catholics of Father Mullan's church overwhelmed me. The applause was deafening.'

The joy shared by both clergymen was shortlived. The Session of Mr Armstrong's Presbyterian Church in Ireland headquarters said yesterday: 'We did not involve ourselves in this local matter but we think when the issue became public the situation changed with certain members of the Session not wanting to be seen to be involved in any move to remove the Rev Armstrong.'

Mr Armstrong said: 'I would call for the evangelical side of Presbyterianism to leave aside the hardening political dimension and to extend the hand of friendship to the Roman Catholic neighbour.

'Protestants have a mental filing cabinet about Roman Catholics and Roman Catholics are filed away in a very predictable folder. Sometimes we speak to Catholics in a patronising way. We don't listen to what they are saying but listen to what we think they are saying.'

Father Mullan said: 'Catholics too could learn from the spirituality of prayers in the Protestant churches. In fact we should learn from each other in a spirit of love.'[25]

What Father Mullan and Rev Armstrong are advocating here is that members of two opposing groups can begin to resolve their differences by changing how they each describe and assess the other. If Catholics describe and assess Protestants in Catholic terms, and Protestants describe and assess Catholics in Protestant terms they do not share a common language within which differences can be amicably discussed and ameliorated. But if Catholics can have an understanding of Protestants in Protestant terms and Protestants an understanding of Catholics in Catholic terms then they do share a language where differences can be discussed. This is a method of psychotherapy which I and many other psychotherapists use. Our task as therapists is not to teach our client our language (as some doctors do – 'You might think you're exhausted with overwork, Mr Jones, but I know that you are suffering from a depressive illness'). Our task is to learn the client's language, his way of evaluating himself and his world ('You describe yourself as exhausted by overwork. Can you tell me some more about this, what it feels like? . . . What do you call overwork? . . . Why is it important to you to work so hard?). The process of discovering the other person's language is quite difficult. It means listening hard, not letting our own perceptions delude ourselves into thinking that we have understood when we have not, and knowing our understanding is never complete. Every act of understanding reveals something more yet to be understood, what we have understood today may change by tomorrow, because the person we are trying to understand is changing in ways which we cannot predict. This knowledge can make us feel very insecure.

How much better, then, it is not to make the effort to understand, or not even recognise that it is possible to make such an effort. Preserve security by not recognising the possibility of insecurity. Be absolutely certain that the way you see the world is Right and True and that anyone who does not see it the same way as you is either mad or bad, if not both. Allowing the possibility that someone else can see something differently from yourself and yet be neither mad nor bad is the first step that a client in therapy has to make in order to find the way out of the predicament which is causing so much pain. Allowing such a possibility is also the first step to resolving the differences between political, racial and religious groups.

However, a perusal of Russian and American newspapers, or listening to the speeches made by Russian and American leaders shows how locked into their own world each side is. The Russian rhetoric of 'imperialisim' and 'capitalism' seem to me to set up an impenetrable wall, while the way the word 'Communist' in America is so blanket a term of abuse that it seems to have lost its meaning in the way the word 'bloody', which once was the oath 'by our Lady', has no meaning other than one of emphasis. Hurling 'imperial capitalist' and 'Communist' at one another is hardly a way to seek mutual understanding. Russian censorship is appalling, but equally worrying is the way, as an American lecturer in Russian studies said to me, 'Americans can understand one another only in their own terms – how much it is like America. They cannot understand another country in that country's own terms.' This was particularly apparent in the *Time* magazine article on life in China written when President Reagan visited China in 1984. [26] This article did not attempt to explain how the Chinese see themselves and how they express their system of values through the way they live. Instead, the article was concerned with how the Chinese are becoming more and more like Americans, that is, for the purpose of President Reagan's visit, if nothing else, the Chinese were being redefined as 'like us' and therefore 'not dangerous'. Such a redefinition does not preclude a subsequent redefining of China as Different and Dangerous.

One potent method of maintaining group cohesion is the writing, and rewriting, of that group's history. The past is not fixed. We can make it whatever we want it to be. A study of this process has been made by Marc Ferro, the Director of Studies in the Social Sciences at the Ecole des Hautes Studies in Paris. In his *The Use and Abuse of History* he wrote of the ways in which various countries and political groups have reinterpreted their history to strengthen their power. Of Russia he said,

> 'Historians are dangerous, and capable of turning everything topsyturvy. They have to be watched': thus Krushchev in 1965, at the time of de-Stalinization. The remark admirably sums up the place of history in the USSR. At the best of times, it is under supervision. The difference with other authoritarian regimes is not just that the Party, rather than the state, is the supervising agent; there is also the fact that the regime claims to incarnate the very movement of history, and to be history's own interpreter. The leadership could never allow historians to produce versions different from its own: if they even try, the Party hurls anathema.[27]

Of America he wrote,

> History is matched with citizens' requirements and education, whether private or public, is dependent on funds from private, municipal or state sources. American society as a mass is more traditional than its academics, and the law of democracy is such that society can more or less impose its views, for better or worse. There is clearly a good variety of teaching, more so than in other countries, whether in the content of the historical material to be analysed or the methods of examination, but there is a common feature, the lack of interest in non-American history. It is of course studied at high school, but it is clearly not part of the pupils' common stock of knowledge. This is true of university students if they are not specialists.
>
> The Americans lead the field in ignorance of the outside world. This can be easily seen in newspapers, which devote only a very small share of their news to foreign countries, unless they have some bearing on American life. The same is true of television. . . . there is an almost insatiable desire to probe questions of urban life, desegregation, or whatever. You can sense this as an almost psychoanalytic need in an anxious society wondering as to its own instructions (since Watergate,

especially) and as to the future.

This probing always comes in the same way, an analysis that amounts to a kind of social narcissism, together with a superiority complex towards the economic, political and cultural systems of other nations and societies. In history, it is obvious that the ignorance of the problems of Islam or the USSR is, except among the academics, as uncomprehending as total. The American myth has led to a supposition that America took in people from the whole world, so the rest of the world is not worth serious attention. The relationship of America to other countries is wholly distorted. For instance, the idea that American imperialism can exist is dismissed as abhorrent, insulting and absurd; and there are few history books that even consider this problem, except perhaps to say that in the era of the 'Big Stick' in 1901, Theodore Roosevelt 'delivered the Cubans from Spanish oppression'.[28]

I could go on and on recounting how a particular nation, race or creed regards the rest of the human race as unimportant, nothing more than objects to be ignored, used or destroyed, or how two nations, races or creeds misunderstand one another and seek to destroy one another. In the end I would have to include every nation, race and creed, even those unaggressive groups like the Eskimos and the Quakers, who wanted to live quietly on their own but who find themselves at the receiving end of aggression because they have something which another group wants or because their mere existence is taken as an affront. It seems that groups of people fight not merely because they want to secure the land they see as theirs and to make themselves wealthier but also because they see the other group as in some way evil and so must be combatted and destroyed. It seems that when we define the Stranger we use not merely objective criteria like 'They have land which is rightly ours' or 'They are richer than us' or 'They want what we have' but subjective criteria which arise within us and with all the force of Revealed Truth show that our enemies are evil and must be combatted and destroyed. When we define our enemies solely in terms of objective criteria we can allow that the situation has changed and that compromise and peace can follow (for instance, after centuries of war, England, France and part of Germany could sink their differences and belong to the EEC). But when all or part of the definition of our enemies is based on subjective criteria then we do not perceive any changes in the situation and we cannot tolerate even the possibility of compromise and peace. The more absolute our views, the more we are defining our enemies by subjective criteria, and we have to go on defending our absolute views because we use them to defend something within ourselves, something so frightening that we dare not acknowledge its existence.

Feiffer's little girl, the one who knew she was bad because good people punished her, often comes to talk to me – in one guise or other. One woman said to me, 'I had to see my mother as perfect because I was so weak and frightened.' Another woman who had fought her way through many of her difficulties so that she could at least see what was happening to her said to me,

> I always feel guilty. I've been like this for as long as I can remember. I could never please my parents. Anything I did, it wasn't good enough for them. When I got a 2:1 degree all my father said was, 'Why didn't you get a first?' When I was a child they both used to beat me and tell me how bad I was. I thought I must have been, otherwise why would they beat me? I never told anyone. At school I thought they'd laugh at me. It's only recently I've talked about it. I can see now that they were taking their bad feelings out on me – they had problems in their relationship – but I still feel guilty.

From my personal and clinical experience I have come to agree with the psychoanalyst Alice Miller that we much underestimate the pain we have suffered in childhood. The current controversy about whether Freud was right when he claimed that his patients' stories of being sexually molested in childhood were fantasies or whether he was failing to face up to the fact that many parents inflict such pain on their children has brought forth many stories from women who only now feel able to talk about what they experienced as children. For instance, Jessica Hallam told of her experiences when she spoke on Radio Three,

> It's a bitter time for a journey, but it's a journey I must make: 'Those who do not remember the past,' goes the saying, 'are condemned for ever to re-enact it.' And so I'm going back now – back to the beach near our house, the bleak beach in winter. I'm five years old and I'm out there on my own, piling the black sand into a castle and crowing it with stones. When my mother finds me she's white and angry and she hugs me and shouts at me, all at the same time: 'Haven't I told you never to go down to the beach on your own? How many times have I told you bad men might get you?'
>
> I remember the cold wind. I remember pulling her hand. 'I was frightened, Mummy,' I said. 'Mummy, I'm frightened. But not on the beach, Mummy, I'm frightened at home. Daddy frightens me.'
>
> 'Nonsense,' says my white-faced mother. 'He loves you. He's the best father in the world. He's kind and he's gentle – Oh darling, I chose him especially for you.'
>
> Two years later, when I was seven, I ran away from home. Never to do things by halves, I tried to take the cat and the boy next door along with me. But the cat would stay in my warm bed, and the boy next door didn't hear me knocking on his window. So I had to face the wet road by myself. For miles and miles and miles, I walked. For miles and miles. I'd got to the common when they found me, and though I thought that was almost the other side of the world, they had me home in five minutes and they sat me on my father's knee. 'My little girl's too young to run away from home,' he said, and stroked my hair. I cringed then, as I've since seen other incest-children cringe – I cringed from the sentimental sneer, the soft, relentless hand, and I lowered my head and wept: another attempt had failed – another attempt to tell my mother and the whole world that no danger out there – no bad men on the beach or rain on the winter common – nothing could compare with the danger that crept like a thief round our house and stole my own heart from me.[29]

I would guess that both Freud and his critics were right. Some of his clients would have suffered assaults like that described by Jessica Hallam while others would have been shamed, humiliated, abandoned and beaten in ways which lead the child to deal with the pain engendered by turning it around into images of desire. Freud's patients were the victims of the harsh and cruel childrearing methods which were popular in nineteenth-century Europe. Alice Miller writes of these methods of what she calls 'poisonous pedagogy' and shows how methods which hurt and humiliate children are still being used today. Her critics say that she exaggerates, that we use much kinder methods of childrearing nowadays. I was in the midst of reading her book, *For Your Own Good* when the following letter was published in our local paper, the *Lincolnshire Echo*.

> Sir, – Having just retired after 32 years of teaching, I consider my views on punishment in schools reflect those of the majority of teachers and parents.
>
> My experience included Head of Physical Education, Grammar School, Head of PE at a 2,000 pupil comprehensive, senior teacher, School for the Blind, deputy warden maximum security Approved School, deputy head, School for Maladjusted Boys, and lastly head of a High School.
>
> In all the schools mentioned caning and detention were used. . . .
>
> The system used to work very well and the majority of the population do not want the 'soft approach'. Since the 1960's the soft core has grown and just look at the results. Let us go back to discipline as it used to be and allow teachers to do their jobs without fear of being taken to court by parents and 'do-gooders' who do not really care about children – teachers do care, let them get on with it.
>
> When I meet ex-pupils whom I had to deal severely with while at school, without exception they hold no malice towards me and in fact go out of their way to speak to me and we still have a mutual regard and respect for each other. The soft approach does not gain respect either way and never will . . .

Leave the system alone, the old system didn't do us
any harm did it?[30]

Why is it that Jessica Hallam, as she got older, did not
complain about her father's treatment of her, why do the boys
whom this teacher had beaten not protest against such humiliating and painful methods of education, why does this
teacher himself deny that any harm was done to him as a
child? The reason, says Alice Miller, is that the memory of
those events is too painful to be borne. So the pain has to be
turned into something else. It is not just that the child has felt
abandoned, shamed, humiliated and unfairly punished. It is
that the child has been forbidden to feel, much less express
any anger over having to suffer so. And more than that, the
child has been ordered to forget that such events have taken
place. Alice Miller lists the individual psychological stages in
the lives of most people as –

1 To be hurt as a small child without anyone recognising
   the situation as such.
2 To fail to react to the resulting suffering with anger.
3 To show gratitude for what are supposed to be good
   intentions.
4 To forget everything.
5 To discharge the stored-up anger onto others in adulthood or to direct it against oneself.

She goes on,

The greatest cruelty that can be inflicted on children is
to refuse to let them express their anger and suffering
except at the risk of losing their parents' love and
affection. The anger stemming from early childhood is
stored up in the unconscious, and since it represents a
healthy, vital source of energy, an equal amount of
energy must be extended in order to repress it.[31]

All young children recognise how dependent they are on
their parents, so they must accept their parents' pressure to
conform to the way of family life as best they can. They learn
to define 'evil' from the way their parents defend against their
own pain and fear. ' "Evil" can be anything which makes their

parents insecure.'[32] The messages which the child receives can be simple, as when during the Second World War the Australian government's propaganda was 'British, American, Russian = good, German, Japanese, Italian = bad.' Or the messages can be subtle and complex. When I was a child I often went barefoot, being either too lazy or too hot to put on my shoes and socks. My mother disliked seeing me barefoot and she would say, 'If you don't wear your shoes you'll end up with blackfellow's feet.' I knew what she meant, even though I was unacquainted with blackfellows, the Aborigines who lived in the distant bush and who went barefoot. Walking in the bush barefoot requires strong feet with toes which can move freely like fingers and soles which are thick and protective, not the kind of feet which would slip easily into the narrow shoes of a well-brought-up white young lady. My mother's ambition for me was that I should be a credit to her, that I should become a quiet, orderly, well-dressed young women who worked in a bank and was a companionable and dutiful daughter. I was showing strong signs that this was not going to be so. I kept disappearing into the bush near our home or away to the beach or into my books, and she would try to hold me back with the threat that if I followed my own inclinations I would be so wild and undisciplined that people would reject me the way that blackfellows were rejected. She was letting me know that inside me was something which was bad, which I should be ashamed of, and which I should keep hidden. Receiving this message I felt pain which I had to live with by feeling shame at the despicable, unlovable person I was or which I could get rid of by projecting my desire for freedom and adventure and unmindfulness for the need for respectability on to the blackfellows and then despising them for having these qualities which I coveted but had been taught to hate. I chose the shame, and withdrew even further into myself.

Had I chosen to hate the Aborigines instead of myself I would now be unable to remember my mother's threat. I would have forgotten how angry she had made me and how much she had hurt me.

The process whereby a child learns to react to pain inflicted by his parents by denying that he feels anger against his parents and forgetting the incident which gave rise to this pain produces obedient and uncritical adults. Of course obedience has a secondary gain. It allows the person to feel that he does not have to take responsibility for his actions. He was only doing what he was told to do. He can be cruel with impunity. Obedience engenders the idea of martyrdom, that if we sacrifice ourselves for some greater power we shall be saved. To achieve the obedience which the parents require the child has to give up awareness and acknowledgment of his own feelings, which means, in the long run, that the person loses touch with these feelings to the extent that he loses touch with himself. He loses himself. He gives up himself in order to go on thinking that his parents, those people who should have looked after him well, are good people – not simply the real people in his home, but the images of those people which he has taken inside himself. But denying feelings, denying that one is as one is does not eradicate those feelings or abolish the knowledge that something valuable has been lost. The unacknowledged feelings arise again in tears and rage and nightmares while the loss of the most valuable part of ourselves is something we mourn forever. But such mourning is too painful and must be defended against. The defence against such mourning is depression. The essence of depression is the belief that one is bad, evil, unlovable. But how can you love something that you do not know, something that has never been loved? The prevalence of depression in all cultures shows how common such child-rearing practices are. Adult society demands that children conform to the rules of that society, and children obey. When they themselves become adults they demand the same sacrifices from their children. Thus, as the Bible says, the sins of the fathers are visited upon the children. Thus are we born to our karma.

Because we deny that as children our parents did not accept our feelings of anger and because we do not wish to acknowledge the damage which was done to us in childhood we claim that the way we were brought up is the way that children should be brought up, and we then proceed to bring up our children in the same way. More than that, many of us expect our children to make up to us what we have been deprived of.

Many good and loving parents will say, 'I want my child to have what I didn't have', and so load the child with gifts (opportunities as well as objects) and the responsibility of using those gifts well, thus taking away from the child the right to be himself and to develop his own future. The parent and child will want different things simply because they are different generations. To my mother going barefoot was the sign of the terrible poverty which was part of her experience – the hard life in the coal-mining villages in the early part of the century and the suffering of the unemployed people during the Depression of the 1930s. But for me, even though I was always being warned about not straying into Happy Valley where poor people lived in shanties and being told how lucky I was that my father had a job, poverty was not a reality and a fear to me. I could not appreciate my mother's need to show that she could afford to keep her children well shod.

However, while I knew that this experience of my mother's wishes clashing with mine had profound effects on me, it did not stop me doing the same to my son. During the protracted and very painful period of the break-up of my marriage and our journey to England I, being unhappy myself, was very anxious that my son should be happy. I kept giving him things with the injunction 'Be happy'. Finally he could bear it no longer and told me that it was difficult enough going through all the changes in living that he had to without the added burden of being happy all the time. I tried to accept this and to let him be unhappy when it was appropriate that he should be unhappy, as it often was then and still is, since he was born into the unemployment generation and has much to contend with. But I still find his unhappiness much harder to bear than my own.

Nowadays, with the greater knowledge we have of how families function and how children develop, and with, in at least some sections of society, the greater interest in self-understanding, some people are able to reflect upon their childhood, to come to understand why they are as they are, and to make changes in themselves so that they can live more easily and more openly with themselves and their family. But such people are still very much in the minority. The kind of people whom Alice Miller describes are still very much with us.

The child has the primary need to be regarded and respected as the person he really is at any given time, and as the centre – the central actor – in his own activity. . . . Parents who did not experience this climate as children are themselves narcissistically deprived: throughout their lives they are looking for what their parents did not give them at the correct time. The most appropriate objects for gratification are a parent's own children. A newborn baby is completely dependent on his parents, and since their caring is essential to his existence, he does all he can to avoid losing them. From the very first day onward, he will muster all his forces to this end, like a small plant that turns toward the sun in order to survive. . . .

In many societies, little girls suffer additional discrimination because they are girls. Since women, however, have control of the newborn infants, these erstwhile little girls can pass on to their children at the most tender age the contempt from which they suffered. Later, the adult man will idealize his mother, since every human being needs to feel that he was truly loved, but he will despise other women, upon whom he revenges himself in the place of his mother. And all these humiliated adult women, in turn, if they have no other means of ridding themselves of their burden, will revenge themselves upon their own children. This indeed can be done secretly and without fear of reprisals for the child has no way of telling anyone, except in the form of a perversion or obsessional neurosis whose language is sufficiently veiled not to betray the mother.[33]

In therapy it is very striking how people who are suffering the most terrible despair are unable to talk even about the ordinary, funny and exasperating things which happen in family life and which would always happen, even in the most happy world. The reason that they cannot remember, or will not allow themselves to talk about these incidents is that at the time they occurred they were forbidden by the adults around them to express their own feelings. One young woman who saw herself being taken over by a mysterious illness of a fast-beating heart, sweating, nausea and headache every time she had to leave her home first described to me her childhood as being 'an ordinary childhood'. Later in our conversation about all these immobilising symptoms she remarked, as an aside, that she had felt as ill as this once before, when her father died. I asked her to tell me more about this, and out came a story of terrible sadness, not just the sudden death of the parent she was closest to, but the way in which she felt so angry that he had betrayed and deserted her by dying, so guilty that she had not been able to make her peace with him before he died, and so brave and sensible because if she was not her mother would be upset. Not upsetting mother seemed to be a family rule, and when there was the opportunity for me to help her look at this rule what emerged then was a picture of a married couple, a quiet, seemingly imperturbable man and a volatile woman who, seeking a response from him, would goad and goad him until he suddenly exploded into violence. My client, as a little girl, would try to stop this by her presence, but often this would fail and she would witness her parents abusing and striking one another. Afterwards she dared not show how angry and frightened this made her, lest she would become the object of their anger. Now her fear of anger, hers and that of other people, and her fear of the symptoms of fear, and the fear of fear itself, keeps her indoors lest, if she steps outside she will be struck by this mysterious 'illness'.

Her tragedy is not just that these terrible things have happened to her in childhood nor that she is experiencing such frightening symptoms born of fear, but that, even as she recounts these events and describes these symptoms, she cannot *see* the connection between these events and the symptoms. She dutifully listens to me and, equally dutifully, reads Claire Weekes' excellent book[34] on this problem, but the connection, and the consequent solution, eludes her. Not only does it elude her, but she is not interested in finding it. She is not curious about herself. It seems that if as children we are not allowed to live our lives in a continuous development of understanding, if we are presented with events which we experience as powerful and dangerous and which we are not helped to master by the adults around us, if we have to repress or to isolate rather than express our feelings of anger and fear, we suffer a deficit in the unfolding and development of our talents. Just as not being allowed to explore music or art or mathematics in childhood can mean growing up without any capacity to understand these areas of knowledge, so not being allowed to discover the full significance of one's childhood world can mean growing up without the capacity to see connections between the past and the present, between mind and body, between events whose overt appearances are different but whose covert meanings are the same. The great tragedy is that while those of us whose education in the arts or mathematics was deficient can recognise this deficit, can be curious about these subjects and seek to remedy our ignorance, those of us who lack the ability to see the meaningful connections in our lives are unaware of this lack. The great tragedy is the death of curiosity.

But curiosity would reveal what must also be kept secret, that forbidden part of the self, the unloved and unlovable self. In therapy it is very striking how unloved is the child the person once was. My client has forgotten this child who wanders like a lonely ghost in his dreams, or remembers him without sympathy and concern. My client may express sympathy and concern for other children, like the starving children of the Third World, but he shows not the slightest shred of compassion for the little child he once was who faced, alone, such fear and confusion. He despises and hates this child whom he sees as weak, frightened and wicked.

Evidence of this wickedness is the anger he feels. He might turn this anger against himself and lacerate himself with guilt, or he might turn it into righteous anger and punish other people for being weak and evil.

Righteous anger is the outcome of the defence of 'identification with the aggressor'. Here the child, having to cope with the pain of being punished and the additional pain and fear of knowing that the person who is doing the punishing is the person on whom the child depends, can reduce this pain and fear by not only saying to himself that he is bad and his good parent is punishing him but also that he is going to be like his parent. He will be a good parent who punishes wicked people.

So we find plenty of people who will say, 'I was beaten when I was a child and it never did me any harm.' They deal with their hatred of their father who beat them by beating their own children. But this second generation of children are beaten not just for their own assumed wickedness but because they remind the parent of those split-off, unacceptable parts of himself which he wishes to punish and obliterate. So the beating goes on, and the human race perpetuates its cruelty – and takes pride in its cruelty.

Jeremy Paxman, reporting for the BBC on the presidential election in El Salvador, told the following story,

> In 1932 Augusto Farabundo Marti, a young middle-class radical, was dragged before a military court in El Salvador. Marti, who was given to wearing badges showing Trotsky's face inside a red star, had led a group of dispossessed peasants in revolt against the military dictatorship then in power. Disorganised and poorly led, with machetes against the rifles of the army, the uprising was soon snuffed out. Whereupon the military began a massacre which set precedents for every fascist in Latin America. Within days, the folklore has it, 30,000 *campesinos* had been murdered, merely on suspicion of having some sympathy with the rebels.
>
> With Marti the authorities went through the motions of a legal process. Sentencing him to die by firing squad, the judges asked whether he had any last words. His reply was characteristically Salvadorean: 'I will not ask you for the slightest clemency,' he said, 'because if I had triumphed, it would be your heads rolling, not mine.' Brutality is attached to El Salvador like a parasitic worm, an inseparable part of the normal processes of politics, a necessary condition of power.[35]

This is the real problem in Central and South America, the unquestioned handing on from generation to generation of cruelty which means that no government, of whatever political persuasion, can establish a stable rule because so many of the people are unable to tolerate the uncertainties and freedom of a democratic government and react against the strictures of a totalitarian government, reminiscent of their harsh and punishing parents, with blind anger and the need to punish cruelly others as they themselves were punished. Military support from Russia and America only perpetuates the legacy of cruelty.

The way we were brought up as children, and the way we bring up our own children gives to the Stranger an essential function. If as children we are convinced by the adults around us that we are unacceptable as ourselves and that if we want to stay in the group (family) we have to change, to get rid of those unacceptable parts of ourselves, we can do this by projecting on to other people, those not in the group, those parts of ourselves which we deplore and despise.

Children are very adept at finding some child who is different from themselves and then despising and persecuting it. They have no understanding of what pain that child may feel under such persecution. As children get older they usually develop some understanding that other people feel pain, but to those groups who are the recipients of their projected despised self they show no mercy. Sometimes they act with great cruelty to this group: sometimes they act with an air of knowing superiority and tell the despised and dangerous strangers how they should behave. Such advice may come from the President of the United States to the despised, ill-informed and wicked communists, or, in a seemingly more benign form, from the staff of a psychiatric hospital to the patients there. None of these 'good' people see what pain they inflict on the 'bad'.

While in Australia recently I encountered far more strong feelings against the Aborigines than I remember being expressed in the 1940s and 1950s. Then, if I remember rightly, little mention was made of the Aborigines, no more than was made of mentally handicapped people – subnormals as they were then called. To many white people the Aborigines were subhuman, of no account. They were certainly not counted in the census. Now things are different. The Aborigines have been granted citizenship. Moreover, they have come to understand the concept of land ownership, and their claims to land sacred to their tribe remind many Australians that white settlers had, not all that many years ago, dispossessed the Aborigines of their land. Few white landowners would choose to return their land to the Aborigines, while in most cases recompense is impossible, since the descendants of the dispossessed Aborigines have died or possess no written records of their descent. Some white Australians want the Aborigines to be enabled to live a decent life, while a few white Australians actively try to help the Aborigines find some kind of justice, but such hopes and actions involve some measure of accepting responsibility for past misdeeds and of seeking forgiveness, all very painful and risky things to do. Far safer are the jokes against the Aborigines, the abuse, the derogatory names. Better to deny guilt and greed and the shame of greed. Those people who choose to do this are those people who praise the virtue of hard work, something they were taught to do by the sternness and punitiveness of their elders. They learned as children to reject those desires to play, to slip, like the vagrant Aborigines, into the timelessness of the bush and water, and to live, not for tomorrow but for today. As their erstwhile prime minister reminded them, they know that they were not put on this earth to enjoy themselves. Life was not meant to be easy, so there must not be any unproductive play, but only competition in sport, wealth, drink and sex, a severe division between what is male and what is female, and, under the jokes and the aggressive good humour and generosity to friends, much anxiety. To bear all this it becomes necessary to despise the Aborigine, the Stranger, to project on to these dark figures the unacceptable parts of oneself. The Aborigines are despised in a way very different from the way 'the Asians' are despised, for while they represent the dark unknown, 'the Asians' represent something consciously recognised and feared – an efficient, hard-working competitor.

Sometimes what is projected on to the Dangerous Stranger are aspects of the person who persecuted the small child, thus making the Stranger more dangerous and less understood. This was what was happening with a young man, Russell, who came to see me because his obsessions were preventing him from carrying on his life with ease and enjoyment. Whenever he drove his car he had to feel that he was certain that none of the pedestrians, cyclists or motor bike riders whom he passed had been injured by him. If he thought that he might have injured someone and not noticed he would have to go back along the road to search and reassure himself. But such reassurance was hard to find and he would spend hours retracing his journey until sheer exhaustion would force him to return home where he would continue to worry. Practical reassurance like, 'If you had knocked someone down someone else would have noticed and the police would be soon around here' had no effect. He would think of good, rational reasons why no one would have seen the accident and why the injured person had disappeared from the scene. There were other cruel and destructive fantasies about which he was reluctant to tell me. Such fantasies, he felt, were evidence of his wickedness. He rejected my explanation that it is through fantasy that we manage to live peacefully together. We can expend our aggression in fantasy and not express it in action. Russell held what Alice Miller called 'the absurd belief that a person can have nothing but kind, good and meek thoughts and at the same time be honest and authentic'.[36] A good person, he believed, never got angry and never fought.

Russell was an introvert. He sought to maintain his identity by seeking clarity and reducing chaos. However, emotion is always chaotic, so he had to try to deal with it by separating it from thought and denying its existence, but it came back in bizarre, aggressive, hate-filled fantasies. Like all the people who use isolation as the preferred method of defence, he despised emotion and over-valued thought. The trouble with learning to value thought above emotion early in childhood is that the childish belief in the power of thought to affect the outside world is never relinquished. A baby in a state of hunger desires a bountiful supply of warm milk. It appears, and the baby, being unable to conceive of an outside world which supplied it, believes that the wish alone produced the result. A small child has to come to terms with an outside world which is indifferent to his wishes, but sometimes coincidence suggests that fantasy alone has an effect upon the outside world. He might be busy hating his older brother who has just taken the biggest piece of cake when his brother, absorbed in devouring the cake, falls off his bike. Seeing this as mere coincidence does nothing for the child's self-esteem. Believing that he has punished his brother through mere thought brings a heady sense of power. (The belief in the power of thought alone to affect the real world, by merely wishing or casting a spell, what we call magical thinking, makes those people who rely on isolation as the means of defence more prone to get out of touch with reality than those who rely on the defence of repression. If actually powerless, they can fall into that state of delusion and hallucination we call schizophrenia, or if given power by the group they can become paranoid dictators.) Of course, if the brother subsequently dies of his injuries, the sense of power is quickly succeeded by overwhelming guilt. Guilt is the fear of punishment, and such punishment can be warded off by acts of reparation. But such acts have to be repeated endlessly for the guilt is always present. So Russell found driving such a torture. His obsessions also interfered with his work in an insurance office where he feared that the smallest mistake on his part could cause a client such distress that the client would die, say, of a heart attack. So he had to check everything he did, often to the annoyance of his boss who wanted the work to be carried out more quickly.

Russell was a very active worker in the Campaign for Nuclear Disarmament, so one day when he came to see me he talked at first about the recent visit of the theologian much concerned with nuclear issues, Jim Garrison. Then he went on to talk about his boss Richard. Richard, he said, was out to get him. 'He is so patronising,' Russell said. 'I have to smile and be pleasant. He doesn't know how much I hate him.' Russell spoke with great passion. I said, 'I suppose the problems you are having with Richard remind you of the problems you used to have with your brother.' Russell was astounded. He had never thought of it, but once I had said it he knew it was true. Quentin, with all the superiority of an older brother, made more powerful by the death of their father, had always wanted to control and dominate Russell. This, Russell felt, was a situation of great peril. Quentin was not merely ordering him around. He was threatening to annihilate him, to wipe him out as a person. If Russell fought his brother his brother would win, thus annihilating Russell. If he conceded without a fight he was also annihilated. As a child Russell had had to deal with this by developing a philosophy of life which rejected all forms of aggression and by taking refuge in the fantasies of the powerless, that by mere thought he could take revenge.

The child who is taught by the adults around him that he is not good enough, that there is something about him, like his anger and his desire to be himself, which is wicked and must be eradicated or kept under control, can come to believe that he contains something which is evil. Russell believed that inside him was some evil force or something which could contact an evil force (like Satan). He rejected this foreign other part of himself. He feared that this evil force could use his fantasies to wreak havoc on those who annoyed him. This belief incapacitated him when he had to deal with people who were quite objectively aggravating. His boss fell into that category of dangerous people 'older men' and could be hated in a way which he could not hate his much-loved brother. But because he saw and did not acknowledge that he saw his boss as being like his brother he could not find ways of dealing with this man other than the ways he used in dealing with his brother, that is, 'Get angry and be destroyed' or 'Kowtow and despise yourself'. (These are like the pre-emptive alternatives of 'Would you prefer to be dead or red?') He found it easy to think of Russians as fellow human beings and not want to destroy them, but Russians were far away and close at home are 'men like my brother' and 'the evil person inside me' who could not be forgiven. (Thus do Muslims fight Muslims and Christians Christians.)

For Russell to find his way out of his predicament he would have to turn and face the evil inside him and see it, not as evil, but as the child his parents and older brother would not allow him to be with the unexpressed pain and anger that child suffered. That this is possible is shown in a case study by Dr Jeremy Holmes, a consultant psychiatrist at University College Hospital. He wrote,

> The patient was a woman in her early thirties, middle class, feminist and she had had a brief childless marriage some years before. She came for help because over the previous weeks she had developed a state of paralysing panic. The basis of it was simple, she said: she was convinced of the probability of nuclear war.

Every time she heard a plane pass overhead she feared that it was a bomber carrying nuclear warheads. Every time the traffic made a loud noise it made her think of invading tanks. Worse than noise was news. She was unable to watch television, listen to the radio or read a newspaper. She could not use public transport in case she saw the newspaper headlines of her fellow-passengers. When she did encounter the media their messages all pointed in the same direction – war was inevitable. Every action of the world leaders suggested it, every local conflict might provide the spark which would light the final conflagration. To survive this nightmare she had built a complicated cocoon for herself in which she was protected from the daily reminders of the holocaust which she was convinced was to come. Yet within her psychological bunker she was far from safe. After feeling a little better one evening, she went to visit some new friends, and was horrified after an excellent dinner to be given a tour of inspection of the house including the cellar which had been converted into a fallout shelter.

By most standards she was a brave woman: she had travelled widely on her own, and had a demanding job which exposed her to much human suffering. Beneath her anxiety and phobias she was clearly depressed (linked to the guilt she felt about a recent abortion).

In therapy she recovered a memory and dared to tell Dr Holmes about how she had, as a small child, hit her baby cousin and thought that she had killed him.

It seemed as though the discovery of this apparently gratuitous aggression, and having the chance to reveal it in an accepting, but not uncritical atmosphere, was a great relief to her. Her panic about the impending end of the world lessened.

Dr Holmes went on to ask,

Can we learn any wider lessons from this case of personal disarmament? The first point is a general one. The difficulty which nations face in trying to disarm is not unlike the problem of the neurotic patient. It may be generally agreed that it would be desirable to disarm, and that nuclear weapons are unacceptably dangerous; the neurotic patient is often prepared to try any measure to rid himself of his symptoms; yet in both cases it is extraordinarily hard to make progress. Rational effort alone seems inadequate. In both, it seems likely that there are powerful unknown forces maintaining the status quo.

What are these forces? No doubt for disarmament these are economic, political and social. They may be psychological as well. The patient's fear was of attack from without. She was frightened of the bomb which would drop on her and her world. Her recovery began when she realized that she was as persecuted by her *own* aggression as she was by any external enemy. She had projected long-forgotten destructive impulses, never adequately acknowledged by her father, on to every passing aeroplane. When she faced up to and could begin to accept her war-like wishes, her peace of mind returned.

Projection is intrinsic to the arms race too. *We* have defensive, deterrent, peace-keeping nuclear weapons, while *they* have aggressive, expansionist, first-strike bombs. By locating all the aggression in the enemy we avoid looking at the threat we pose to them. The remoteness of nuclear weapons and the 'unthinkability' of nuclear war provide excellent vehicles for such projections. . . .

There are two aspects to the process of projection. First there is the projection itself, then there is the content or nature of the projection. This is often a primitive and distorted fantasy. The patient imagined that her little cousin was dead, that she annihilated him: in fact she had simply given him a nasty bruise. In adult life her violent inner wishes were transformed into horrifying images of nuclear attack, which paralysed and terrified her. When she took the projections back into herself and saw them for what they were – the residue of childish feelings which she had outgrown –

their spell was broken.

Similarly, each of the superpowers sees in its opponent an image of its own ambition, expansionism and desire for absolute superiority. The terrifying vision of the enemy then fuels the race for more fearsome deterrents on each side. In this atmosphere of mutual projection it is impossible for each side realistically to assess the threat which the other poses. For example, commentators seem to have great difficulty in gauging the likelihood of a Russian invasion of Great Britain. If each side were able to acknowledge its *own* wish to attack and humiliate the enemy, rather than steadfastly insisting that its armaments were merely defensive, it might then be easier to look at how great the actual threat is, and whether it is more or less dangerous than possessing nuclear weapons. Unfortunately there is an important difference from the neurotic patient. Her childish fantasy of the damage she had done far exceeded the reality. It was reassuring for her to realize this. Nuclear weapons, on the other hand, are almost certainly *more* damaging than we imagine, despite the efforts of the military to 'normalize' our attitude towards them.

To summarize: an important impediment to disarmament lies in the fiction, fiercely held by both sides, that neither has aggressive intentions towards the other. The moral argument for disarmament turns on this point, since it questions the rightness of being prepared to destroy a civilian Soviet population – the very basis of deterrence.

Dr Holmes went on to describe three other points of similarity between an individual's neurotic conflict and the mutual fear between the two superpowers – (1) how the conflict absorbs vast amounts of energy (resources) (2) which could be used in more creative ways and (3) how the original aggression sprang from envy. Just as the patient envied her little cousin so

there is a great mutual envy between the superpowers, and both have in common an envious attitude towards

Europe, towards its cultural history and hegemony. For the USA this is towards the parent culture, while for the USSR, Western Europe is like an older sibling with whom one can never catch up. For both there is an attitude of contempt and a primitive wish to destroy the envied rival.

He concluded,

The inbuilt response to fright is flight or fight. There are two situations in which we can do neither. The first is when the threat is internal. That is the problem for neurotics, who in the end cannot escape from themselves even though they frequently try to do so. The second is when the threat is all-pervasive. That is the case – at least in the Northern Hemisphere – with nuclear weapons. We may run the risk of destroying ourselves with them, but cannot run away and hide. The threat can be dealt with initially by projection. The problem was eliminated by the patient by externalising her aggression, projecting it onto a threatening world; in the arms race it is done by locating the threat entirely in the 'enemy'. This works for a while, but not for ever. Eventually the repressed aggressor returns, becomes a persecutor, incapacitates. We are becoming socially and morally incapacitated by the arms race. At this point there is only one solution: to face the reality of the threat. As in the legend of the Medusa, the defensive shield has to become a mirror. By reflection, the Gorgon's head can be removed. This is dangerous enough. The risk of failure is greater: to be burned and blasted and irradiated to stone.[37]

Other psychotherapists give the same message. Alice Miller wrote,

The stockpiling of nuclear weapons is only a symbol of bottled-up feelings of hatred and of the accompanying inability to perceive and articulate genuine human needs. . . . Adolescents' 'heroic willingness' to fight one another in wars and (just as life is beginning) to die for someone else's cause may be a result that during

puberty the warded-off hatred from early childhood
becomes reintensified. Adolescents can divert this
hatred from their parents if they are given a clear-cut
enemy whom they are permitted to hate freely and with
impunity. Contempt for those who are smaller and
weaker is the best defence against a breakthrough of
one's own feelings of helplessness; it is an expression of
the split-off weakness. The strong person who knows
that he, too, carries this weakness within himself,
because he has experienced it, does not need to
demonstrate his strength through such contempt.[38]

Thus are our macho men the weakest of them all.

I was writing this chapter in the weeks of the run-up to the
1984 Presidential election in the USA. The English media
were very interested in how this election which is so crucial to
the future of the human race had become a television event,
and so we were treated to many images of Ronald Reagan and
his campaign. Television consists of simple ideas presented
simply. So the vast complex of nationalities and races which
comprise the USSR was presented as a brown bear plodding
through the forest with a voice over telling us that the bear
could be dangerous and that we should defend ourselves.
When Reagan spoke he did not try to explain how he planned
to deal with the complexity of problems which are the responsibility of the president but merely uttered platitudes of
sentimentality and patriotism. Sentimentality is the cloak
which hides unacknowledged hate, and patriotism rests on
the definition of the group in terms of the Dangerous Stranger. My despair at the sight of such stupidity was increased by
the knowledge that had I been watching the leader of any
other country in the world talking to his subjects I would have
been presented with the same images of sentimentality and
patriotism. Such images may make us feel secure, but if we
believe them and continue to act in accordance with them
then we shall bring upon ourselves even greater suffering
and, eventually, our extinction.

The question is, can we change?

Chapter 7

SHALL WE GO THE WAY OF THE DINOSAURS?

The dinosaurs evolved a way of living which served them well for many millions of years but which, in the end, could not alter and adapt to the changes in their environment, and so they perished. All species of the dinosaur became extinct.

The human race is now living in conditions which could render it extinct. Unlike the dinosaurs, we have created the conditions which threaten us with extinction.

The mode by which we live is the mode by which we shall die, *unless we are capable of change*.

To summarise:

Necessary conditions for our existence are

1 To perceive anything we must be aware of a contrast, e.g. black/white, good/bad, empty/full, friend/foe.
2 We create ourselves and our world out of structures which, when threatened, we defend with aggression.
3 To become and remain a person we must be a member of a group.

We define our groups in terms of the contrasts we perceive,

me/not like me,
us/not like us.

We define 'not like me' and 'not like us' in terms of

> objective differences
> and
> subjective differences.

Objective differences are those which are there in reality and which all people can perceive, e.g. older/younger, male/female, living here/living there, has legal ownership/does not have legal ownership.

Subjective differences are those projected attributes understood only by those who do the projecting, e.g. good/bad.

Thus we define ourselves in terms of

us/the Stranger

The more the Stranger is feared, the more cohesive is the group.

The human race has lived for all of its existence in terms of Us/the Stranger.

The opposition of Us/the Stranger has created competition for resources and wealth. Such competition has often been carried out by fighting and war.

The opposition of Us/the Stranger has now produced

The Nuclear Bomb, which can destroy all the major forms of life on the planet.

The Debt Bomb, which can destroy all systems of commerce and trading on which we all depend.

The Population Bomb, which means too many people competing for the world's resources and many suffering irreparable mental and physical damage through starvation.

The Ecology Bomb, which will make the planet uninhabitable by humans.

These 'Bombs' are not separate impending disasters but are intimately related to one another and have developed from the way human beings function as members of a group.

Can we change?

Are we trapped and doomed by the necessary conditions of our existence?

Or can we reflect upon the necessary conditions of our existence and choose to change them?

Chapter 8

CHANGE AND COURAGE

When we grow up we realise that there are no referees.
                                        Dennis Staniland

When Dennis said this to me he was emerging from a depression where he had been mourning his father who had died when Dennis was twelve and whose advice and support Dennis longed for now, at 32, close to the age at which his father had died, when he had to face the problems of the recession and unemployment.

How we long for referees! Someone who will tell us what is right and what is wrong. Someone who relieves us of the responsibilities of deciding. Someone who can be blamed for the consequences. Someone, though stern, who sets and maintains the rules, who provides a fixed framework, an Eternal Reality, in which we can live secure. Someone who will always meet our need to *amaeru*. When we were children our parents and teachers were our referees. We might have reacted against them, but they were *there*, holding up the sky and imposing order on chaos. Fearing to lose our referees as we got older, we looked to people in authority to take their place in an even grander, stronger way, but all the time we were in danger of discovering that they were human beings just like us, prone to error and uncertainty. We looked to God for absolute security, and found a mystery which we can only take on trust. We find that we can have referees only if we remain children. If we want to grow up we have to recognise and accept that there are no referees, just ourselves. Growing up means recognising, as Sheldon Kopp said, *We are totally responsible for our life over which we have only partial control.*[1]

We are totally responsible for the way we define ourselves. We are totally responsible for deciding which group we belong to. We are born into a family, but we can decide whether or not to remain in that family and how to define our family in relation to the groups to which we belong. We are born in a particular nationality, but we can decide how central that nationality is to how we define ourselves. We might be born an extrovert or an introvert, but we decide just how we shall define ourselves as a member of a group or how we shall seek clarity.

Our family, our nationality, our inherited physical characteristics, are events over which we have no control. Yet we are responsible for what we make of these events. We are responsible for how we define these events and how we use our definitions to decide upon our actions.

In arguing that as adults we are responsible for ourselves I am saying that we are responsible for how we define the Stranger. I say this in hope rather than in certainty. For each of us our physical inheritance determines that we can never know something unless there is a contrast. If there were no darkness we would never know light. If there were no death we would not know that we were alive. If there were no Stranger we would not know ourselves. The question is how we define the Stranger. If it is fixed and beyond our control that we can define the Stranger only as the Enemy and Unforgiven, then we, as the human race, are doomed. Sooner or later we shall destroy ourselves, either by a nuclear holocaust or by the destruction of the resources of the planet. I hope that this is not so, that it is possible for human beings to choose to define the Stranger as different, not dangerous, and from that we can learn to live together, and when, in millions of years, the sun threatens to swallow the earth we can together move house to another planet. I hope I am right. I shall act as if I am.

But there are many people who believe in the immutability of human nature. Some people who believe this, like certain psychologists and psychiatrists, have a vested interest in this belief since it is the basis of what they claim as their special expertise. Some people believe this because it is a labour-saving device. It saves them from the effort of reflecting on their actions and beliefs and having to deal with uncertainty. But whatever reasons people have for believing that human nature cannot change, even if this is only a belief and not a scientific fact, if sufficient people hold this belief it has the force of reality. If we believe that we cannot change then we cannot change, and so we are doomed, as a species, to suffering and death. As Einstein said, *'The unleashed power of the atom has changed everything except our way of thinking . . . we need an essentially new way of thinking if mankind is to survive.'*

If we believe that we are capable of change then we have to deal with the problem of forgiveness. We have suffered at the hands of the Stranger. How can we forgive? Jesus recommended forgiveness, but apart from exhorting us to love God, He did not describe the process by which forgiveness grows within us. As a topic of study forgiveness has attracted no attention from psychologists and psychiatrists, and, indeed, psychologists and psychiatrists show themselves to be no different from the rest of the human race in their ability to fight among themselves and not to forgive. So I have had to begin my understanding of forgiveness by looking at myself.

From my earliest childhood I was presented with contrasting attitudes. My mother neither forgave nor forgot, while my father followed the precept 'Never let the sun go down on your wrath'. He had, by the greatest of luck, survived as a soldier in the First World War, and this experience helped him sort out what in life was valuable and to be cherished and what was dross and unnecessary. So when some years ago I was faced with the full force of the question of forgiveness, whether I should spend my life resenting what had happened to me or whether I should put that behind me and get on with changing myself and my life, I was able to draw on my father's wisdom. But what made forgiveness easy for me was that I went on to lead a much more interesting and satisfying life than I would have had if my original life plan had come into fruition. Had I failed to achieve what I have achieved forgiveness might not be so easy.

But that was forgiveness of other people. What I have

difficulty in forgiving is myself. As a parent I realised too late the hurt I had done to my child, how, as Alice Miller described, I had done to my child some of the painful things which had been done to me. Like most loving parents of grown-up children I can plague myself with, 'If only ... ' If only the mistakes we parents make hurt only ourselves and not our children.

But that is forgiveness of the past. In the present matters are different. I have little difficulty in having noble, forgiving thoughts about people who are far away. I can look at the line up of the old men of the Kremlin or at Reagan being Tremendously Sincere, and think nothing worse than, 'Stupid old goats'. I watch on television the people of the Third World or in the Middle East starving or being destroyed by war and I feel anguish and pain for them and try to understand what is happening and why. But, like the couple in the Punch cartoon

*"We've been forgiving our enemies like
mad, Reverend. What's the story
on friends?"*
PUNCH March 16 1983[2]

when the problem is right here in my everyday life I have difficulties.

A typical instance was when some years ago I had to work with a consultant psychiatrist whose ignorance and bad manners were of quite breathtaking proportions. All of us who had to work with him were continually confounded, frustrated and angered by his lack of co-operation and by his personal abuse of each and every one of us. When we would talk together about the problems we had with this man one fact was always present in our discussion, even if we did not state it. This man was not British.

As I tried to deal with the continual problems this man created I was always aware of the temptation of venting my anger and frustration by resorting to the Hate the Stranger attitudes which are part of my experience. I remember the attitudes of my father's friends who had been soldiers stationed in this man's country. Moreover, I was a child in the latter part of those years when the Australian government followed the White Australia Policy which barred any person whose skin carried the slightest trace of inborn brown, black or yellow. Australians then had, so they believed, excellent reasons for excluding such persons. I can remember these attitudes. When pressed, it was a temptation to slip back into them, to sneer and laugh at, to ignore and hurt this man, not because of what he did but because he was not a member of the group to which I belong.

So, what did I do to try to overcome this problem? First, I had to say to myself my problem was *him*, not his nationality. What was he doing and why did he do it? I observed him closely the way I observe anyone I am trying to understand and I thought about what I saw. I learnt from this that, even allowing for the fact that English was not his first language, that he was not particularly bright. He was slow in absorbing new material, particularly abstract ideas, and his way of doing this was to repeat back to people the facts and ideas which he was trying to absorb. We got impatient and bored with this, and each of us, in our own way, shut off from listening to him when he started to talk at length. If the boredom became excruciating or we became anxious about what he was saying we would make jokes. We included him in these jokes, but that was worse than excluding him, because he had never grasped the way we made jokes about one another. Such jokes he took as a personal affront. He did not understand joking as a way of affirming group solidarity and affection and concern for one another. He felt attacked, and so attacked us. He withdrew to a position of power and used it to frustrate and injure us.

I could see all this. I could see how anxious and uncertain he was, how the more threatened he felt the more he talked, the more he boasted of his wealth and power, the more violent was his abuse, the more dogmatically and destructively he used his power as a consultant to destroy what we were trying to create. I could see clearly his fear and his need for the support for which he could not bring himself to ask, and I suspected that his grandiosity was a defence against depression. Had he come to me as a client I could have, very gently, acknowledged my awareness of his pain and weakness and my concern for him. But he had not come to me as a client. He needed nothing from me except my obedience.

In his system of values I was a mere thing. He despised psychologists and all matters psychotherapeutic (but under this he was scared that I used the mysteries of psychotherapy to penetrate his secrets), while women were objects of no more value than meeting his needs. I was an old woman (same age as him) so I was of no sexual interest to him. If I gave him a cup of coffee he received it graciously. If I offered advice he dismissed it. If I disagreed with him, however politely, he was furious.

My problem was that although I could, with effort, see him as a Stranger and Different he saw me as a Stranger and Dangerous. Without some acknowledgment from him of what was actually happening, how could we ever have some kind of meeting where we could share our difficulties and reduce our fear? We needed someone whom we both respected to bring us together and act as a conciliator. I hoped that one of our senior administrators would do this, but unfortunately none of them had these skills. They (all men) were trained to organise and conciliate on practical matters – money, development of the health service, conditions of work, building requirements. They had no skills for dealing with emotional issues, the fears, angers, jealousies and passions which underlie all our practical activities. They were trained to resolve all ambiguity. They could not cope with situations where ambiguity was of the essence, where people feel both hate and love, fear and contempt, power and dependence. So they stayed safe in their offices and issued communiqués, or chaired fruitless meetings, and we lost the opportunity to explore and discover better ways in which a diverse collection of people can work and live together. Instead, we continued stumbling on from disaster to disaster.

If the human race is to escape the terrible fate which awaits it we have to develop new skills. We have some knowledge of the process whereby we come to forgive those who have injured us, become reconciled and get on with our lives without dragging the burden of unforgiveness and revenge with us, but our knowledge of this is limited. We have never regarded it as an area of knowledge worth expanding. We know how to get to the moon but not how to reach our neighbour, the Stranger. There is large research literature on the processes whereby crises arise and may be resolved, and conciliation services have been developed in marriage and divorce and in industry and trade unions. There are many therapists who understand how the way out of the predicaments in which many individuals find themselves begins with self-forgiveness. So a basis of knowledge is there for us to build on. What we need are many skilled conciliators.

We need conciliators, not referees. Referees follow a rule book. All they have to do is to apply the rules which someone else has created. Conciliators have no rules, just wisdom. Wisdom that it is better to preserve our lives than destroy them. That love is better than hate. That we create our own worlds, and as we are free to make our worlds so we are free to change them. That while there are many differences between us there are many things that we share. If we start from what interests we have in common we can generate ideas about all the many ways we could resolve our differences. A conciliator is someone who has no personal interest in the dispute, who can understand each person's point of view, empathise with each person's point of view while at the same time observe it objectively, dispassionately, and see it within the framework of the overall situation. A conciliator understands both the internal and external reality of each of the disputants and gives each reality equal weight. The conciliator helps each disputant to confront his own fear, greed and envy and does not let him hide behind bluster and sentimentality. The conciliator helps each disputant to see the other disputants as people, not objects, and to accept the reality of their fears. The conciliator is not in the business of getting people to love one another, or even just to like one another. The conciliator is in the business of getting people to see that argument and fighting are self-defeating and that the amicable resolution of disputes is an act of enlightened self-interest.

Listing the tasks of a conciliator makes such people sound like a race of superior beings, like something out of *Star Trek*. We cannot rely on such beings turning up in the nick of time to save us from our folly. We have to develop the skills of a conciliator, each of us, and be prepared to use them whenever necessary. I shall conciliate for you, and when I get into dispute, then you will conciliate for me.

We are all quite good at picking up new skills, but we only do so when we are convinced that a new skill will be useful to us. I ignored computers steadfastly because computers were concerned with numbers and numbers never interested me. I was sure that I could never understand computers. But as soon as computers dealt with words and could do the things that typewriters do, only much better, I started taking notice of them, and, once I had one of my own, the very first computer I had ever touched, I taught myself word processing in a matter of days. Computers had become important to me. The reason that we have never developed and acquired the skills of a conciliator is because we do not value them. We do not value forgiveness and reconciliation.

We have been taught that not forgiving is good, that it is a sign of strength to vow revenge and heroic to carry it out. Forgiving and forgetting is soppy, weak and feminine. Not that women are any better at forgiving than men. They may not spend much time hating their nation's enemies and fighting them but they do spend a lot of time not forgiving their relatives and the neighbours who have offended them, and they teach the art of not forgiving to their children. Because forgiving is despised it is not understood. Forgiveness and the understanding which must precede it are confused with condonation. Those of us who are in the business of trying to understand why people behave as they do are always being told that we are 'do-gooders', something we ought not to be.

(Presumably those people who call us do-gooders are themselves do-evillers, which is a curious thing to want to be.) Researchers into the cause and cure of cancer are not accused of doing good. Somehow, trying to understand the process whereby cancer kills does not mean that cancer is condoned, whereas trying to understand the process whereby we hurt, maim and kill one another means that hurting, maiming and killing are condoned. How strange. How stupid.

If we are to save ourselves we have to define forgiveness as good, an act of strength, not of weakness. Not forgiving is easy. It means not having to think. It means not trying to imagine what it is like to be someone else. It makes us feel better. It wards off the pain of mourning the irreparable injury we have suffered. By not forgiving we can hide our immediate blind wish to destroy anything that causes us pain or frustrates us behind righteous anger ('It distresses me to do this but I am beating you for your own good'). By not forgiving we can try to force the world to conform to our wishes ('If you disobey me I shall never speak to you again'). By not forgiving we can indulge in the excitement of arguing and fighting. We fear that a world of universal love and understanding would be very dull and boring.

Arguments and fighting can provide excitement without threatening change. The insults which spouses and nations hurl at one another are usually part of a situation which both participants want to keep from changing. Fighting is a way of maintaining the status quo. Forgiveness is dangerous because it always means change. We have to see things differently. Forgiveness means freedom, and many people prefer security to freedom.

What many people want is to have the security of believing that they know everything that they need to know about their enemy and that their enemy never changes. They do not want to be made to feel insecure by discovering that their beliefs are wrong, that their enemy is not as they thought, that their enemy has changed, as everything changes over time. That is why nations try to prevent their people from finding out too much about the nation's enemies and why individuals refuse to have any contact with the neighbours who offend them.

To forgive we have to be able to comprehend the

circumstances of our enemies' lives. This means not just seeing how they are like us but how they are different. To do this we have to be able to understand ourselves.

The process of understanding and forgiveness requires us to carry out the following tasks:

1   We have to take the other person as seriously as we take ourselves

That is, we have to see the Stranger, our Enemy, as a *person*, not as an object. Objects are things which we can use, abuse, and destroy because they have no feelings and do not suffer pain. Persons have feelings and suffer pain.

2   We have to separate the act from the actor

If we say, and believe, 'That is an evil person' or 'I am an evil person' then we make ourselves helpless. Evil construed as a mysterious and powerful force which inhabits and controls a person cannot be combated in any way. But if we say, and believe, 'That person does evil things' or 'I do evil things' then evil ceases to be a mysterious and powerful force and becomes something which we can understand and, through our understanding, change. We can understand the process whereby we learn to see our enemies or the people whom we want to control as objects which we can use, abuse, torture and kill. Understanding this process, we can help those people who carry out these evil acts to understand what they do and to choose to behave differently. Understanding this process we can prevent children from experiencing the kind of punishments which lead them to carry out evil acts. But to separate the act from the actor and to understand the processes of hatred, envy and cruelty which manifest themselves in evil acts we have to accept the reality of evil acts wherever they occur. We have to accept that they happen close to us as well as far away and that we connive with their evil intent when we refuse to recognise them. Our friends commit evil acts as well as our enemies. Moreover, to understand the processes of hatred and cruelty which manifest themselves in evil acts we have to recognise and own as our own the processes of hatred, envy and cruelty within ourselves.

3 We have to know that we do not know

This means giving up the superiority of claiming that we know all that needs to be known. We all like to feel that we understand other people. We all like to claim to be 'a good judge of other people'. The truth is, we are not. We cannot be, because we each inhabit a separate world and we cannot literally enter another person's world. We can do so only *figuratively*, by an act of imagination. Even then we can get it wrong, and even if we get it right, what we get right is only a fragment of that world and only temporary. Knowing that we do not know makes us realise the importance of the next task.

4 We have to create a shared language

This means trying to understand another person *in his own terms*, not in our terms. It means giving up saying things like, 'I don't know what the youth of today are coming to. When I was a teenager I knew how important it is to work hard and get a good job' and actually talking to young people so as to discover what it is like to be young in the world today – something very different from being young in all previous decades. It means finding out more about the problems and difficulties which other people face. Creating a shared language can mean having to give up in-jokes about the people we see as Strangers and Enemies. For instance, Australians, many of whom are descended from the eighteenth-century poor of Great Britain who suffered much at the hands of their lords and masters, retain a disdain for the English whom they call 'the Poms'. There is another popular name for the Poms – 'The Great Unwashed', and this is the source of many jokes amongst Australians, who are a compulsively clean people, forever leaping in and out of showers and changing their clothes. They despise the English for not sharing this compulsion. What they do not realise is that the Australian compulsive cleanliness is a result of the hot, humid climate where most of them live and that personal cleanliness has other dimensions in a cold, damp climate. One winter of poverty in a London flat changes many an Australian's understanding of the Great Unwashed.

Creating a shared language means understanding how the other person's language came about, that is, understanding the history of that person and that nation. As individuals we do not talk to the Stranger and so discover how his history has shaped his system of values. As nations we learn, and do not realise that we learn, our history from one point of view, the one which holds us together as a nation and gives us an inflated view of our virtue and importance, and we do not learn about the history of other nations, and certainly not our history from another nation's point of view. (I shall never forget my shock when I sat in a library in Sligo, County Mayo, and read Australian history from an Irish point of view.) Only by creating a shared language and understanding the history of the Stranger can we appreciate the feelings of the Stranger.

5   We have to understand the reality of the Stranger's fear of us

We know that we are afraid of the Stranger, but we protect ourselves from our fear by hurling abuse at our enemy and by denying that our behaviour has made our enemy afraid of us. After all, objects don't have feelings, so objects can't be afraid. Because we are ignorant of the history of our Enemy we do not understand what he fears. Each nation has special fears about the repetition of past disasters – like the Russian fear of another devastating war fought within their borders, the Israeli fear of another, more successful attempt to wipe them out as a race, the American fear of being a helpless captive of a powerful state. Some of these fears are supported by recent events, some are the traditions of ancestors handed down generation after generation. None of such fears are unreal, though they might be exaggerated, because they are interpreted by each individual as a metaphor for the fears of annihilation which we all carry within us – the fear of being expelled from the group which maintains our identity or the fear of being overwhelmed by chaos. We need to understand how we experience our existence and how we experience our annihilation, both in personal terms and in terms of the group to which we belong. We need to be able to see why we fear most the Stranger who is closest to us, who threatens the stability of our group. We can see the threat as one of being overwhelmed by a stronger power; we can see the threat as a matter of greed and envy, our greed and envy as well as that of the Stranger; we can see the threat as the Stranger nearby being able to show up our pretensions as the hollow sham that we know and do not admit they are. How can we claim to be the brightest girls in our school if the class next to ours is just as bright? How can we claim to be the Master Race when there lives within our borders another race which would be, if we let them, as superior as we are?

6 We have to understand the nature of anger

It is as unrealistic to expect people to all like one another as it is to expect that they will never get angry with one another. What we have to do is to come to a better understanding of anger, to see it as a natural response to frustration. Our task, as members of a society, is not to pretend that we never get angry, or to control our anger through fear so that it bursts out in uncontrolled rage, or to turn our fear into righteous anger by which we justify our cruelty, but to acknowledge and understand our anger so that we can find ways of expressing and resolving it. This means accepting anger, our own and other people's, in the knowledge that experienced and expressed anger is self-limiting, while repressed anger waits the opportunity to wreak its vengence. Perhaps it may even be possible for us to come to understand that reacting to anger with anger may not be a proof of manhood but simply a proof of weakness.

7 We have to understand that forgiveness cannot be coerced into being but, like love, arises spontaneously

We cannot teach people forgiveness but only show it by our own behaviour, just as we cannot teach people to love but only show it by loving them.

If there is to be any effective change in the way we define ourselves and the Stranger we must *all* make the change and not just a few of us. There have always been good, peaceful people, much more forgiving and able to turn the other cheek

than I could ever be, but their example has not been followed.
Usually they have been destroyed by the forces of reaction or
they have been elevated to sainthood and so safely ignored.
(Now that Gandhi has become Gandhiji, a revered Hindu god,
few people remember and try to follow his teachings.) The
importance of seeing the Stranger, not as Dangerous but as
merely Different, must be universally recognised and put into
practice by our leaders. As I write this, and think of Reagan's
'empire of evil' speech and the dour old men of the Kremlin, let
alone the militant Muslims, the IRA and Ian Paisley, my
heart sinks. For it is not just the desire for activities like wars
and genocide which must disappear. More subtle changes
have to be made. We cannot afford leaders who boast that
they neither speak a foreign language nor need people with
such language skills on their staff, nor can we afford leaders
who pride themselves in deciding that they know all they
need to know about a person in the first five minutes of
meeting that person. The first of these is said about Ronald
Reagan; the second about Margaret Thatcher. To understand
people who speak a language different from our own we need
to have some knowledge of how that language divides up
reality and evaluates it, while the understanding and knowledge of another person can never be complete. But perhaps
we get the leaders we deserve.

When I was discussing the matter of forgiveness with the
Reverend Keith he pointed out that

> Where one finds conviction one also finds intolerance,
> while where there is tolerance there is usually a failure
> of faith and nerve. The former is illustrated by Northern
> Ireland, while this country (U.K.) provides a model for
> the latter contention.[3]

I would argue that we need to operate on the conviction that
life on this planet is worth preserving and that we intend to do
this. We should not tolerate the actions of people who wish to
destroy the life on this planet. But we should not hold unchanging convictions about how we can achieve our aim of
preserving life. We should not claim that there is only One,
True and Right way of gaining our ends, for if we do, we shall
have defeated our own ends by our intolerance. There is a

multitude of ways in which we can live peaceably together. Every situation always presents us with a multitude of alternative ways of assessing it and acting upon it. Anyone who says that there is no alternative is either a fool or a liar, and probably both.

Keith went on to say that the Church has difficulty in dealing with forgiveness since 'the virtue most valued by the institutional Church is loyalty, above those of faith, hope and charity, on which forgiveness depends.'[4] Faith requires trust, and hope a tolerance of uncertainty,while charity, an old word for love, is very complicated. How do we love others when we have suffered so much at their hands?

For my depressed clients to find their way out of the prison of depression they have to learn to forgive themselves and their parents. In childhood they have suffered loss, abandonment, humiliation. They have been beaten, but they have not been starved, or seen their parents murder or be murdered, rape or be raped. They have not been bombed or turned out of their homes by marauding soldiers. The painful events of their childhood took place in a setting of national security and modest sufficiency. Yet the images of their childhood still arouse such terror and despair that the person must resort to not forgiving to defend against the pain. How much greater the terror and despair, how much more implacable the not forgiving for those children in Central America, the Middle East, Northern Ireland, Uganda, Ethiopia, Namibia, the Chad, for those children whose families are persecuted by military forces led by ruthless dictators or who see their families starving in a rich world. It is not enough to send food to the starving and to sermonize about 'innocent children' in wartorn countries. Such children are not innocent. They are in the process of discovering that to survive as a person they must have enemies. They must hate and never forgive. To deflect such children from perpetuating the cruelty and self-seeking of their elders a great deal of very skilled help is required. The enormity of this problem is not being recognised. Hunger prevents many millions of children from completing the basic physical development necessary for mental development. Poverty forces many millions of children to work and so to lose their childhood, when, through play, children ordinarily master the tasks necessary to become a whole human being. In wealthy countries, where schooling is compulsory, many children who suffer at the hands of their parents find respite and support in their school, and their education offers a chance of escape from the family and to create a life of their own. This is not available to the children in the Third World.

Psychotherapists working with severely deprived children here in England have reported how hard it is to reach these children, much less help them change. The child tries to be completely self-reliant, but in ways which are life-defeating rather than life-enhancing. As one young lad was described,

> Martin suffered not only the deprivation inflicted on him by external circumstances but he deprived himself further by his crippling defences which made him so hard to get in touch with. . . . He had a numb, unreachable quality which the therapist found very hard to get through. In Martin's words to her, she was 'talking to a brick wall'. This brick-wall quality was very hard to penetrate and, although expressed differently, had a quality of forceful projection of unpleasant and violent feelings into the therapist. . . . There was a menacing quality, with a continual threat of violence, suggested by the wearing of knuckle rings, the production of knives and remarks such as, 'We'll have to get a new Mrs Henry.' Again the need seemed to be protection from the painful feelings of dependence. 'You can get your face wet with rain, with tears, with blood, and yours is going to be wet with blood before mine is wet with tears.'[5]

Severe deprivation interferes with the child's ability to deal with experience both emotionally and intellectually.

It could be that girls react rather differently from boys to the lack of a mother's holding arms and caring preoccupation when they are very tiny. The therapists' observations of the kinds of relationships which some of the girls make over a period of time, in psychotherapy, suggest that not having been 'held' at a crucial stage of development may lead to an impairment of the capacity to take in, grasp and hold on to thoughts, feelings, memories, and experience – the 'in one ear and out the other' kind of phenomenon. There is no feeling of depth or of an inner world or space. Everything falls out or is dropped, sometimes concretely expressed by soiling. We can see how they might grow up to have difficulties with mothering their own children. It must be hard to be a mother who can hold and care for a child when you do not have a feeling of a good internal mother to sustain you. It is hardly surprising if these girls grow to be mothers who let their own children slip into care, so perpetuating the cycle of deprivation.[6]

Assessment of these children shows that

on the Weschler Intelligence Scale for Children a familiar pattern of scores emerges: average non-verbal IQs but lower scores on tests of general knowledge, vocabulary, arithmetic and often coding. This evidence of failure to take in information, perhaps because their environment has been impoverished, may also be due to their poorly developed listening skills and inability, described so vividly by therapists, to concentrate, to hold on to and make sense of the events and experiences in their lives. Occasionally the test pattern is reversed and children of average verbal ability show unusual difficulties with Block Design, Object Assembly and Picture Arrangement Tests. They may have neat writing and copy shapes accurately; the problem is not perceptual or motor but seems to be one of integrating fragmented pieces into a whole. . . . The puzzle of a face also seems to present undue difficulties. . . . The Draw a Person Test also produced a very characteristic omission of arm or hands even in drawings which were otherwise quite detailed. This seemed to me to be an expression of helplessness, of an inability to act, but has also been interpreted as characteristic of children who have had little experience of being held.

Projective tests with older children are often unproductive; the less defended violence and deprivation of earlier years is replaced by emptiness and denial. They convey a restricted emotional life and little capacity to think about themselves. Their difficulties in thinking and making links, already evident in their response to the intelligence tests, are also reflected in their apparent inability to link feelings to events, past, present and future. They seem to experience life as random and arbitrary.[7]

Unsatisfactory experiences, of violence, abuse and neglect, unmodified by loving and supportive reality experiences, may leave residual memories which are difficult to assimilate and digest. These may constitute intrapsychic configurations which are liable to be triggered off and re-enacted when an external situation seems to match the early memory. . . . It throws light on the tendency for the early tragedies to repeat themselves, for the abandoned child to become the abandoning parent and for the cycle of deprivation to be perpetuated.[8]

The only way the child can break out of this repetition is, somehow, to retain a sense of outrage and loss and not give way to a cynical disbelief in any real goodness, but this means remembering what terrible things he has suffered at the hands of other human beings. For this a child needs the holding experience of a wise therapist.

Shirley Hoxter, writing about the feelings which are aroused in the therapist trying to help these children said,

Such extreme vulnerability requires such sensitivity in the timing and wording of any approach and, for some children, one mistake may carry the threat of unbearable pain. As Donald Meltzer has said, sometimes one needs to 'tiptoe up to pain'. The injured child's capacity for feeling love and the need for love is so fraught with vulnerability that it is no wonder that his communications abound with images such as armoured vehicles, brick walls, ice walls or hedgehog spikes and snail's shells and similar means of warding off exposure to the pain of contact. Such children express their own attempts to make contact in terms such as fingers being pinched in doors and splinters jabbed in old grazes, and tears are admitted only as painful grit in the eye. A few children seem to perceive the very nature of contact in a relationship as being inevitably a matter of sadistic and perverse mutual mutilation. With these children sensitivity in modulating their pain goes hand in hand with much restraint and patience in modulating the offer of a possibility of being in touch with human warmth; the worker will ache with a longing to give while being obliged to recognise that compassion can only be received as though it were an attack.

It is very painful for us to perceive suffering in children. We want to take action to remove the pain or at least to achieve a causative understanding which makes the pain more tolerable, more forgiveable. But historical explanations can sometimes obscure the essentials rather than help us in our search for understanding. Often the simple truth is that our client, be it child or parent or substitute parent, is desperately unhappy, right here and now. It is this raw pain that requires our attention; it cannot be explained away, it has to be attended to and encountered in ourselves. We can never observe emotional injury; we can only observe the adaptations and maladaptations which each individual utilises in attempts to cope with pain. The pain remains unseen, our only perceptual organ for it is that most sensitive of instruments, our own capacity for emotional response. By maintaining our sensitivity without being overwhelmed or resorting to withdrawal or attribution of blame, we may then be better able to provide the answer which brings relief: the experience of a relationship with someone who can be relied upon to attend to suffering with both receptivity and strength.[9]

It is very hard just to stay with another person who is in pain, hard to stay with our own helplessness and not rush into doing something, however futile, hard to let someone else's pain remind us of our own. Such reminders can come at any time. The other evening when I was taking a seminar with postgraduate education students I told them of Alice Miller's contention that we have all been hurt, in some way, by the way were brought up as children and that we repress the memory of this injury. One member of the group, an experienced counsellor himself, said,

> While you were talking about Alice Miller I became
> aware that I had become terribly sad. You know, I can't
> remember anything of my life between four and six
> years. There are tiny fragments, but nothing coherent.
> All I do remember is that at six, when I went to school, I
> had become a very clean, neat, obedient child.

Parents who have been robbed of the confidence to be themselves by their parents feel that they cannot possibly know what is best for their children and so they turn to 'experts'. Judy Dunn, a psychologist and mother of three, who has made a special study of the upbringing of young children, has commented that, 'I'm afraid people do want to be told (what to do). I think they get the best advice from other parents of small children, and from health visitors, but very rarely from doctors.'[10] In her study *Sisters and Brothers* she reports that research shows that emotional and financial stress in a family produces particularly quarrelsome children and that parents who use physical punishment to discipline their children have children who are themselves more physically aggressive.[11] So unhappiness produces unhappiness and aggression aggresssion.

However, we should not assume that an unhappy childhood necessarily does *irreparable* damage. Human nature can change. Colwyn Trevarthan, reviewing the research into the function of attachment commented,

> Epidemiological evidence shows beyond reasonable
> doubt that early deprivation of love can potentiate
> emotional illness. But extraordinarily recuperative
> powers inhere in the structure of human affection and
> companionship, and substitute relationships can bring
> recovery from past deprivations.

He went on to comment on the results of the research on the relationship between the mother and baby. 'Clearly, the "bond" is a negotiated contract – not a reflex.'[12] Contracts are something which can be revised and rewritten. The first group to which we belong and the desires and needs which that group generates and may satisfy, the desire and need to *amaeru*, is something which is capable of change.

As much as we try, we can never give our children entirely peaceful and secure lives. Even if we could, it may not be wise to do so, for a completely peaceful and secure childhood, with no opportunity to face difficulties and hardships and to discover how to overcome them, would not be a realistic preparation for adult life. But when parents meet disasters and difficulties how much should we let our children see of the emotions these disasters and difficulties arouse? Any parent whose spouse has died or deserted knows how violent the emotions of anger and grief can be and how children can be frightened by seeing their parent so strangely disturbed. So a parent will try to hide these emotions and run the risk of frightening or alienating the children who, at some level, know that they are not being told the truth. Anger can be dealt with more openly, because, if we see anger as the natural human response to frustration and so accept our children's anger and help them learn good ways of managing their anger and coping with other people's anger, then our children will, to some extent, accept our anger. It is fear that is the problem.

If we show our children that we are afraid, then we not only teach them to be afraid but we also undermine their total security. Anxious parents have anxious children. The solution is for parents to become brave. We need to teach our children that though the world has many dangers and difficulties these can be met bravely with a sense of courage and mastery. To teach a child not to be afraid of life parents, as Erik Erickson said, must not be afraid of death. To be courageous the first step is to acknowledge one's fear. Parents who deny that the human race is in peril are themselves afraid of death, and, as such, they cannot give their children the courage to face life.

Family life is a microcosm of the life among nations, and settling disagreements in family life can be no easier than settling disagreements between nations. Different people want different things and not all needs and desires can be met. Sharing has to be taught by example, not by precept, but husbands and wives do not always accept and value their spouse's desires and interests. When children quarrel it is not enough to preach forgiveness. Doing so will probably achieve nothing except make the child resentful and jealous. We need to acknowledge the child's anger and hurt, and then help the child work his way through this to a place of reconciliation. To teach this point it is often necessary to go through a period of what I call 'creative unforgiveness', that is, not withdrawing, hurt, to nurse one's resentment, but actually working on the problem to find some kind of resolution. Such work can be fuelled by the unforgiveness which might, in the process, burn itself out.

I came across an example of this creative unforgiveness some time ago when I was asked to visit a self-help group of people who were or had been depressed. The meeting was held in the home of one of the members. Dinah was a woman in her late sixties. As we settled ourselves in the living room I noticed several pictures of a handsome, smiling young woman. This was Pat, her youngest child. Dinah's older children had left home but Pat had stayed with her mother because she had Downs Syndrome and, though capable in many ways, could not earn her own living. All her life she had suffered with bronchiectasis, an unpleasant lung condition. She rarely complained of being ill, so one day when she told her mother that she was in pain her mother was greatly concerned and sent for the doctor. It was many hours before the doctor came, and when he did it was not their usual doctor who knew Pat well. This doctor, without consulting Pat's medical notes, gave her an injection to reduce the pain. She went to sleep, and never awoke.

The doctor denied negligence. Dinah told me that when the vicar came to see her the day after Pat's death he wanted to say a prayer to ask God to help Dinah to forgive the doctor. But she said, 'Don't expect me to forgive him. I'll never forgive him, never.'

However, instead of retiring into a bitter depression Dinah took positive action. For years she had been a nervous, agoraphobic woman, yet with this anger inside her she confronted the doctor. Far from apologising or expressing sympathy, he told Dinah that as Pat was a mongol she wouldn't have lived long anyway. This further hurt spurred her to greater efforts. She took the matter to a tribunal and presented her case herself. Confronting the closed ranks of the medical profession is no easy task. Dinah is not likely to receive any real satisfaction, except the knowledge that she has entered into the fray to defend Pat. What she did was creative unforgiveness. Uncreative unforgiveness would be shooting the doctor.

We should not teach our children to hate, to define themselves in terms of a dangerous Stranger who must be hated and fought to the death. We should try to stop them feeling so weak and in such peril that they need to vow lifelong revenge and carry the habits of revenge with them into adult life. They should not be forced to maintain their pride by resorting to magical thinking, like one man who said, when I suggested that he go to our local bookshop to buy Phillip Hodson's book, 'I can't go in there again. I had a row with the manager there, and I vowed never to go there again – it's a kind of curse – I'd lose my soul.'

We should allow our children to protest about the world they have been born into. When I was last in Boston, Mass. the *Boston Globe* carried a story about a group of high school students who planned to hold an antinuclear rally. One of the students, Emily Borman, was quoted as saying how the idea grew out of the viewing of the film *The Day After*. 'It made us feel helpless. We wanted to do something. We wanted something where kids could come and learn about the arms race, because the teachers don't teach it in school. But we also want something that would be fun. To celebrate life.' Another student, Karen Crawford, said, 'When I started a STOP chapter at Boston Latin, I was so embarrassed standing outside the door waiting to see if students would show up for a meeting. Kids would tease me and call me "liberal". They think we're going to eat wheat germ and yoghurt and talk down to the government.' If anyone did any talking down it was the *Boston Globe*. The patronising headline on this article was *The antinuclear kids*.[13]

The peril which our world is facing is not something which can be hidden from children in the way that adults have tried to hide all knowledge about sex from children. When there is poverty, children are the first to suffer. When there is war children are not exempt.

> For many centuries in Europe and perhaps around the world, it was considered barbaric to kill children – and women – in war which was mostly a male affair. Following this tradition, in the first world war, only five per cent of deaths were civilian. Then in the 1930s, from Guernica on, the fascists started bombing civilians. Hitler's aim was to lower enemy morale by such bombing. Although it was proved to heighten enemy morale, Britain adopted civilian bombing in 1942. Fifty per cent of the casualties in the second world war were civilians. (In Hiroshima, more women than men were killed.) So only in the last half century has war involved deliberately killing children.[14]

The only way that children can live with the danger of being the victim of a war or a terrorist attack or with the evidence of how unfair life can be is that they have a chance to talk about these things, to ask questions and get their questions properly answered, to protest about the injustice of it all. This way they can come to understand that life is not straightforward and simple, a contest between the goodies and the baddies, the forces of good and the forces of evil, but is composed of paradox and irony. There is the paradox that total security is total immobility and therefore total helplessness. To be in charge of your life you have to understand, as any skier or rally driver knows, that successful movement means letting go, controlling and yet not controlling the flow from one state of being to another. There is the irony that if we become so powerful that we can force the world to approximate to what we want it to be, if we try to get other people to accept our construction of what the world should be, then we find ourselves totally alone, because there is no one else in our world who will confront, argue and share with us. Getting your own way means being completely alone.

One evening I had dinner with Rachel and Richard and their mother Glenda. Rachel is eleven and Richard twelve. They know all about the devastation of nuclear weapons – the explosion, the fire, radiation and the nuclear winter which would follow. It was the radiation which worried Rachel the most – how it got inside you and what happened then. Richard said, 'I don't want to be alive afterwards. I'd rather be killed.' Rachel agreed with him. 'I wouldn't want to go into a shelter. That would be awful.'

Glenda said, 'But we shouldn't give up in the face of death. You know those lines your father's always quoting,

> "Do not go gently into that good night,
> Rage, rage against the dying of the light." '

Rachel and Richard talked about how foolish men were to struggle for power and put life on earth at risk. They saw that there could be no end to this danger until all people learned to live peacefully together, but they could not see this happening because fighting was so much part of people.

'Look how fights break out in the playground,' said Rachel.

I asked Richard how he saw his future. He looked very serious. 'I think there won't be a nuclear war. I don't know why, but I don't think there will be.'

I asked Rachel the same question. She said, 'I know it might happen, but I don't think there will be a nuclear war.' And then she said, 'Can't we talk about something else? I think if you think about it too much you forget all the nice things here right now and you never enjoy yourself. That's silly.'

Rachel is right. In thinking about the possibility of a nuclear war we can forget the nice things that are here right now. But even as we enjoy the nice things we need to keep somewhere in the back of our mind that these nice things are too valuable to lose. We must keep the nice things, and we must continue to enjoy them.

Can we go on enjoying the nice things and at the same time ensure that they, and us, are not destroyed?

To do this we would have to see the world as one place. We need to realise that the Nuclear Bomb has not preserved world peace. Some of us have managed to avoid being involved in a war, but since 1945 16 million people have died in military and paramilitary activities. Many millions more have died of starvation brought on by the spending of money on arms rather than on food production and distribution and combating drought, floods and soil erosion. When aid is given to poor countries the aid is organised by men and given to men, even though in underdeveloped countries it is women who do the growing and harvesting of food. Men guard the cattle and their manhood; men control the world's finances. Two-thirds of the world's food is produced by women; women own only a small fraction of the world's wealth.[15] Men need to reflect upon themselves, and change.

The four Bombs which threaten to destroy us and which we have created out of our way of defining ourselves and our groups are each part of the one predicament, our greed for ourselves and our fear of the Stranger. All four Bombs could disappear by the simple expedient of all nations ceasing to spend their resources on arms and using the money so saved to provide adequate care for *all* the peoples of the earth. But we cannot do this – we cannot even want to do this – until we make enormous changes in ourselves. Every aspect of how we see ourselves, how we bring up our children, how we form groups and choose our leaders would have to change.

A leader, if we are lucky, can be someone who accepts the responsibility of leadership without wanting the power which goes with the leadership. If we are unlucky, and we usually are, we choose, connive with, or have thrust upon us a leader who wants power, and what is power but the opportunity to insist that other people put our ideas, our constructions of our world before their own. Parents define the world for their children; dictators define the world for their subjects. In a democracy the theory of government is that many alternative constructions of reality can exist, but in practice politics reduces to two apparently simple alternative constructions and the electors have either to take sides or to ignore the whole business altogether. When the political parties of a democratic country are led by people who understand that alternative constructions not only exist but are the means by which creative compromises can be achieved then we can live in peace together and enjoy some measure of justice. But when the political parties are led by people who insist that they alone possess the Truth and in the imposition of this Truth no compromise is possible then peace, co-operation and justice within the group (country) diminishes and the group fragments into smaller groups, each of which is held together by fear, anger, greed and envy. When we have leaders who prefer conviction to compromise we then discover that conviction and cruelty go hand in hand.

This is not surprising. Not one of us knows, or can ever know, what reality really is, not one of us is intelligent enough to comprehend the vast complexity which we call life. Anyone who claims to have such knowledge is deluded. The structure that each of us creates in an attempt to approximate reality and to give some meaning to life can be no more than a fragment of imperfect understanding. If we do not realise this, if we try to impose our constructions on other people, other people ignore us, because they have their own constructions. We can recognise this, respect the constructions of other people, and then try to create some shared constructions. But this means changing our own constructions, and if we refuse this compromise and continue to wish to impose our constructions on other people then we have to resort to force, to some form of cruelty, to get other people to accept our constructions. So we beat our children, give greater powers to the police, send in the army to destroy those who oppose us, collect and use guns, bombs and the instruments of torture.

Those people who seek power in order to impose their beliefs upon the world are themselves people who, as children, had the views of others imposed on them with strictness and cruelty. They sought refuge from the pain of this by identifying with the cause of their pain, and they embarked upon a lifetime of trying to prove their worth, despite the hidden badness they felt within themselves, and of finding objects (people) against whom they can vent the unacknowledged hatred they have of those who caused them such pain and cruelty in childhood. Such leaders perpetuate the definition of our group in terms of the feared and hated Stranger. The human race can no longer afford such leaders.

To outgrow our need for leaders who express our own projected fear of the Stranger we would have to extend our knowledge of ourselves knowing that gaining self-knowledge is a continuous process and never comes to an end. We would need to discover and face the harm that was done to us as children, to endure the pain such remembering brings, to turn our guilt into sorrow, to mourn and not fall into despair nor hate the people who did this harm. We would need to learn how we experience our existence and, if we are extroverts, that there is no danger in self-enquiry, and if we are introverts that some loss of control can be risked. We would need to revise the Myth of the Hero so that it serves to preserve life and not to destroy it.

We would need to learn more about how we understand others. After all, how can you love someone you don't know? Do you know your loved ones as they really are, or only as you see them because they are there to fill your needs? We can never change our enemies by hurling abuse at them. Like all people so attacked, they close ranks against us. But by learning about them, using whatever ways we can find to get to know them as people, similar to us in many ways but different in others, we could reduce the fear we all have of one another. We could reject any leader who demands that we must hate and fear the Stranger.

We could learn better ways of informing ourselves about what is happening in the world around us. We could always ask 'What advantage does this person, government, organisation, get out of doing or believing or expecting us to believe this?' We need not be taken in.

We could practise living with uncertainty and ambiguity and we could give up trying to make everything certain and absolutely secure. That way we can continue to hope.

A belief that there is some Power beyond this need not make us turn away from the present, from this world and the people around us, to seek solace and certainty. Religious belief and experience need not be based on homesickness, a longing for another place, but on a sense of immanence, the sacredness and holiness of the world we have been given. Those of us who believe that it is God's plan that the world will come to an end should remember this story,

The time was the 19th of May, 1790. The place was Hartford, Connecticut. The day has gone down in history as a terrible foretaste of Judgement Day. For at noon the skies turned from blue to grey and by mid-afternoon had blackened over so densely that, in a religious age, men fell on their knees and begged a final

blessing before the end came. The Connecticut House of
Representatives was in session. And as some men fell
down and others clamoured for an immediate
adjournment, the Speaker of the House, one Colonel
Davenport, came to his feet. He silenced them and said
these words: 'The Day of Judgement is either
approaching or it is not. If it is not, there is no cause for
adjournment. If it is, I choose to be found doing my duty.
I wish, therefore, that candles may be brought.[16]

We could learn to keep our candles lit and to continue caring
for our planet Earth.

We could learn to accept our own anger, and not turn it into
righteous, destructive anger.

We could learn not to despair. We could learn to accept
death but not side with it.

We could learn to face reality and not deny it.

We could realise that we are not helpless. Concerted action
overcomes tyrants. When Bishop Thomas Gumbleton visited
England recently he was interviewed by Susan Thomas of the
Guardian. She asked him,

What if you encounter something as evil as Hitler? He
looked weary. It is the question everyone asks pacifists.
'Pacifism could have worked in Germany if only the
church had given a lead, but it didn't. If you have
sufficient resolve you can prevail. Take Norway. Hitler
put in a Quisling government and attempted to change
the whole school system to teach the philosophy of
Aryan supremacy. But 12,000 unarmed school teachers
refused to cooperate and the government had to
capitulate. In Denmark when the Jews were ordered to
wear the Star of David so they could be identified and
shipped to concentration camps, the King put on the
Star and so did the rest of the citizens and the plan
failed. Non-violent, passive resistance can work.'[17]

We need a society where there is a wide range of opinion so
that the excesses and limitations of each point of view can be
restrained and counteracted. Conservatives are always good
at criticising what they are against but not very good at

justifying what they are for, while those people who want radical change do not always see the precise steps necessary for effecting such change and the wider implications that such change will have. All range of opinion needs to be able to talk to one another.

To understand the interconnectedness of our lives on earth will require new concepts. To date in the West we have excelled in generating concepts which separate and divide – the reductionism of science, the splitting of mind and body. Fine though the holistic concepts of the Eastern philosophies are, they do not have that precision and predictiveness which allow them to be used to understand and act upon the world we live in. We need words not just for Us and Them but for what connects Us and Them.

We need to give up the idea of once-and-for-all solutions and see the process of dealing with the problems of living as something which is co-existent with living. And living, we hope, never ends.

And we need to learn more about forgiveness. If we are to maintain relationships with other people and to live harmoniously with ourselves we must be able to forgive. Without forgiveness we have to drag the heavy burden of the past along with us wherever we go. Without forgiveness we can never be free to try again. Without forgiveness we can never love another person for what that person is, and loving a person for what that person is and not for what we want that person to be is the only kind of love which allows us to live freely without the demands and expectations which cripple and isolate us. Forgiveness and love are inseparable. We cannot have one without the other. We cannot live in relationships with others unless we can forgive others and forgive ourselves.

Each of us structures and so creates our own world. Because we are free to create our world and ourselves we are free to change our world and ourselves. We can choose to see ourselves as capable of change, and, doing so, the future opens up before us in an infinite array of possibilities. Or we can choose to see ourselves as unable to change, forced to live our lives as we have always lived them. Making this choice we are thus doomed to repeat our errors until the culmination of our errors brings the extinction of a species more intelligent but less wise and adaptable than the dinosaurs.

Oh, the sorrow and the pity of it all.

EPILOGUE (FROM BBC RADIO 3)

Biologist, geologist and historian of science, Stephen Jay Gould of Harvard University discussed with Colin Tudge the strengths and weaknesses of modern Darwinian theory.[1] Gould emphasised the distinction between evolution and progress. 'I don't deny,' said Gould, 'that if you go way back into the pre-Cambrian period three billion years ago you only had bacteria, non-nuclear creatures, and now you have flamingoes, hippopotamuses and people. In a sense, that's progressive. But there is no story of slow, steady, increasing, gradual, accumulated advance. What you basically have is one great burp called the Cambrian explosion, 600 million years ago, in which virtually all the major groups of organisms evolved, and the history of life since then, as I see it, has been largely a running of variations on these basic themes.

'I do not see gradual, predictable, accumulative progress in the history of life – I don't think you'd expect that: Darwin's theory is about local adaptation: it's not about cosmic advance. I think the idea of progress is very much a cultural bias, based on the desire to read the history of nature as the history of perfection, gradually increasing and leading to the late evolution of humans as dominant and dominating creatures by right.'

'*You're very excited,*' asked Colin Tudge, '*by the modern suggestion that in fact cataclysmic changes in the development of the world have been a major force in evolution?*'

'Yes, it's one of the main arguments, by the way, against progress, to put it in the most forceful and dramatic way. There's now reasonably good evidence that mass-extinctions cycle at a 26-million-year period. There's a strong suggestion that the frequency of those large impact craters which can be dated – there aren't many of them so the data are not fully persuasive – correlate with the extinctions and the cycle at the same rate. There's evidence at least of the Cretaceous/Tertiary boundary, when the dinosaurs became extinct, for extraterrestrial impact in the form of an element iridium which is not present in high abundance in Earth rocks, but which comes in from the outside.

'So it all seems to be converging – though it sounds like a science-fiction scenario – upon the notion that not infrequently in the history of the Earth we get that ultimate of unpredictable and random catastrophes, namely, major impacts of extraterrestrial bodies on the Earth's surface. What that means for the history of life and the notion of progress is that patterns of life are fundamentally being set at reasonable intervals by an event to which organisms can't possibly be adapting and preparing. You can't prepare for the 26-million-year cometary showers.

'Let me give you the best example of how you must look at the development of the complexity of human intelligence as a lucky random event, and not as a predictable consequence of accumulated progress. Most people don't know that mammals evolved at the same time as dinosaurs. They both evolved in the late Triassic period. Mammals lived for 100 million years – that's two-thirds of their existence – always as tiny little creatures in the interstices of the dinosaurs' world. They didn't dominate, they didn't get bigger; they lived as little rat-like creatures. Then along comes this cosmic catastrophe at the end of the Cretaceous period, wipes out the dinosaurs, and mammals take over because space is cleared out.

'Now suppose that hadn't happened. Dinosaurs had lived for 100 million years, mammals had never got anywhere. It's only been 65 million years since; there's no reason to think that dinosaurs wouldn't have survived. I think, had it not been for that cometary shower or whatever, dinosaurs would still dominate; mammals would still be tiny creatures. For 100 million years dinosaurs were not moving towards intelligence; I think they would be now what they were then. That's what they were for 100 million years. And we wouldn't be sitting here. Our potential ancestors would be little rats scurrying around among the dinosaurs.

'There is no predictable progress to human intelligence. A cometary shower may have been the *sine qua non* of our own accidental evolution. Now I really do look at human evolution as glorious. Consciousness is the greatest invention in the history of life; it has allowed life to become aware of itself and to recognise the facts of its own evolution, at least in one species. But it sure as hell wasn't a predictable consequence of universal progress.

'One interesting political or social spin-off to these extinction theories is the development of the nuclear winter scenario as a powerful additional argument against nuclear war. It's fascinating that the scenario envisaged in nuclear winter – getting very cold and dark thanks to a dust cloud thrown aloft by nuclear explosions, dust and soot – is in fact the same scenario that many people are proposing for the Cretaceous extinctions. It was a recognition that an asteroid packs more megatonnage than all the world's nuclear weapons which lead to that scenario. I often think it is a delicious irony (if in fact the cometary shower by wiping out the dinosaurs allowed our own evolution) that perhaps it's the recognition through the establishment of nuclear winter of the same scenario which is one small aid in a larger struggle that would contribute to our own survival now.

'*If we manage to wipe ourselves out by our own catastrophe, what succeeds this?*'

'I see no reason to predict that consciousness would evolve again. I don't want to say never, because there's billions of potential years to go before the sun explodes, and 13 million years, by the way, before the next cometary shower or whatever – we're in between them, so don't worry when you hear about the cycle. I see no reason to predict the evolution of consciousness again. I think it was a glorious, unpredictable, evolutionary accident. There's no mammalian lineage that seems to be moving in that direction. We've been around for a long time. That's no reason even to think that the great apes would be moving again in that direction – they've been around a long time. So I think it probably wouldn't happen, so we better stick around, if we like the invention.'

ON Days when I have had a FIGHT WITH JASON, Nigel has had A TEMPER + TANTRUM at KINDie, AND THE crème BRULÉE burned, I REMEMBER THE NEUTRON bomb AND THEN i don't feEL so baD...[2]

Once MY wiFe discoVEreD that it took plutonium 239 24,400 years to DECAY To HALF its activity, sHE DeCiDED sHe WANTeD a DIVORCE AND is PResENTly engAGeD in gAmBlinG HER LiFe savings in LAS VEGAS[3]

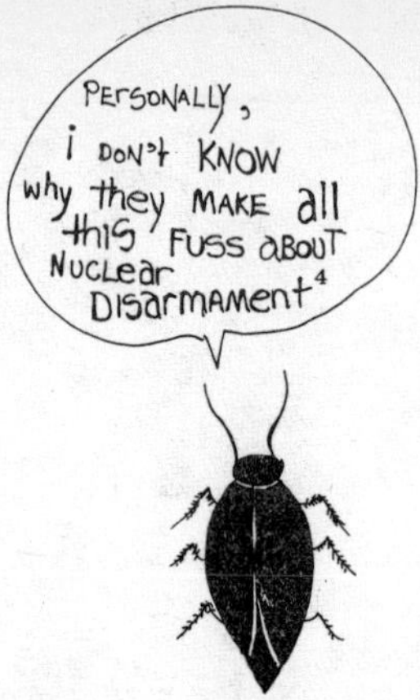
PERSONALLY, i DON'T KNOW why they MAKE all this FUSS ABOUT NUCLEAR DISARMAMENT[4]

NOTES

Preface

1 Dorothy Rowe, *Depression: the Way Out of Your Prison*, Routledge, 1983.
2 Marjorie Ballard, personal communication, 30 January 1984.
3 Paul Erlich, contrasting the effects of nuclear winter with the continuing devastation of the planet, said, 'present trends will simply take us in 50 to 150 years where a nuclear war could take us in 50 to 150 minutes. Ending the nuclear madness is the first step, but it is only the first step.'
'The nuclear winter: Discovering the ecology of nuclear war', *Amicus Journal*, Winter, 1984, p. 30 (quoted by Derrick de Kerckhove, 'On nuclear communication', *American Journal of Diacritics*, Johns Hopkins University, 1984).

The death toll caused by the world's natural disasters – floods, droughts, earthquakes, hurricanes and volcanic eruptions – is on the rise.

A new report, analysing data from the U.S. government and the International Red Cross, found that in the 1970's the average number of natural disasters recorded per year was 75, a 50 percent increase over the previous decade. But, comparing the same two decades, the estimated deaths caused by these events climbed fivefold, to 114,000 per year. During the average year of the 1970's, disasters caused disruptions in the lives of an estimated 44 million people.

Many relief officials are beginning to feel that emergency assistance today is 'like trying to bandage a wound that is constantly growing', as expressed by Anders Wijkman, secretary general of the Swedish Red Cross, which sponsored the study.

The increase in casualties, occurring in Africa, Asia and Latin America, is attributed to three main factors:

deforestation, erosion and other ecological stresses are reducing the land's resilience to climatic extremes; poverty is forcing more people to live in disaster-prone areas, and the population is growing rapidly.

While acknowledging that improved reporting may account for some of the rise, the authors of the Swedish report argue that the trends revealed are 'so marked that they may be considered as strong, fairly reliable indications'. Ecologists and geographers who have studied the issue agree that disaster casualties are climbing, as are numbers of economically marginal people and the stripping of forests in developing countries. They add that preventative measures that could reduce the impact of disasters are not receiving adequate priority.

The rise in death and destruction from disasters appears to be continuing. Numerous floods and droughts, especially in Latin America, made 1983 'a banner year for disasters,' in the words of one development official. Drought-related famines are unusually widespread in Africa this year.

The problem is not that nature has become more mercurial, according to seismologists and climate experts, but that the number of vulnerable people has increased. Earthquakes and unusual weather are not labeled as disasters unless people and property are adversely affected.

Throughout the Third World, as prime farmland becomes scarce, more rural families are forced to scratch a living in drought-prone areas, in flood plains and on steep hillsides where the risk of landslides is high. Substandard housing is built for the urban poor on the only plots available – on the sides of ravines, along known geological fault lines and in low-lying areas that frequently flood. Heavy storms, meagre rainfall or modest earth tremors can thus cause far more damage.

At the same time, ecologists argue, the degradation of the forests, pastures and soils has led to increases in the frequency of floods and droughtlike conditions. The deforestation of hillsides, mainly a result of the spread of farming, lets rainwater rush off slopes rather than being absorbed for later percolation. The result is an increase in flash floods in the rainy season and water shortages in the later months as the springs and streams dry up.

In many semiarid zones, a reduction of plant cover and organic matter in the soil because of overcropping, overgrazing and tree-cutting has meant a decline in the effective use of rainfall. The result is drier soils and an intensified catastrophe when a serious drop in rainfall does

occur, as it has repeatedly in parts of Africa in the last 15 years.
Erik Eckholm, *International Herald Tribune*, 2 August 1984, p.8.

Now the world population exceeds 4.8 billion on the most likely projections, growth is unlikely to have halted before 2100 – by which time the total will have passed ten billion . . .
'Unless we succeed in increasing the production of basic necessities to meet growing human needs,' warns Dr Normal Borlaug, Nobel Peace Prize winner and the instigator of the Mexican green revolution, 'the world will become more and more chaotic and social and political systems will collapse.'

Jim Crace 'Can we survive a population bomb?' *Weekend Australian*, 18–19 August 1984.
4   Derrick de Kerckhove, *op.cit.*

Chapter 1 'I wake up crying'

1   Norman Myers, 'Why is no one afraid of the dark?', the *Guardian*, 1 March 1984.

Dr Norman Myers, an environmental consultant based in Oxford, was one of the 20 scientists who contributed to a study of the long-term biological consequences of nuclear war, published in the US magazine on December 23, 1983. Other contributors included Carl Sagan, Paul Ehrlich, Edward Ayensu, Thomas Eisner, Stephen J. Gould, and Robert M. May.

2   Marjorie Ballard, personal communication, 12 February 1984.
3   'True Stories', *Private Eye*, 10 February, 1984, quoting *Mirror on Sunday*, 11 December 1983.
4   Jill Tweedie, 'Mummy, why do you go to Greenham Common?' *Guardian*, 7 February 1984.
5   Joanna Macy, *Despair Work*, Interhelp pamphlet, 1983.
6   Brick, *Beyond a Joke*, Spokesman, Bertrand Russell House, Gamble St, Nottingham NG7 4ET, 1983.
7   Alex Hutcheon letter to the *Guardian*, 26 March 1984. (Monseigneur Bruce Kent was then General Secretary for the Campaign for Nuclear Disarmament.)
8   Leeds City Council, *Leeds and the Bomb*, 1983.
9   Jonathon Schell, *The Fate of the Earth*, Pan Books, London, 1982, p. 139.

Chapter 2 'It'll never happen'

1   Joanna Rogers Macy, *Despair and Personal Power in the Nuclear Age*, New Society Publishers, Baltimore, p.4.
2   Raymond Briggs, *Where the Wind Blows*, Penguin, Harmondsworth, 1984.
3   Otto Fenichel, *The Psychoanalytic Theory of the Neuroses*, Norton, New York, 1945, p. 144.
4   Heath cartoon, *Punch*, 8 December, 1982.
5   Otto Fenichel, *op.cit.*, p.181.
6   Marjorie Proops personal communication, 8 February 1984.
7   Barry Katz and William Ringle, 'India may test second nuke bomb', *USA Today*, 3 May 1984.
8   Ripley, *Believe It or Not*, Channel 7, New York, 6 May 1984.
9   Robert Jastrow, 'How to make nuclear war obsolete', *Science Digest*, June 1984.
10 Jules Feiffer, *Marriage Is an Invasion of Privacy*, Andrews McMeely and Parker Inc, New York, 1984.
11 Stephanie personal communication, February, 1984.
12 Brick, *Beyond a Joke, op.cit.*
13 James Adams, 'Strangers and Brothers', *Sunday Times*, 15 April, 1984, pp.33–4.
14 Brian Tully, personal communication, 16 April 1984.
15 John Marks and Patricia Greenfield, 'The CIA and psychological tests', *Psychology News*, Nos 35 & 36, 1984.
16 Elizabeth Bishop, 'The Country Mouse', in *Collected Prose*, Chatto & Windus, London 1984, pp.32–3.
17 Dorothy Rowe, *The Construction of Life and Death*, Wiley, Chichester, 1984, p.105.
18 Myra Burgess, personal communication, 12 May, 1984.
19 Otto Fenichel, *op.cit.*, p.144.
20 Dorothy Rowe, *op.cit.*, p.130.
21 Phillip Hodson, personal communication, 14 February, 1984.
22 Robert Jay Lifton quoted in Craig Newnes, 'Facing the reality of nuclear death', *Changes*, July, 1982.

Chapter 3 'There's nothing I can do'

1   Pat's poem when she was depressed.
2   Dennis Friedman review of *Depressive Disorders in Different Cultures, Report on the WHO Collaborative Study on Standardized Assessment of Depressive Disorders*, World Health Orga-

nisation, Geneva, 1983, in *British Journal of Psychiatry*, No. 144, 1984, p.560.

3 George Brown and Tirril Harris, *Social Origins of Depression*, Tavistock, London, 1978.

4 George Winokur, *Depression: The Facts*, Oxford University Press, 1981, p.v.

5 Phillip Hodson, *Men: An Investigation into the Emotional Male*, BBC Books, London, 1983, p.21.

6 Elisabeth Kubler Ross, 'A philosophy for living – and dying', *The Listener*, 3 May 1984.

7 Jules Feiffer cartoon, *Observer*, 20 February, 1977.

8 Mary Boston and Rolene Szur (eds), *Psychotherapy with Severely Deprived Children*, Routledge & Kegan Paul, London, 1983, p.9.

9 Donald Winnicott, quoted in Madeline Davis and David Wallbridge, *Boundary and Space*, Penguin, Harmondsworth, 1983, p.45.

10 *Ibid.*, p.58.

11 W.R. Bion, *Learning from Experience*, Heinemann, London, 1962.

12 Gianna Henry, 'Difficulties about Thinking and Learning', in *Psychotherapy with Severely Disturbed Children*, *op. cit.*, p.84. See also D. Meltzer *et al.*, *Explorations in Autism*, Clunie Press, Perthshire, 1975.

13 Gianna Henry, *op.cit.*, p.87.

14 Alice Miller, *For Your Own Good*, Faber, London, 1983, p. 265.

15 Melkamu Adisu quoted in *The Listener*, 24 May 1984.

Chapter 4 'There is something beyond this life'

1 Jonathon Schell, *The Fate of the Earth*, Picador, London, 1982, p.26.

2 Lal, L., 'The Preserver Preserved', *The Times of India*, 10 April 1983, p.8.

3 *On Making Peace in a Nuclear World*, British Council of Churches, London, 1983.

4 Catholic Bishops' Pastoral Letter, quoted in *On Making Peace in a Nuclear World*, *op.cit.*

5 Pope John Paul II, *Appeal for Peace*, Hiroshima, 25 February 1981.

6 Ronald J. Sider and Richard K. Taylor, *Nuclear Holocaust and Christian Hope*, Hodder & Stoughton, London, 1982, p.97.

7 Scully cartoon, *Punch*, 20 April 1983.

8   Taylor cartoon, *Punch*, 22 June 1983.
9   Billy Graham, 'Whatever happens, Christ is going to win', *The Listener*, 19 April 1984, p.19.
10 Ronnie Dugger, 'Reagan's apocalypse now', *Guardian*, 21 April 1984, reprinted from the *Washington Post*.
11 David Blundy and Hirsh Goodman, with additional reporting by John Barnes, 'Bombers in pursuit of Armageddon', *Sunday Times*, 30 September 1984.
12 Margaret Ballard, personal communication, 12 February 1984.
13 Genesis 1: 26.
14 Melvin J. Lerner, *The Belief in a Just World. A Fundamental Delusion*, Plenum Press, New York, 1982.
15 Jim Garrison, *The Darkness of God: Theology after Hiroshima*, SCM Press, London, 1982, p.213.

Chapter 5 'We need the bomb'

1   Charles E. Osgood, in *The Liberal Papers*, ed. James Roosevelt, Quadrangle Books, Chicago, 1962, reprinted in Alistair Mant, *The Leaders We Deserve*, Martin Robertson, Oxford, 1983.
2   Sophie cartoon, *Guardian*, 1 May 1984.
3   *Space* phone-in, BBC Radio 4, 17 April 1984.
4   Brian Easlea, *Fathering the Unthinkable*, Pluto Press, London, 1983, p.96.
5   Edward Teller, quoted in *Living and Dying*, Robert Jay Lifton and Eric Olson, Bantam Books, London, 1975.
6   Phillip Hodson, *op.cit.*, pp. 95, 19
7   Arnold Palmer, 'Legend of the Links. Master in the Game of Sportsmanship', *Regent Magazine*, 1984.
8   Tony Wilkinson, 'Marathon mentality – the risks sportsmen run', *The Listener*, 31 May 1984.
9   Phillip Hodson, *op.cit.*, pp. 95, 100.
10 Judi Marshall, *Women Managers: Travellers in a Male World*, Wiley, Chichester, 1984.
11 *Punch* cartoon 1 February 1984.
12 Alistair Mant, *op.cit.*, p.18.
13 Alistair Mant, *op.cit.*, p.8; also T.W. Adorno et al., *The Authoritarian Personality*, Norton, New York, 1969.
14 Alistair Mant, *op.cit.*, p.18.
15 Alistair Mant, *op.cit.*, p.19.
16 George Hyatt, in *Man Enough* by Yvonne Roberts, Chatto & Windus, London, 1984, p.100.
17 Michael Howard, *The Causes of Wars*, Unwin Paperbacks, London, 1984, p.15.

18 Tom Wolfe, *The Right Stuff*, Bantam Books, London, 1983, pp. 18, 22, 26.

19 Ian Moffitt, *The Retreat of Radiance*, Collins, Sydney, 1982, p.46.

20 Jeremy Seabrook, 'The inheritance of despair: unemployment in the eighties', *Changes*, vol. 3, no. 1, 1984.

21 Otto Fenichel, *op.cit.*, pp. 149, 500.

22 Jules Feiffer, *Marriage is an Invasion of Privacy*, Andrews, McMeely and Parker Inc, Kansas, 1984.

23 Alice Miller, *The Drama of the Gifted Child*, Faber, London, p.129.

24 Personal communication, May 1984.

25 Brian Lee, 'Records in the Sands of Time', *Quantas Airways Inflight Magazine*, July/August, 1984, p.22.

26 Walter T. Anderson, 'Faraway lunches consume Central American forests', *Los Angeles Times*, 27 August 1984.

27 Anne Woodham, 'If a woman is tortured, then her whole family is tortured', *Guardian*, 16 October 1984.

28 Jorge Valls Arango interviewed by Graham Fawcett, 'Speaking with a voice made of bubbles of blood', *The Listener*, 26 July 1984.

29 Phillip Hodson, *op.cit.*, p.18.

30 Phillip Hodson, *op.cit.*, p.23.

31 Dale Spender, *Man-Made Language*, Routledge, London, 1984, p.12.

32 Bev Roberts, 'Ockers and malespeak', *Australian Society*, 1 August 1984.

33 *Survive* Series, Channel 4, UK, 17 May 1984.

34 John Metzger Editorial, *Survive*, June 1984.

35 Ian Mather, *Observer*, 26 February 1984.

36 Donald Trelford, *Observer*, 1 April 1984.

37 Phillip Hodson, *op.cit.*, p.135.

38 Yvonne Roberts, *op.cit.*, p.11.

39 John Carey and Mary Bruno, 'Why cynicism can be fatal; *Newsweek*, 10 September 1984.

40 Gibbard cartoon, *Guardian*, 31 May 1982.

41 Editorial, 'Death hits a boom market', *Guardian*, 14 March 1984.

42 Steve Wright, 'The hard sell', *Guardian*, 21 June 1984 extract from *The Export of Repression — a New Case for Arms Control?*, Richardson Institute for Conflict and Peace Research, University of Lancaster, 1984.

Chapter 6 Must we always fear the Stranger?

1 Reverend Michael Dougherty, in Whitley Strieber and James Kunetka, *Warday and the Journey Onward*, Hodder & Stoughton, London, 1984, p.145.
2 Banx cartoon, *Punch*, 8 June 1983.
3 Mary Douglas, *Purity and Danger*, Routledge & Kegan Paul, London, 1966.
4 E.P. Thompson, *Beyond the Cold War*, Merlin Press, London, 1981.
5 Clyde Haberman, 'Japan smooths over its imperial past', *New York Times*, 2 September 1984.
6 Robert Christopher, *The Japanese Mind*, Pan Books, London, 1984, pp.40, 45.
7 Frank Gibney, *Japan: The Fragile Superpower*, Charles E. Tuttle Company, Tokyo, 1975, pp.148, 149.
8 Takeo Doi, *The Anatomy of Dependence*, tr. John Bester, Kodansha International, Tokyo, 1981, pp.121,127.
9 *Ibid.*, p.74.
10 Frank Gibney, *op.cit.*, p.74.
11 Frank Gibney, *op.cit.*, p.77.
12 Chie Nakene, *Japanese Society*, Charles E. Tuttle, Tokyo, 1984, pp.3, 4.
13 Takeo Doi, *op.cit.*, p.28.
14 John Bester, in 'Foreword' in *The Anatomy of Dependence, op.cit.*, pp.7, 8.
15 Takeo Doi, *op.cit*, p.30.
16 Takeo Doi quoted by Frank Gibney, *op.cit.*, p.127.
17 Chie Nakene, *op.cit*, p.102.
18 Frank Gibney, *op.cit.*, p.148.
19 Robert Christopher, *op.cit.*, p.63.
20 Frank Gibney, *op.cit.*, p.76.
21 Yoshiya Ariyoshi, quoted by Robert Chistopher, *op.cit.*, p.225.
22 Robert Christopher, *ibid.*, p.49.
23 Sudhir Kakar, *The Inner World*, Oxford University Press, Delhi, 1981, pp.117, 124, 125, 135, 136.
24 Matthew 5 38:48, Authorized Version.
25 *Observer*, 29 January 1984.
26 *Time*, 30 April, 1984.
27 Marc Ferro, *The Use and Abuse of History*, Routledge & Kegan Paul, London, 1984, p.114.
28 *Ibid.*, pp.224, 225.
29 Jessica Hallam, *The Listener*, 9 February 1984.
30 Letter to the editor, *The Lincolnshire Echo*, 24 December 1983.
31 Alice Miller, *For Your Own Good – Hidden Cruelty in Child-*

Rearing and the Roots of Violence, Faber, London, 1983, p.106.
32   *Ibid.*, p.138.
33   Alice Miller, *The Drama of the Gifted Child*, Faber, London, 1983, pp.21, 90.
34   Claire Weekes, *Self Help for Your Nerves*, Angus & Robertson, Sydney, 1984.
35   Jeremy Paxman, *The Listener*, 22 March 1984.
36   Alice Miller, *For Your Own Good*, op.cit., p.265.
37   Jeremy Holmes, *Bulletin of the Royal College of Psychiatry*, vol. 6, no.8, 1982.
38   Alice Miller, *For Your Own Good*, pp.144, 171; *Drama of the Gifted Child*, pp.88, 89 op.cit.

Chapter 8 Change and courage

1   Sheldon Kopp, *Back to One*, Sheldon Press, New York, 1981, p.180.
2   Punch cartoon, 16 March 1983.
3   Keith, personal communication, 1984.
4   *Ibid.*
5   Mary Boston and Rolene Szur (eds) *Psychotherapy with Severely Disturbed Children*, London, Routledge, 1983, p.86.
6   *Ibid.*, pp.24, 25.
7   *Ibid.*, pp.70, 73, 74.
8   *Ibid.*, p.60.
9   *Ibid.*, pp.130, 131.
10   Judy Dunn, *Guardian*, 12 November 1984.
11   Judy Dunn, *Sisters and Brothers*, London, Fontana, 1984.
12   Colwyn Trevarthen review of *The Place of Attachment in Human Behaviour*, C.M. Parkes and J.Stevenson-Hinde (eds) London, Tavistock, 1982, *British Journal of Psychiatry* 1984, vol.145, p.560.
13   'The Antinuclear Kids', *Boston Globe*, 11 May 1984.
14   Clare Cherrington, 'The Greenham Children', *Guardian*, 21 September 1984.
15   Alistair Cooke, 'Getting away from it all', in *Letters from America*, London, Rupert Hart-Davis, 1951, p.20.
16   Susan Thomas interview with Bishop Thomas Gumbleton, the principal author of *The Bishop's Pastoral Letter on War and Peace in a Nuclear Age, the American Catholic Church's statement of policy*, *Guardian*, 9 June 1984.

Epilogue

1 Stephen Jay Gould, 'Cosmic catastrophe', *The Listener*, 20 September 1984.
2 Fiona Buckland, 1985.
3 Fiona Buckland, 1985.
4 Fiona Buckland, 1985.

INDEX